Workers' Self-Management
in the United States

Workers' Self-Management in the United States

CHRISTOPHER EATON GUNN

CORNELL UNIVERSITY PRESS

ITHACA AND LONDON

Copyright © 1984 by Cornell University Press

All rights reserved. Except for brief quotations in a review, this book, or parts thereof, must not be reproduced in any form without permission in writing from the publisher. For information, address Cornell University Press, 124 Roberts Place, Ithaca, New York 14850.

First published 1984 by Cornell University Press.
First printing, Cornell Paperbacks, 1986.

International Standard Book Number 0-8014-1644-2 (cloth)
International Standard Book Number 0-8014-9376-5 (paper)
Library of Congress Catalog Card Number 83-45937
Printed in the United States of America
*Librarians: Library of Congress cataloging information appears
on the last page of the book.*

*The paper in this book is acid-free and meets the guidelines
for permanence and durability of the Committee on Production
Guidelines for Book Longevity of the Council on Library Resources.*

TO HAZEL

Contents

Preface

The term *workers' self-management* has been used in the United States in various and conflicting ways. This book explains the concept of workers' self-management in historical and theoretical terms and in light of the actual working experience of men and women in this country today. The focus on the United States is not meant to lessen the importance of French, Yugoslav, Israeli, Spanish, or any other example of this phenomenon. It was chosen to facilitate study of workers' self-management by grounding it in the social, economic, and political institutions of one country. It was chosen also in the hope of advancing the knowledge and practice of workers' self-management in this country.

Although workers' self-management exists only in isolated and tentative forms in the United States today, one of the fundamental assertions of this study is that it has existed, in partial forms and as an objective, in various American industries at different times in our history. Attempts at self-management have taken the form of a quest for greater autonomy on the shop floor, demands for some voice in the pace and direction of technological change, and resistance to the fragmentation of work tasks. They have also taken the form of rejection of the very premises of the conventional organizations of production and attempts to construct new, more cooperative productive organizations. Most of these attempts have taken place under the pragmatic assumption that the American economic system would continue largely unchanged and that alternatives were possible within that system. Some have been based on the premise that they could contribute to changing the system itself.

Part I of this book defines workers' self-management and briefly summarizes its historical precedents. A set of defining and facilitating conditions is then developed which summarizes theoretical and empirical evidence concerning worker-controlled and self-managed firms and serves as a framework for analysis at the level of the firm. Part II consists of case descriptions and evaluation of several firms and groups of firms that are wholly or substantially self-managed. They are the forest workers' cooperatives, the plywood cooperatives, and two firms that had operated as conventional businesses before they were taken over by their workers. Case material describes the histories of these firms, and their financial and organizational structures in 1982.

Part III broadens the level of analysis of the study. It includes a reevaluation of the conditions used in analysis of cases, a related summary of industrial characteristics that lend themselves to the development of self-management, and a historical analysis of U.S. workers' co-ops. It then addresses macroeconomic, social, and political conditions that would support the development of self-management in this country, initiatives that could help establish those conditions, and methods for achieving them.

Self-management can work in the United States, but for reasons that will be made clear in the text that follows, creating and maintaining self-managed firms are arduous tasks. Liberals and pragmatic advocates of self-management generally believe that it is a viable alternative in the capitalist economy, and the cases presented in Part II of this book provide some evidence for that belief. These cases, however, also point to significant barriers to development of workers' self-management. They indicate that self-management may be possible at the fringes of this economy, but that it could flourish only in a considerably more hospitable environment. The concluding chapters of this book address the relationship between that environment and self-management and the potential relationship between workers' self-management and social change.

CHRISTOPHER EATON GUNN

Trumansburg, New York

Acknowledgments

The text that follows has benefited from many and diverse contributions. People who have been directly involved in development of the worker-controlled and self-managed firms described in Part II of this text deserve special thanks both for what they have done and for so willingly sharing their experiences. Over the past four years conversations with forest workers in Oregon and Washington, particularly Roscoe Caron, Dave Straton, Laurie Patterson, Greg Nagle, Tim Schottman, Valerie Jaffie, Fred Miller, Rick Kovan, Steve Marquardt, and Jonathan Walker, have been helpful and enjoyable. I am indebted to several of these people, and to Gerry Mackie and Hal Hartzell, for reading and commenting on drafts of material that became Chapter 3.

Many members, managers, and workers at plywood cooperatives in the Northwest contributed to this book by their generous sharing of time and insights into that group of co-ops, and their work in them. My thanks also go to Katrina Berman for sharing her considerable knowledge of the plywood co-ops in reading and commenting on a draft of Chapter 4.

At Local 46 of the United Food and Commercial Workers International Union in Waterloo, Iowa, Chief Steward Charles (Chuck) Mueller and then-President Lyle Taylor shared insights and details of takeover efforts at Rath Packing Company which were indispensable to construction of that case study. Chuck has been a special friend in his effort to keep me informed of what has happened there. My thanks to Herbert Epstein, Leroy Grittmann, and other past and present Rath staff members for sharing their knowledge of that remarkable attempt to save a firm.

Discussion several years ago with Steve Johnson, a key actor in the formation of Denver Yellow Cab Cooperative Association, sparked my interest in that co-op, and more recently his comments improved my understanding of it. Tom Hanlon and others at Yellow Cab and Ed Cassidy, president of the Independent Drivers Association in Denver, were also very helpful.

This book is in part a product of classroom discussion of self-managed firms which I have had over the past several years with students of Hobart and William Smith Colleges, and I am thankful to them for those good experiences. I am also indebted to Hobart and William Smith for a sabbatical that allowed me time for writing, and for research funds that helped pay travel expenses.

I owe a longstanding debt to Jaroslav Vanek of Cornell University. My several years as his student and research assistant were an intellectual and human adventure that graduate students rarely get to enjoy. Conversations with students and faculty members of and visitors to the Program on Participation and Labor-Managed Systems at Cornell have clearly shaped this work. I am also grateful to Peter Miovic, who introduced me to the philosophy, theory, and international history of workers' self-management a decade ago.

Two friends read a draft of this manuscript and gave me the benefit of their considerable knowledge in response to it. Special thanks to Chandler Morse, professor emeritus of economics at Cornell and to John McConnell, former dean of the Graduate School and of the New York State School of Industrial and Labor Relations at Cornell and past president of the University of New Hampshire.

My clearest debt in this endeavor is to my wife, Hazel Dayton Gunn. Her encouragement to do this work, keen insight in many conversations about the material, astute editorial comments, and continual assistance in development of the manuscript made this project possible. Projects of this kind take time and energy from other endeavors. I owe Hazel untold hours of support for the projects of her life.

Finally, I thank Carol Betsch of Cornell University Press and Allison Dodge for their editorial contributions to this book.

C.E.G.

PART I

DEFINITION, THEORY,

AND EVIDENCE

CHAPTER 1

Workers' Self-Management

This book has to do with an unusual way to organize and control the work we do as human beings. It describes and analyzes firms that are managed democratically by the people who work in them. Work is more commonly organized and controlled by owners and managers, or perhaps by managers who report to a government agency or a board of trustees. The organization in which most people work operates hierarchically; regardless of the style of its management, somebody at the top has a controlling voice in its operation. The subject of this study is an organization without externally imposed management and hierarchy, that is, a self-managed firm.

Workers' self-management refers to the collective process of self-governance and democratic management within an organization that produces goods or services. It eliminates employee-employer relationships and provides an extension and reinforcement of democratic principles fundamental to modern Western thought. Workers' self-management refers to an environment that encourages human growth by stressing cooperation and participation by all those actively engaged in the productive process. It can contribute to increases in material productivity and to greater output. It can also stimulate productivity in the fullest human terms—in people's more complete growth and development through their work.

The term *workers' self-management* defines *who* is managing in this process of self-governance. It is well known that in a predominantly capitalist economy and society, workers typically do not manage. From the days of Adam Smith's early analysis of capitalism it has been accepted wisdom that workers ultimately carry out orders and directives, whether they are delivered in congenial or hostile terms. Capital, and today its cadre of professional assistants, manages. Capital conceptualizes and plans work; labor executes those plans. This book deals with how that traditional arrangement can be and has been dispensed with.

The very use of the terms *capital* and *labor* involves fundamental tensions. Notions of class do not come easily to the American mind, even though we routinely discuss capital and labor, the rights of each, and how protection of those rights is negotiated. We are encouraged by mainstream social science to understand class in socioeconomic terms and to think of it largely in terms of annual income flows and their likely implications for our lives. The study of workers' self-management is based on an older and more political understanding of class, one that derives from people's relationship to the means of production. Capital has maintained its right to manage production based on the property rights that attend capital ownership, and those rights stem from the power that accompanies ownership. Workers have not managed because they did not own or control the production process or its product. At times they have little control over whether they work or do not work, much less over how the work is planned, organized, and executed. Issues of class, power, and control are inseparable from the topic of self-management. Workers' self-management is defined from a premise that there is no inherent right of capital to participate in management. It locates the right to participate in the management of work in work itself, not in capital ownership. It is based on the premise that all who actively contribute to production, at whatever level of skill or scope of competence, have the fundamental right to manage that production.

Issues cutting close to the substance of workers' self-management have not been absent from American industrial history. Skilled workers have hotly contested issues of control over production with their employers (Montgomery 1979). The Industrial Workers of the World, a radical labor union with a taste for workers' control in syndicalist form, caused far more official concern than its numbers seemed to warrant (Boyer and Morais 1972, ch. 6; Dubofsky 1971). Several clusters of worker-owned and -controlled companies have operated for extended periods in the U.S. economy (Jones 1979, forthcoming).

But interest in forms of workers' control over production is not simply historical in nature. Several recent economic and social phenomena have stirred renewed interest in them. For example, threats of economic and social dislocation brought on by plant closings have prompted questions about how firms would be run if they were taken over or reopened under worker and community control. Corporate managers seeking to bolster productivity have designed programs to encourage worker participation in management. Why have these programs been so controversial, and what is the limit to their expansion? The last two decades have also produced numerous experiments in alternative ways of working in small, countercultural organizations. What makes them unusual, and what can be learned from them? These questions can be answered more easily with a fuller understanding of workers' self-management. Discussions of future directions of the U.S. economy or solutions to its malaise often include references to industrial or economic democracy, increased worker autonomy on the job, or providing workers with stronger feelings of a stake in the success of America's business organizations. Again, these debates could be sharpened with a clearer understanding of how, and if, workers' self-management works.

People about to throw themselves into a plant takeover or formation of a workers' cooperative sometimes have only fragmentary ideas about how the firm they plan to create will actually function. Many times they share a misconception that they have to work by intuition and trial and error. That is not the case; there are flesh-and-blood examples of success and failure to learn from.

Defining Workers' Self-Management

Before proceeding, it is essential to define workers' self-management as clearly as possible. Workers' self-management has already been defined as a collective process. That definition assumes common goals among people, not only at the level of assuring continued material reproduction for society but at the level of the unit of production. The focus of this study is primarily the latter. Theorists have been challenged to define the common goals of people joined together in a collectively managed unit of production. One of the most basic objectives that can be assumed by these organizations is maximizing income per worker. That objective serves to ground some theoretical inquiry, but in the real world it could hardly be the only goal of a collective of men and women whose concerns are not purely economic. A broader common objective could be achieving a satisfactory mix of income, longer-term economic security, satisfaction from work, sense of community at work, and contribution to the broader community. Some of these objectives may best be realized at a larger social level than that of the firm. Yet they can also serve as common objectives bonding those who come together to produce. Whatever the mix of common objectives, they help to define the self-managing organization.

Second, the *self* in *workers' self-management* does not refer to the individual within the organization. The expression should not be taken as referring to a vehicle for maximizing personal individual freedom of action. Self-management refers to the relative autonomy of the organization to conduct its affairs, to determine its course of action. That autonomy presupposes an absence of *direct* external control, either by capital owners or by an autocratic governmental hierarchy. A self-governing organization of production cannot, of course, exist in isolation. It is a part of a broad social community and of a more immediate local community. The range of actions it can take are conditioned, constrained, and mediated by that social existence. In the concrete world, a self-governing firm can operate in either an economy in which goods and services are exchanged through markets or one in which a form of planning for material needs that allows significant autonomy for producers has been achieved.

Finally, workers' self-management is a process based on democratic principles—rules and procedures that allow all participants an equal voice in the management of the organization. Democratic practice may take several forms. Small organizations or subunits of larger organizations may be able to practice full or modified forms of consensual decision making. Larger groups may function best with a workers' council form of democracy in which all workers participate, particularly for decisions involving major policy matters. Other democratic organizations may use a representative democratic process for many decisions. If democratic principles are to be meaningfully employed, it is likely that this representative form will be used cautiously, with built-in safeguards such as rotation of representatives, day-to-day direct contact between representatives and the working community, and rights of recall. Such safeguards emphasize democracy as people's government, one that must involve all those affected by the process.

A commitment to democracy conjures up images of long meetings, full disclosure of information to all concerned, and lots of give and take in reaching decisions. That image is antithetical to a world that values quick decisions, tight control over information in the competitive world, and control over subordinates in a business organization. In part, the image is incorrect. Nothing precludes a democratically run enterprise from setting up an efficient management structure to take care of much of its day-to-day coordination of activities. Many self-managed firms designate members as managers, and some bring individuals with specific management skills into the organization. But even in those situations, *the people working in the firm* have determined what is best for them, and they, of course, retain the power to modify or nullify any arrangements they have made.

Democratic processes take time. Several fundamental arguments can be offered for them. Pragmatically, it has been demonstrated that there are economic benefits to be won with their use. People have demonstrated the benefits of direct involvement in decision making through increased satisfaction, improved productivity, and greater commitment to the organization. Philosophically, there is broad commitment to people's right to a role in their governing process and to ultimate control over their governing institutions. There is no reason why that commitment has to be abolished at the office door or factory gate. Realistically, there is no better method by which people can equitably govern themselves.

Workers' self-management shares some features of, but also must be differentiated from, workers' participation in management, workers' control, and worker ownership. Investigation of the relationship between these terms can help further define workers' self-management as an ideal and as economic, social, and political reality.

Workers' participation is a truncated form of workers' self-management. Workers' participation generally involves spreading some management functions to a broader mix of people working in an organization. Most typically the process begins with decision-making power being granted to workers over the details of their immediate tasks such as scheduling a predetermined work quota, rotating certain tasks among themselves on the shop floor, or modifying some aspects of the production process. The next level of involvement might include workers having greater responsibility for quality control, participating in the selection or dismissal of fellow employees, or determining how to meet production targets. But it is precisely the status of workers as employees that sets limitations on the issues in which they can participate. Employees are hired by capital owners to contribute to the expansion of that capital. For the logic of the system to hold, those decisions that most directly affect profit must remain the province of those who work in capital's interest. The fact that the wage bill in the traditional firm is a cost to capital, that it diminishes profit, is the most obvious source of conflict between the aims of capital and workers. The quest for profit can also pit workers against capital and its managers on issues such as health and safety on the job, the organization of the work itself, and when and under what conditions the worker is expendable. It is reasonable to assume that in a traditional firm workers' participation will be introduced when it serves capital's interests, and that it will be expanded within limits set by those interests. Workers' self-management has a fundamentally different premise—that all members of the organization fully participate as a result of their direct productive activity in the organization. The right to manage stems from work, not from capital ownership.

Full-fledged workers' self-management is sometimes linked with the term *workers' control*. For a productive organization, rather than the economy as a whole, there are important distinctions to be made between these terms. Workers' control simply specifies that all people who work in an organization control it, while providing no indication of how it will be managed. Workers' self-management specifies a nonhierarchical form of organization and a democratic process for management. *Workers' control, then, is a necessary condition for workers' self-management.* It stands in sharp contrast to capital's control of a firm and to direct control by any other outside interests.

Worker ownership has received considerable attention in the nation's press, in Congress, and among business leaders in recent years. It has been promoted as a means of saving jobs by raising new capital for a firm, transferring a small firm from proprietor to workers, or gaining more employee commitment and higher productivity and as a possible strategy for combating labor organizing. Some forms of worker ownership involve schemes to use workers' capital in order simply to tie them financially to the firm that employs them. Many employee stock ownership trusts (ESOTs) do this without passing to workers the voting rights of stock owned by their trust. Other worker ownership plans limit the amount of stock available for employee acquisition to such a low percentage that worker-stockholders have virtually no impact on the firm's operation. Worker ownership can be related to workers' self-management only when there is enough ownership to place control in workers' hands. Even then, workers will have gained control through rules of capital ownership, not through principles consistent with self-management.

If workers manage to buy the right to control their firm, they still face the challenge of determining how to run it. They may opt for a continuation of the work organization and management processes that were in place before their acquisition. To do so implies unquestioning acceptance of their new status as owners, and of the logic and property rights they have just used in acquiring control. That thinking may also lead them to employ other workers who do not own a part of the firm, further diminishing any potential for development of self-management. The other possible outcome of worker ownership with control could involve a fundamental change in the firm's management processes and the organization of work. That change could be motivated by a desire to produce as a community of workers, rather than as capital owners seeking profit and workers earning a wage. In short, some form of workers' self-management may be made possible through acquisition by workers of a majority ownership position: by buying control. Whether any real form of workers' self-management materializes depends on the strength of a group's consciousness, commitment, skills, and knowledge of how to organize for a more cooperative form of production.

Critical to the development of workers' self-management is a collective vision of preferable forms of productive organizations. Development of that vision requires thinking about, debating, and struggling toward new ways of working together. It means becoming familiar with what others have tried, how they have failed, and what they have achieved. It means gathering strength through resisting what is, at the same time that the people involved are working toward what could be. This is not a new effort, but it is one that is being rekindled under changing conditions in this country.

Why Now?

Mainstream and radical economists and other observers of the U.S. economy agree that it is in trouble; the golden era of American capitalism appears to have come to an end. Beginning with the 1969–70 recession, and especially in the more severe 1973–75 downturn, it became clear that the U.S. economy was losing its dominant position internationally and that it had lost any supposed ability to operate without downturns or crises.

Periods of crisis lead to debate over paths to recovery of past stability. They also can stimulate more trenchant critiques of the existing order, and they may provide fertile ground for thoughts and actions toward alternatives. The economic and social turbulence of the past fifteen years has been largely responsible for bringing the issue of workers' self-management to growing numbers of American people. With plant closings, rising unemployment, and declining growth in productivity, once accepted institutions and practices have been called into question. At the same time, alternate work organizations initiated over a decade ago are surviving and becoming better known. Lastly, participants and researchers are beginning to distill the lessons of new forms of organization and management, increasing awareness of them and enabling others to learn from them. Each of these trends will be reviewed briefly here.

Recent economic crises have affected working men and women in many ways. Most common have been diminished growth in real wages, a general increase in the threat of unemployment, diminished expectations for the economic future of their children, and heightened anxiety over prospects for secure retirement. One of the most visceral experiences for many Americans has been the threat or actuality of losing their jobs because of plant shutdowns. Beginning in a few industries and geographic regions, shutdowns became harbingers of major problems in the economy. During more dynamic periods in the economic history of the country, new capital investment helped alleviate the shock to a community of losing one of its principal employers. Despite the human suffering involved, Joseph Schumpeter's "creative destruction" worked in its crude way; weaker firms and declining industries were cleared away, replaced by vital new economic activity. At least three modern phenomena make that process less acceptable than it was in the decades immediately following the Second World War. Two have to do with technological change. First, as technological change occurs more rapidly, people in the labor force find that the job skills that served them (and their employer) in their old jobs may not serve them in finding a new one. As people's skills become obsolete, they fall victim to structural unemployment. They are faced with the choice of gaining new training to acquire currently needed skills or accepting a job with lower skill requirements and, typically, lower pay. Second, technological change frequently involves a mix of more machinery with fewer workers: an increasing ratio of fixed capital to labor. In a growing economy, new jobs offset some of this loss to mechanization. In a stagnant economy, though, far fewer jobs are created. Third, in today's economy, the new jobs that are created may be on the other side of the globe. International competitive pressure and the lure of lower costs in a system in which wages reduce profits to capital owners mean that new jobs may not be available to those losing the old ones. Plant closings may once have been perverse signs of health in the economy, but recently they are more likely disastrous to the people and communities affected by them.

The specter of plant shutdowns has left workers and whole communities feeling increasingly threatened over the past decade. Newspaper and television reports of them reach us daily. Analyses of the situation have revealed some cold facts: that the problem is one affecting not only the old industrial heartland, but the South and far West of this country as well (Bluestone and Harrison 1982); that American investment overseas grew at a rate more than twice that of private domestic investment during the period 1950–74 (Bluestone, Harrison, and Baker 1981, p. 16); and that less than 1 percent of domestic jobs created in the period 1969–76 occurred as a result of investment by the 1,000 largest firms in the United States (U.S. Congress, House, 1978).

Responses to these conditions have been many and varied. Some communities have stagnated in resentment and frustration, while others have actively competed with each other for any new job-creating investment they could get. Some have succeeded in attracting new industry. Still others have been moved to take action to keep a plant operating or attempt to reopen it if it has been closed. Those plans, from large cases such as that of the Campbell Works of Youngstown Sheet and Tube Company in Ohio or a smaller one such as Library Bureau in Herkimer, New York, often include calls for some form of worker or community ownership and control. Workers and community leaders share a desire not to be caught again by a decision made in some distant corporate headquarters that will cut off a part of their lifeblood. A vague notion that business can or should be run differently is often a part of these plans, but it is generally characterized by unspecific allusions to worker or community control, to management that answers to the work community, or to forms of workers' self-management. The threat of economic dislocation has started many working Americans imagining a different way of running their industries and organizing their work.

Managers also feel the pressures of economic stagnation. They, too, are affected by shutdowns and by the fear of them, although they may be less threatened than production workers by a plant closing or layoffs. People in management positions tend to have skills that are less firm- or industry-specific than those of production workers. As a group, they also have probably been more conditioned to changing jobs and geographic locations during their careers. Nevertheless, people in managerial positions may join with workers and community leaders to maintain jobs in their community.

Organized labor has been rocked by plant shutdowns. Many unions have been forced to abandon their usual approaches to obtaining better pay and working conditions for their members in favor of more defensive job security measures. More important, the bargain struck between labor and capital after the turbulent 1930s has been called into question. Collective bargaining took place for almost four decades under the assumption that jobs would be there, that capital would be invested in continued domestic production. But one of the most basic elements in the post–World War II accord between labor and capital was labor's acceptance of the managerial right to make capital investment decisions. By accepting that tenet of capitalism, labor left itself open to the day when capital approached the globe as both market and arena of production. With the arrival of that day in many industries, the strength of domestically organized labor unions has been diminished. So, too, is rank-and-file faith in the collective bargaining process. After four decades its premises are shaken.

Economic stagnation in the United States has been accompanied by decreasing growth rates in the productivity of industry, and corporate managers at first turned to dramatic new programs in their attempt to satisfy workers and return growth in productivity to earlier levels. The early 1970s brought an explosion of interest in worker participation programs. They were seen as a means of dealing with not only sagging increases in productivity, but absenteeism, falling quality of product, and other manifestations of worker-management discord and worker dissatisfaction. Increasing worker participation in management seemed to provide a way out of these workplace problems. A widely read report of the Special Task Force of the Secretary of Health, Education, and Welfare entitled *Work in America* (1973) pointed to the benefits of expanded participation. Social scientists rediscovered and examined decades of literature on the subject, and one reported that "there is hardly a study in the entire literature which fails to demonstrate that satisfaction in work is enhanced or that other generally acknowledged beneficial consequences accrue from a genuine increase in workers' decision-making power" (Blumberg 1968, p. 123). One of those beneficial consequences was increased worker productivity. In the United States, firms such as General Foods and Procter & Gamble initiated bold programs designed to reap the benefits of this new management technique. Others watched warily, waiting to see the results of both U.S. and international experiments, including the highly publicized adoption of humanization and participation programs by Volvo, Sweden's largest auto producer. The immediate results were, in most cases, impressive. Productivity increased, and turnover, absenteeism, and other signs of malaise diminished.

But by the late 1970s, it was difficult to find much news of these programs. Some, including General Foods' "Topeka System," had been quietly dismantled after workers sought even more participation, which proved threatening to some managers and a good many of their superiors (Zwerdling 1978, pp. 19-29). Other corporations apparently decided that allowing workers to participate in management was too costly, not in hard accounting terms but in terms of turmoil within the corporate structure. Observers of the international experiments reported less dramatic gains in productivity, measured against the added cost of new plant designs, than had been anticipated. It also became increasingly clear that the gains of Volvo's Kalmar plant came at a price that did not have to be paid except in a society, such as Sweden, in which labor wielded more power than it did in the United States. Cumulative effects of the slump in the United States, particularly in heavily unionized basic industries like autos, left labor attempting to re-place losses in workers' real purchasing power or even just to save jobs.

Market forces alter the positions of both labor and management, and by the early 1980s broad-based workers' participation in man-agement was not high on either's list of priorities. Back-to-back recessions and increasing unemployment levels have induced peo-ple to work harder and have diminished pressure for more im-aginative approaches to problems of the workplace. What remains of many of the bold plans of the 1970s is implementation of much more limited quality of worklife (QWL) programs, labor manage-ment committees, and worker ownership schemes. They constitute an attempt on management's part to reap some of the benefits of broader participation programs while avoiding their difficult ques-tions concerning worker involvement in decisions that affect prof-itability and private capital accumulation.

Yet experiences with participation over the past decade cannot be wiped away. Management knows there are gains to be won as long as these programs can be structured in ways that limit the rise in workers' expectations and the threat to mid-level supervisors and managers. A number of workers, through experience with these programs, have come to envision a different way of working that involves new challenges and responsibilities, new understand-ing of various aspects of the production process, and new pride in work. Labor leaders have begun to strip away some of the blinders created by decades of collective bargaining in a world in which management prerogatives were sacrosanct. They are concerned about issues of work process, technological change, and capital investment. Perhaps more significantly, people who have been affected by these participation programs have begun to sense the limits of these programs in organizations in which the programs are ultimately offered or scrapped according to the interests of capital. They may also have been tempted to think of how a pro-ductive organization might be structured if it were fully partici-patory, if those who did the producing organized and managed themselves.

There is another way the impact of economic forces may have contributed to a growing awareness of workers' self-management in this country. It has been argued that countercultural social experiments of the late 1960s and early 1970s were made possible in part by the relative affluence of the 1960s or even by a cumulative effect of the long boom that culminated in that decade. If that is the case, then that period can also be credited with providing a base of experience for efforts to develop more democratic work organizations. During that time most states and major cities across the country became home to various forms of workers' cooperatives, new-wave consumer co-ops, and work collectives. How much of a role relative economic affluence played in triggering this development remains a matter for debate. It is clear that the period provided a social environment conducive to experimentation with non-traditional work organizations. Many of those experiments sought less hierarchy, fewer or less formal control systems, and less overt interpersonal competition than traditional organizations. Generally, nontraditional work organizations were initiated by the children of professional and managerial families in society who emphasized a quest for personal growth and an environment that would be supportive of personal fulfillment. Affluence may have provided a breeding ground, but the seeds stemmed from contradictions within traditional work organizations and fundamental questions concerning their very objectives.

The feminist movement directly influenced these alternative work organizations. Particularly by the 1970s, politically active women played a major role in shaping them, perhaps because they knew well the significance of hierarchy and dominance on the job and at home. Their job prospects were more limited than those of their male counterparts; they could not as easily escape to an interesting or challenging job within a traditional organization. Neither could they have many illusions about their ability to change those organizations from the positions they held in them. By working together through consciousness-raising and feminist awareness groups, women discussed and confronted issues of power, hierarchy, and dominance. They learned the importance of process in decision making—how it could be used to maintain positions of power and how it could be modified to open up opportunities for sharing power. Alternate work organizations provided important arenas where newly articulated beliefs could be actualized and further ideas developed. Through the development of these organizations women had an opportunity to grow in keeping with their values, gain new skills, and share a sense of community in the process.

Some of the alternate work organizations of this period have disappeared. Others have undergone extensive change, gained more structure, or become more traditional in their operation. But their ideas and ideals have continued. The cooperative awakening of the late sixties and early seventies provided the basis for an array of alternate businesses today. Many are found in towns and urban areas where a liberal or progressive atmosphere has prevailed—the Boston area in the Northeast and the Bay Area on the West Coast; Eugene, Oregon, and Ithaca, New York; Austin, Texas, and Amherst, Massachusetts. Others are more scattered in rural areas such as eastern Tennessee, western Virginia, or the Ozarks. They do not constitute a significant part of a local economy in monetary terms, but in many of these areas they constitute an important part of a local alternative community. In many cases people came together knowing what they did not want in their new organization: hierarchy, sexism and racism, production for profit rather than use, lack of ability to participate in decision making, and lack of ties and responsiveness to their broader community. Among the goals they shared were openness of information, more equal sharing of economic risks and rewards, and a greater integration in their lives as citizens, producers, and consumers. These alternate work organizations have been laboratories for development of processes of workers' self-management.

Finally, people who have observed or been involved in these efforts have written about them, made films about them, and generally helped make others aware of them. A growing body of knowledge from domestic and international experiences has enabled people to move more confidently in initiating and modifying these organizations.

As groups have worked to structure new work organizations to meet these ideals, they have discovered that others had shared them before. Both in their own country and abroad, sometimes prompted more by freedom and other times more by necessity, people had charted some of the waters that many recent participants thought were being discovered for the first time. A brief history of those ideas and efforts concludes this chapter.

Domestic and International Precedents

The roots of modern thinking on workers' self-management can be traced to critical reactions to industrial capitalism. Early utopian socialists such as Charles Fourier in France and Robert Owen in England advocated autonomous communities that would be organized and governed by those who worked in them. In France, a nineteenth-century thinker by the name of P. J. B. Buchez developed philosophical and theoretical justification for "workmen's associations" that would establish a "republic in the workshop" (Vanek 1975a, p. 17). Communities inspired by Robert Owen's New Lanark in Scotland and New Harmony in the United States experimented with cooperative ideals and methods. By the mid-nineteenth century England had a working example of an alternative to industrial market outlets of the day in the form of the Rochdale consumer cooperatives. Owen moved from organizing cooperative communities to encouraging the newly legal Builders' Union in England to take over the entire building industry in that country. That work anticipated strategies to be advocated by French syndicalists and later British guild socialists such as G. D. H. Cole.

Two other figures vital to the development of the idea of workers' self-management emerged in the mid–nineteenth century. The first of these was Pierre-Joseph Proudhon, who beginning in 1840 advocated a series of radical reforms that included revised property rights, workers' associations for artisans, and industrial associations for larger-scale production. His influence was felt throughout Europe and the United States in the form of "mutual aid" societies and more importantly by participants in the Paris Commune and later anarchist and syndicalist movements. His thinking was fundamental to the "workers' control" thrust developed by these movements.

The other nineteenth-century figure whose thinking played a significant role in the development of ideas of workers' self-management was, of course, Karl Marx. There is much in the writing of Marx and Friedrich Engels that inspires a vision of production by "self-managing producers" rather than through "wage slavery" under capitalism. That workers, those who produce, should control production was central to Marx's thought. For him that out-

29

come was possible only after the working class had overthrown all forms of capitalist oppression. The method by which management of production would take place was a minor concern to him compared with the fundamental struggle required for workers to win control.

More recent international forms of broad workers' participation and self-management have been many and varied. They include workers' soviets created in the early days of the October Revolution in Russia; workers' councils in Germany in 1918; the workers' control movement in northern Italy after World War I; the anarchist collectives of Spain's civil war years; some aspects of the Israeli kibbutz movement; and most notably Yugoslav self-management of the past thirty years. Other forms of worker participation outside the United States include codetermination in current German industry; development of worker-managed firms in Chile during the Allende years; expansion of the social property sector in Peru in the late 1960s; expansion of participation on communes and in factories in China during the 1960s; and the network of workers' cooperatives that has developed over the past several decades in the area of Mondragon, Spain.

In the United States, the history of workers' cooperatives dates from 1791, when striking journeymen carpenters formed a co-op in Philadelphia (Wilson 1975, p. 3). Since then hundreds of others have been formed (Jones, forthcoming). Some have existed as clusters of co-ops grouped in various industries and regions of the country. An example is the cluster of cooperage co-ops developed by skilled barrel makers in the Minneapolis area before the turn of the century (Jones 1979). Others have had a common initiator, such as those formed by the Knights of Labor in the 1880s (ibid.). More recently, clusters formed in the West. They include cooperative shingle mills created in the Northwest at the time of the First World War, plywood cooperatives formed in that same region and operating today (see Chapter 4), refuse collection co-ops currently operating in the San Francisco area (Perry 1978), and most recently the forest workers' cooperatives (see Chapter 3). These clusters have been augmented by other more scattered examples of worker-initiated and -controlled firms, including the recent wave of co-ops formed in this country.

The variety of philosophical roots and practical experiences cited here are evidence that many people in many lands have pursued workers' self-management. These people share a belief that working people should organize and control the work that they do. Lessons on how that might be done are distilled in the next chapter.

CHAPTER 2

Defining and Facilitating Conditions

Formulas for the success of traditional capitalist firms are well known; they are taught in business curricula at many educational levels and are disseminated by branches of government such as the Small Business Administration of the U.S. Department of Commerce. They are the subject of much of the theoretical investigation and empirical research of the country's economists, not to mention the continual search for better ways of doing business within firms themselves. Formulas for successful worker-controlled and self-managed firms are, by comparison, in their infancy. Only in the last decade has research begun to shed light on how these firms might be structured for survival in a less than supportive environment.

This chapter presents research findings that bear directly on the operation of these firms. The findings are organized in a framework of defining and facilitating conditions for workers' self-management, a management process that can be common to both workers' co-ops and worker-controlled firms. The conditions have in many cases been developed in response to past structural deficiencies of these organizations, but they are written as positive statements that can serve as criteria by which attempts to create self-managing organizations may be evaluated. Based on the research findings cited below, workers' cooperatives and worker-controlled firms that tend to fulfill these conditions can be assumed to have a greater likelihood of survival than those that do not.

No attempt has been made to develop some form of quantifiable measure of an organization's "fit" with these defining conditions. Workers' cooperatives and worker-controlled firms in the United States are so few and so diverse at this time that such a measure would be of little value. It might also tend to imply that knowledge about how to structure these organizations is complete, that these conditions are in some way both necessary and sufficient. That is not the case, and any pretension to that level of understanding would be misleading. Knowledge about them has developed to the point that people attempting to establish a self-managed firm do not have to proceed only by trial and error; they can use these conditions as a guide, modifying them to suit their particular needs.

Sources

Attempts to create self-managed firms here and abroad have provided fertile territory for recent research on conditions that lead to their successful creation, and those that seem to lead to failure. These self-managed firms vary from the worker-managed firm in Yugoslavia to the neighborhood alternate business in the United States. Broadly shared objectives of these organizations are stable and sufficient income to members, internal control of the organization by those who work in it, and some form of democratic decision-making process.

The framework of analysis used in this study is based on surveys of evidence from historical cases and on the theoretical and empirical research of three prominent students and writers on workers' self-management and workplace democratization. Jaroslav Vanek, Paul Bernstein, and Branko Horvat each have sought to understand the factors that contribute significantly to the successful operation and survival of these firms. They have summarized the findings of their own and other researchers' work and presented them as necessary conditions for workplace democratization and self-management (Vanek 1975a, pp. 33–36; Bernstein 1980; Horvat 1976a, 1976c, pp. 179–188). This study is based on a synthesis of those conditions. Both the original conditions and the way in which they were combined are explained in Appendix 1. The synthesis of conditions serves as both a detailed description of self-management, and as a framework of analysis for current U.S. workers' co-ops and worker-controlled firms.

The three authors have also formulated macro or society-wide conditions for successful self-management, but these conditions are not considered in this chapter. Instead, the chapter focuses on how workers' control of their productive endeavors may be achieved within the current social and economic environment of this country. Many aspects of that environment are serious impediments to achievement of workers' control. To set aside these broader social and institutional conditions is not to argue that they are unimportant, but simply to place manageable limits on the empirical portion of this study. The third part of this book will investigate the relationship between the firm and its macro environment.

The Conditions

The ten conditions that define and facilitate the existence of workers' self-management are presented in the following chart. A summary of the theoretical rationale and empirical evidence that support each condition is presented below. Their use as an analytic framework is explained at the end of this chapter. The conditions vary in character, and they are grouped into categories. The first condition is treated alone, as it is both fundamental and multidimensional in character. Following Condition 1 is a group of conditions that deals with economic and financial characteristics of the self-managed firm in an environment like that of the United States today. The next group has to do with the firm's democratic management structure. The last pair of conditions deals with the survival and development of this kind of firm in an unsupportive environment.

CONDITION 1

This most vital of conditions encompasses issues of the rights of producers to be self-governing, internal versus external control of the firm, and how the firm is to be controlled. It has philosophical, political, economic, and social dimensions.

Condition 1 places the control of productive organizations squarely and fully in the hands of those who work in them. It is clearly a normative condition, emphasizing control of the firm by *workers* rather than by *capital owners*. The United States is a country where the dominant mode of production is private enterprise. Its citizens are taught explicitly and implicitly that private capital owners have the right to control productive enterprise and that equity capital

Defining and facilitating conditions for workers' self-management

Condition 1   Control and management of the enterprise is the right of all people who work in it, and this right is based on their work role, not on any requirement of capital ownership. Management is based on direct or both direct and representative democracy and equality of voting power among all who work in the enterprise.

Condition 2   Income earned by the enterprise, after payment of all costs and taxes, belongs to those who work in it. Decisions concerning its distribution among members, including social valuation of individual members' contributions to the organization, individual needs, and the division between collective and individual forms of income, rest with the members of the organization.

Condition 3   Funding of capital assets for the enterprise can be obtained from a number of potential sources: members' loans, other debt financing, or some source of social or national funding. Members should retain individual claim on their contributions of capital, and collective funding should result only from some part of retained surplus.

Condition 4   Private or institutional sources of finance capital do not command any right of control, but capital is entitled to a scarcity-reflecting remuneration in the form of interest.

Condition 5   To encourage growth and development of self-managed firms, rents to capital (and land) should be reinvested in new capital assets within the firm or in a fund for capitalization of new self-managed firms. As a general rule, rents accruing to members who have supplied funds to the firm should be distributed at the time of the members' departure or retirement from the firm.

Condition 6   All information concerning the firm must be available to all its members, and managerial and task skills must be shared and disseminated as fully as possible.

Condition 7   Members of the firm assure each other individual rights corresponding to basic political liberties.

Condition 8   An internally representative and independent judiciary acts to settle disputes over infractions of rules, safeguard basic rights, and protect the bylaws of the organization.

Condition 9   A democratic and participatory consciousness is essential to the firm, and educational efforts to develop the philosophy and practice of self-management are important in developing and maintaining this set of values and attitudes.

Condition 10   Support organizations that can serve as advocates, technical assistance providers, and funding conduits for self-managed firms are vital to their long-term development.

NOTE: see Appendix 1 for sources.

suppliers have the determining voice in how the firm is run. That notion is equally normative.

Capital's control over enterprise has a long history. It is closely linked to legal arrangements over rights of property ownership in many Western societies (Tigar and Levy 1978) and to the long-standing belief that benefits accrue to a society when each of its members seeks individual gain (Smith 1937). The belief that capital should control enterprise is more than familiar to citizens of Western capitalist societies; it is with us daily in our legal and commercial codes, the teaching of our schools and textbooks, and most of our work. In this society it is easy to forget that "not by logic, but by history, owners of capital have become owners of the enterprise" (Lindblom 1977, p. 105).

Condition 1 argues that the people who are most involved in producing goods and services should have control over that production. People are the active agent in production. Capital is inert.[1] Capitalist society encourages and protects private capital ownership, and it also provides the framework within which those who own capital can hire and fire those who work with it. Condition 1 does not require the abolition of private ownership of capital, but it does call for altering the rights that go with ownership. Rather than capital owners hiring workers, this condition argues that workers hire capital, regardless of whether it is privately or socially owned.

Workers' control of production can lead to greater community control over it. Workers constitute a community in their productive work, which in turn is part of the community they live in. The two communities are likely to have many common interests. The same cannot be said for the relationship between a community where a firm is located and capital owners, who may have no living connection with that community. Of course, workers who control a firm in their community and others who live in that community may have conflicting as well as common interests. Direct communication between community constituencies and the working community provides opportunities for conflict resolution and for development of more complete linkages between people's lives as producers, consumers, and citizens.

The second issue addressed by this condition is *how* the self-managed firm is to be controlled, directed, and managed. The condition calls for a democratic process, with equality of voting power among participants. Participants include all who work in the organization, from the newest hired or least skilled to those with greatest longevity or highest levels of skill and knowledge. An organizational objective is equal opportunity for all members to participate democratically in directing the affairs of the organization.

Hierarchy in an organization is necessary primarily for purposes

1. See note 1 of Appendix 2 on use of the word *capital*.

of coordinating its functions around externally derived and imposed goals. Given internal definition of goals, coordination can be accomplished by cooperation among the actual producers. The process for this coordination that can best assure that a rigid new internal hierarchy of control does not develop is broadly participatory democracy. Most vital to the worker-controlled firm are forms of direct democracy, not the more common "competition among leaders (elites) for the votes of the people at periodic, free elections" of representative democracy (Pateman 1970, p. 14). Rather than simply choosing who will make decisions for the firm, the members of the broadly participatory firm are actively involved in its day-to-day operation and in determining its very method of operation. This is not to say that every worker must be involved in every decision, but every facet of the firm's operation should be open to the informed participation of all members.

Participatory democracy as a practical method of decision making counts all members of the firm as participants in its process. It requires the reorganization of large and complex organizations into subunits and work-team units in which communication can take place, with representative democratic bodies to coordinate the activities of these units, set policy, and make long-term decisions for the organization as a whole (Vanek 1976, ch. 5). Work-team units, in which face-to-face discussion and consensual decision making can take place, might number twenty-five to thirty participants. Research suggests that the next larger unit, in which members of the organization can still share a common sense of purpose, be made up of 300 to 500 members (Horvat 1976b). If a firm consists of more members than that, decentralization into subunits and work-team units of approximately these sizes would enable direct democratic practice to continue, augmented by representative forms.

What benefits could be claimed for a society that produced by means of democratically controlled firms? The same democratic skills that workers developed at all levels of their work institutions would also apply in their roles as citizens. Adults spend approximately half of most days working in institutions that are fundamentally undemocratic. A deep tension exists between private, hierarchical control of production and the supposedly democratic nature of society. Broadly participatory firms offer an environment where "maximum input (participation) is required and where output includes not just policies (decisions) but also the development of the social and political capacities of each individual, so there is 'feedback' from output to input" (Pateman 1970, p. 43). A democratically controlled firm contributes to the development of democratic society, rather than potentially eroding democratic consciousness and practice. The important role for direct, participatory democracy in reconciling citizens' private and public interests is captured in the following paragraph:

> The theory of participatory democracy is built round the central assertion that individuals and their institutions cannot be considered in isolation from one another. The existence of representative institutions at national level is not sufficient for democracy; for maximum participation by all the people at that level socialisation, or 'social training,' for democracy must take place in other spheres in order that the necessary individual attitudes and psychological qualities can be developed. This development takes place through the process of participation itself. The major function of participation in the theory of participatory democracy is therefore an educative one, educative in the very widest sense, including both the psychological aspect and the gaining of practice in democratic skills and procedures.... Participation develops and fosters the very qualities necessary for it; the more individuals participate, the better able they become to do so. [Pateman 1970, pp. 42–43]

The workplace, that "other sphere" where broad participation has historically been discouraged, can provide the arena for this human development.

Theories of democracy have fueled debates in political science for several decades. Arguments for participatory democracy as a system by which society governs itself draw on the classical theories of Mill, Rousseau, Dewey, and Cole. Counterarguments, built in part on Schumpeter's *Capitalism, Socialism and Democracy* constitute much of modern mainstream political science (Pateman 1970, ch. 1). Political scientists in the United States spend much of their time arguing directly or indirectly against either the feasibility or the desirability of participatory democracy (Greenberg 1981a, p. 966n). They seem largely motivated by a concern for social stability or manageability and a fear that the goals of organizations in modern society and of participatory democracy are incompatible.

For more than a century, socialist thinking has addressed the issue of workers' self-management. In addition to rejecting the notion that those who own capital should control the firm, socialist thought directly challenges the premise that productive property should be privately owned at all. In socialist terms capital in all its forms is seen as value that has been appropriated from those who produce. The process of private accumulation by those who own capital may be more subtle than it was under slavery or feudalism, but it is an analogous process. Historically an emerging capitalist class made itself indispensable to the productive process by gaining a dominant position in organizing that production and by developing more efficient ways of producing and gaining a share of the social surplus (Marglin 1974). Part of that process involved diminishing the role of the skilled craftsperson by reducing production tasks to their simplest component parts and substituting machinery and less skilled workers for them. That development stretches from the pin factory described by Adam Smith, to scientific management of Frederick Winslow Taylor, to the fast food restaurant of today. The separation of manual and mental labor, of those who make decisions and those who carry them out, has been a part of that history.

Several currents in socialist writing address the topic of workers' self-management and of this first condition for its existence. One is identified with Antonio Gramsci, the Italian theorist whose work from earlier in this century has gained new attention in the past decade. Gramsci focused on overcoming capitalism in advanced industrial countries through struggles at the point of production (Gramsci 1971, 1977; Anderson 1976; Fiori 1970). He envisioned the development not only of factory councils to run production but of parallel neighborhood councils to further expand a class-conscious process of self-governance. Gramsci viewed both as crucial steps toward socialization of workers' lives and as vital to the creation of a working-class counterhegemony to the dominant institutions and processes of capitalist society. Gramsci's factory councils were a part, then, of a strategy for the larger transformation of society. They were not solely an end in themselves (Greenberg 1981b, p. 30n).

More recent Marxist theorists also envision a role for self-managing forms of production. Notable among them is analysis based on Marxist (not mainstream sociological) notions of alienation and self-management of production as an important component in "progressive disalienation," or overcoming estrangement from the products and processes of work and from other workers in a society divided among and within classes (Mandel 1971, ch. 11). Again, the move to self-management at the level of the firm is only a part of a more thorough and integrated theory of social transformation. In addition, socialist writing on workers' control of the workplace can be as critical of centralized or Soviet-style socialism as it is of production controlled by capital. Whether hierarchical external control serves the interests of private capital accumulation or a state-controlled accumulation process, it is antithetical to the development of workers' self-management.

Numerous Yugoslav thinkers have created theoretical premises for workers' self-management over the past three decades (Horvat et al. 1975). These are based on a reading of Marx that emphasizes constructing a socialist society in which "self-government of the producers" could be realized. Elaboration of that theory has coincided with a lengthy experiment with market socialism and what may be described today as a decentralized, self-governing form of socialism. Development of the Yugoslav self-managed firm has provided further inspiration for theorists from around the world, and those firms serve as a focal point of ongoing empirical research.

In addition to this socialist thought, elements of social democratic thinking have stressed the importance of forms of worker participation, if not control. Eduard Bernstein and other German social democrats were instrumental in this development. England's Fabian Socialists, reflecting especially the influence of R. H. Tawney, envisioned an evolutionary road to "economic democracy," in which capitalism would eventually give way to public ownership and management by "professionalized" workers (Martin 1982). Social democratic regimes today generally advocate forms of worker representation, most typically on tripartite national councils with representatives of capital and government. It is a matter of debate whether that representation imparts to workers any direct control over production or simply a very distant voice in an institutionalized national governance process.

Discussion of the rights of workers to control their enterprise typically leads to questions concerning the ability of a self-managing firm to produce efficiently. Mainstream economists have contested the matter for many years. Alfred Marshall argued that gains could be realized when workers served on boards, but he shared reservations with other economists of his day concerning the efficiency of any more direct forms of democratic management (Jones

1974, pp. 7–14). In work by Ward (1958) and Domar (1966), the same neoclassical economics that is used to demonstrate the allocational efficiency of the capitalist firm was used to set the stage for a major development in the theory of a labor-managed firm. The labor-managed firm is an autonomous unit of production that is fully controlled and managed by its workers. Extending the work of Ward and Domar, Vanek (1970) demonstrated that the economic efficiency of the labor-managed firm was at least the theoretical equivalent of its capitalist counterpart. Vanek used an objective function of net revenue (value added) per worker for the labor-managed firm and demonstrated that it can fulfill the same conditions of optimal resource allocation that made the capitalist firm so appealing to mainstream economists. The economic theory of the labor-managed firm is outlined in Appendix 2 at the end of the book, and a note on the relevance of neoclassical analysis to non-capitalist firms is included there as well. A less detailed summary of the theory follows.

For simplicity, the labor-managed firm is assumed to be guided by the objective of maximizing income per worker. A broader array of objectives can also be assumed (Steinherr 1978, pp. 132–133; Stephen 1982a, pp. 21–24; Vanek 1982). The firm is modeled through use of a production function that specifies a mix of factor inputs and the resulting output. Illustrating the most basic objective for the labor-managed firm, it maximizes income in the following way:

$$\text{maximum income per worker} = \frac{\text{gross income} - \text{all costs including capital costs}}{\text{total number of workers}}.$$

This stands in contrast to profit maximization in the capitalist firm, where the objective of capital owners is assumed to be:

maximum profit =
gross income − all costs, including labor costs and capital costs.

In the case of the labor-managed firm there is no profit, only income to be divided among members. Without employees the labor-managed firm does not have a wage bill, and labor costs are not counted among the expenses to be subtracted from profit, as they are in the capitalist firm. This very simple explanation assumes that all members get an equal share of income. Distributional questions will be addressed under Condition 2 below. The neoclassical economics of the capitalist enterprise assumes that labor is a factor of production to be purchased from the labor market. By contrast, the labor-managed firm does not hire labor. It is a collective of workers that hires capital and necessary materials.

Vanek demonstrated that the labor-managed firm tends to reach normal operating equilibrium at a smaller size than its capitalist counterpart would under similar conditions. In the ideal world of the competitive model, that is a positive attribute. When tested under general equilibrium conditions approximating an economy made up of labor-managed firms, the model reaches conditions of Pareto optimality in which nobody in the economy can be made better off without making someone else worse off. By the test, then, of neoclassical or capitalist economics, an "ideal" labor-managed economy would operate as efficiently as an "ideal" capitalist economy. That finding refuted arguments against the labor-managed firm which had been made on the grounds of pure economic efficiency.

Specific characteristics important to a theoretical understanding of the labor-managed firm compared to the capitalist firm have been debated over the past decade. A summary of those debates can be found in Stephen (1982a). Some have contested the potential efficiency of the labor-managed firm on theoretical grounds. One argument offered for greater potential efficiency of the capitalist firm contends that its hierarchy serves to reduce its cost of transmitting internal information as well as the costs involved in achieving worker compliance with the organization's goals (Alchian and Demsetz 1972). According to another argument, workers actually desire discipline exercised on behalf of capital because it prevents some workers from shirking, which can diminish the capitalist firm's product and ultimately the workers' wages (Stiglitz 1975). A third argument says that because workers' preferences are not identical, the labor-managed firm will have monitoring and control problems that will push costs of production above those for a conventional firm in the same industry (Jensen and Meckling 1979).

Countering these negative theoretical arguments is a growing body of empirical literature that is generally supportive of claims for the economic efficiency of the labor-managed firm. Much of this literature focuses on productivity, frequently finding it to be positively correlated with increasing levels of participation (Cable and Fitzroy 1980a, 1980b; Jones and Backus 1977). Studies that encompass a range of issues broader than the purely economic also tend to support claims for the efficiency of labor-managed and worker-controlled firms (Espinosa and Zimbalist 1978; Blumberg 1968). In addition, studies that compare the economic performance of groups of traditionally and worker-controlled firms point to the stronger performance of the latter (Espinosa and Zimbalist 1978; Melman 1970; Bradley and Gelb 1982).

Comparison of performance between conventional and labor-managed firms is difficult, and the measurement of productivity itself is no easy matter (Levin 1982). Theoretical arguments have frequently been based on different specific models of firms, encompassing various levels and forms of participation, sharing of income, and rights for workers. On balance, theoretical debates have done little to shake the basic case for the efficiency of the labor-managed firm, and empirical findings have tended to support that case.

Recent work in organizational theory bears directly on issues raised in Condition 1. Traditional large organizations of production exhibit bureaucratic behavior that is similar to that of military, governmental, educational, and religious organizations in society. The large enterprise is a tool of those who control it, even when control operates through protocol, rules, impersonality of social relations, individual material incentives, or other Weberian characteristics. Recently developed theory of collectivist democracy provides insight into a firm that is controlled in a more egalitarian manner by those who work in it. In this situation workers are able to develop organizations based on substantive or value rationality, rather than bureaucratic formal rationality (Rothschild-Whitt 1979). Whereas the formal logic of a purely economic objective could be translated into a bureaucratic organization by a community of workers, economic gain is unlikely to be the sole objective valued by such a community. Human growth and development, pleasant relations with fellow workers, and leisure time are other objectives the working community may have. Self-management allows the organization to pull away from Weberian rational-bureaucratic behavior and to develop toward one in which value-rational social action shapes the organization through belief in a value for its own

43

sake. Defining collectivist democracy based on substantive rationality as a polar opposite to monocratic, formal bureaucracy, and using recent examples of small work collectives as empirical examples of collectivist democracy, recent research has begun to identify the contours of organizations shaped by a strong commitment to participative democracy (Rothschild-Whitt 1976, 1979).

Fully participative organizational democracy is an ideal, and obstacles to its attainment include not only organizational size, but social values that bestow privilege or disproportionate amounts of esteem on specific groups (men or the well educated, for example) within the organization. Those problems can be remedied in the firm only through a sharing of skills and knowledge and a broad-based commitment to a democratic ideal. Several of the conditions discussed below are specifically aimed at counteracting these potential barriers and improving chances of maximally democratic structure and process. First, however, conditions having to do with income distribution, capital structure, and reinvestment policies for the self-managed firm are explained.

CONDITIONS 2 THROUGH 5

Theoretical and empirical justification for Condition 2 follows from arguments for Condition 1. Production is organized and managed by those in the firm who produce, and the net income of the productive organization, after any socially determined taxes, belongs to them alone. Labor hires capital (the fruit of past labor) with which to produce. Capital supplied to the firm is entitled to a scarcity-reflecting rent, a payment for its use, which can vary with risk.[2] But capital does not perform any other function, and it has no claim on the earnings of the enterprise. Entrepreneurship is a collective function undertaken by those who will produce, not

2. Capital in its many forms (plant and equipment, finance capital, etc.) is recognized as scarce. Whether it is privately or publically owned, it is paid a rent which reflects that scarcity, and which can vary with the risk that accompanies business undertakings. Given the neoclassical heart of this economic analysis, a price for the use of capital allows calculation of optimal allocational outcomes in the economy. The term *scarcity-reflecting rent* is used in place of the more common term *interest* because the latter carries with it the notion of income flowing to a nonproductive group of rentiers in society. The term *scarcity-reflecting rent* serves as a reminder that even publicly or socially owned capital is scarce, that it is in society's interest to allocate it to users well, and that that can be done by placing a price (rent) on its use even if the rent accrues to public coffers.

a task to be separated from production and undertaken by those who own capital in any of its forms. *The economic category of profit does not exist in the labor-managed firm,* as it does in the capitalist firm where wages are a cost to be subtracted from gross income before a residual profit is determined. The fundamental difference in the two organizations of production is, of course, that a market wage for the sale of labor is not set in the case of labor-managed production. Labor is not purchased by this firm. Income shared among all producers is net income generated by the firm: the total of value added by human labor applied to the means of production, less payment of all costs of production and any reserves for depreciation of plant and equipment.

This model has thus far assumed that income is distributed to members of the self-managed firm, without specifying how that distribution will be determined. The rest of Condition 2 makes clear that decisions on distribution are the province of the organization's members, and they are accomplished through the organization's democratic decision-making process. The range of options facing members is wide: present versus future consumption, individual versus collective forms of consumption, distribution according to need or ability, whether to take into account existing market wage rates that may exist outside the firm, and others. Social valuations and interpersonal welfare comparisons do enter into this process. It requires time, effort, and debate on the part of the organization, but once a basic formula is adopted, subsequent adjustments can be relatively simple. It is also a process that can help overcome the divisive impact that market wage rates can have on a work organization. Overall determinants of income for the group are tied, in the end, to the performance of the firm.

There is evidence that the methods of distribution chosen by worker-controlled or self-managed firms are more egalitarian than distribution according to market precepts. The Mondragon group of workers' cooperatives in the Basque Provinces of Spain has generally followed a principle of three-to-one maximum differential between highest and lowest levels of before-tax income in a firm. Supplemental rules have at times expanded the differential to 4.5 to 1. In a sample of 2,500 members of those firms, the ratios of the top one, five, and ten percent of income earners relative to median income levels have been found to be, respectively, 2.1, 1.8, and 1.6 (Thomas 1982, p. 149). Moreover, the Mondragon group has overcome much of the interindustry earnings differentials normally found in a market economy. Compensation in organizations as diverse as factories, schools, and banks is now linked to a common standard, diminishing incentives to move among these cooperative activities for monetary reasons (ibid., p. 148).

Decisions concerning income distribution in the United States take place in smaller firms than those of the Mondragon group, but they reflect the same emphasis on egalitarianism. On an hourly basis, officers and office workers of the Hoedads forest workers' co-op earn a rate equal to the average hourly income of members working in the field (see Chapter 3; Gunn forthcoming). Owner-members in the plywood co-ops are paid the same amount per hour, and most of those co-ops seek to equalize the number of hours each member works in order to equalize annual income (see Chapter 4; Berman 1982a, b; Gunn 1980a). Forms of collective consumption and special welfare considerations abound in U.S. work collectives. For example, the Starflower food distribution co-op in Eugene, Oregon, has utilized monthly allowances for dependents, work clothing, and even bicycle maintenance if workers commute to work by that means, in addition to a basic wage differential of less than two to one.

Conditions 3 and 4 are closely related and reinforce each other. They clarify the separation of control of the firm from capital ownership so that the source of capital funding is not, theoretically, a significant issue for the firm. The firm can be thought of, in the simplest sense, as one that is fully debt financed by bonds or debentures whose holders have no internal voice in the firm or as one funded through fixed rate preferred stock that also carries no voting power.

The second part of Condition 3 is very significant. Development of a theory of finance for the labor-managed firm followed from the economic model outlined in this chapter (also included in Appendix 2 at the end of the book). This theory of finance can shed light on the reasons for the historical tendency for labor-managed firms to undercapitalize, and to exhibit small size relative to cost minimizing scales of production for their industries. One of the most prominent of those reasons has been the attempt to create workers' cooperatives and self-managed firms in market economies using uncompensated and nonrefundable start-up capital. It is logical that those assets would be provided by members, but such use of members' assets can cause problems. First, members acting as rational managers of their scarce liquid assets in an environment where other income-producing uses for those assets are available will invest only if they stand to gain sufficient return on the investment relative to other possible investment options. If invested capital cannot be recouped, those returns can consist only of increased income generated from members' greater productivity using new equipment that their invested capital has enabled the firm to acquire. Young workers, or those who plan to stay with the firm for an extended period of time, may find this a suitable incentive for investment. But those who plan either to leave the firm or to retire in the near future probably will not find sufficient incentive in this scheme to prompt their investment. If those who are reluctant to invest outnumber those who favor new capital investment, this democratic organization will not undertake new capital investment. If those favoring investment commit nonrecoverable funds and others are allowed not to make that commitment, the end result has historically been unequal conditions of membership. In an extreme case, if a capital replacement (depreciation) fund were jeopardized by internal conflict over financing, member incomes would tend to decline because plant and equipment would be consumed through normal use and depreciation. In an attempt to counter that tendency, members could intentionally diminish their numbers, perhaps simply by not replacing departing members, in an effort to maintain a constant capital-labor ratio with diminishing fixed assets. The historical result has been that both capital value and membership diminish as what have been called "self-extinction forces" eat away at the collectively financed firm (Vanek 1975b, p. 448). Such a situation can be avoided if members structure their firm so that any funds they invest from their own savings can be withdrawn when they depart. Members can then respond more rationally to incentives to maintain, and perhaps expand, the value of the equipment with which they work.

Uncompensated and nonrefundable financing also presents a problem if growth in membership of self-managed firms is desired. Again, income in the firm is in part tied to the amount of fixed assets that each member works with. Once the firm reaches a desired capital-labor ratio and the workers reach a desired income level, the addition of new members must be accompanied by the addition of new equipment to keep up the capital-labor ratio and

47

maintain incomes. Without new investment there are strong disincentives to growth in membership. With nonrefundable financing working against new investment, membership growth is unlikely.

The second part of Condition 4 stipulates the payment of a scarcity-reflecting rent on capital used by the firm. Payment of this rent is the only way that nonaltruistic outsiders can be induced to invest in a firm in which they can receive no share of income. It is also an incentive for members of the firm. Members whose behavior is explained by conventional investment theory will have a time preference for consumption in the present, rather than in the future. Some rate of return (interest) on unspent income (savings) compensates for that time preference. Increased annual income could result from otherwise uncompensated investment, but if that potential increase did not satisfy enough members' time preferences the result would be underinvestment in the firm (Vanek 1975, p. 449).

Co-ops that have been financed through uncompensated and nonrefundable contributions have traditionally been small and undercapitalized, and Conditions 3 and 4 can help overcome those problems. Self-managed firms operating in today's market economy may not be able to eliminate all obstacles to successful operation, but they can at least benefit from these recent theoretical insights.

Several empirical studies have supported this theoretical analysis. Research on two New Guinea copra plantations that were operated as agricultural producer cooperatives demonstrated that although productivity of both co-ops increased under cooperative management, work force membership declined after rents on land were eliminated. Rents had been used to pay off a government loan that helped the co-ops acquire their land, but those who contributed to the initial purchase of the land were uncompensated (McGregor 1977, p. 484). In six years one co-op's membership declined 15 percent, while its income per member more than doubled. At this same co-op, nonmember workers were increasingly used for unpleasant tasks, and they received less pay than members received (ibid.). The other, younger co-op, had begun to use nonmember workers as well. In addition, the older co-op turned down the opportunity to increase its landholdings at very favorable terms. Members argued successfully against foregoing current income in order to expand, even though expansion would almost certainly have meant increased revenue in the future. This case was cited as *prima facie* evidence of the underinvestment force at work (ibid., pp. 484–485).

In a more exhaustive study of British footwear industry producer cooperatives that utilized unrecoverable and uncompensated forms of finance, Jones and Backus (1977) found that the smaller of these firms did tend to operate in the inefficient, increasing returns-to-scale zone of their production functions (p. 496). They had not grown to a level of output that would minimize the unit cost of their product. Comparing their sample of cooperatives to capitalist counterparts in the same industry and over the same period, Jones and Backus found that the growth performance of the producer co-ops lagged significantly behind that of the capitalist firms (ibid., p. 499). These same collectively financed co-ops experienced declines in work force over the period of study, while the work force of capitalist firms in the sample grew slightly (ibid., p. 501). Jones and Backus also demonstrated that average capital investment for the co-ops, and their capital-labor ratios, were lower than those of capitalist firms in the industry. These figures support the tendencies toward underinvestment identified in Vanek's theory.

Support for the validity of Conditions 3 and 4 can also be found in the performance of the Mondragon group of workers' cooperatives. The first workers' co-op of the Mondragon group was begun in 1956. By 1979, they numbered seventy firms with relatively high capital-labor ratios and with a combined membership of over 15,000 workers (Thomas 1982, p. 130). Those firms were part of a larger complex consisting of a cooperative credit union and development bank, food and service co-ops, and education and training institutions. Not one of Mondragon's industrial workers' co-ops has failed. Their financial structure includes provisions for a required but recoverable capital investment and for portions of annual surpluses to be held in individual accounts for members. A loss from an accounting period can also be allocated against these accounts. Individual accounts not only earn interest, but are revalued each year to compensate for inflation in the Spanish currency. These individual accounts are not paid out to members until they retire or leave the cooperatives. Surplus generated in any year is distributed in a ratio of 10 percent to social (community) contributions, a minimum of 20 percent to collective reserves, and a maximum of 70 percent to individual accounts. This surplus distribution does allow for building collectively held reserves, but they are built from surplus, not from paid-in capital. The theory of finance for the labor-managed firm was developed after the Mondragon group was established, but before it was known in this country. Future empirical work on those co-ops should help refine both the theory and development of further conditions for effective financing of self-managed firms.

Condition 5 is more general than the previous conditions in this group. It is important when capital is in very short supply relative to the needs of the firm or sector. It also serves to alleviate some of the distributional problems that can arise from payment of rent to capital.

An agreement by members of a firm essentially to lend the rental income (interest) that each receives on funds that they have loaned to the firm as well has two benefits for the firm. First, it can cushion early capital-short years from a drain on funds through external interest payments. Second, it provides a means of increasing funds available to the firm without routinely contracting for more debt financing. Under such an agreement, members would receive rents on their paid-in capital not as cash payments, but the rents would accrue to each member's individual account as a form of savings and reinvestment.

Reinvestment of rents also helps alleviate some of the possible internal tensions and ideological dilemmas of paying rent on capital to members. Income to privately owned capital is nonlabor income. Yet it may be very important for the firm to encourage members to commit part of their personal savings to the enterprise. Wide variation in asset holdings by members, particularly in economies where significant intergenerational wealth transfer in the form of inheritance is allowed, provides a potentially difficult source of annual income inequality within the working community. But members' knowledge that rents to capital loaned by working members remain in the firm, where they benefit the entire membership, could help alleviate this source of tension. Members can be encouraged to lend their savings and the income that it generates for them to their own firm, with the knowledge that on departure from the firm they will be able to claim those accumulated funds. There can be no confusion over the amount due lenders because the value of funds to be withdrawn is clearly the principal and accrued rental income. Those funds could be repaid in lump sum or over a period of several years beginning with the members' date of departure.

Self-managed firms may be inclined to structure a retirement or pension program around an actuarially determined contribution of income over the period of a member's work. Those funds would then be paid back, again either in a lump sum or over a period of time, upon the member's retirement. One negative aspect of such a program is that it would combine risk associated with the stability of regular earnings resulting from the firm's performance with the risk associated with savings intended for retirement income. Depending on what other savings, investment, or income deferral programs a member chose, that concentration of risk could be undesirable. Participation in such a program might therefore be optional, or risk could be spread through the portfolio of an agency that invested in multiple labor-managed firms (Vanek 1977, p. 227).

Conditions 3 through 5 delineate options available for financing the self-managed firm. Both theoretical reasoning and empirical evidence argue against financing through unrecoverable and uncompensated donations by members of those firms. The conditions suggest several more appropriate options. One involves debt financing, either through funding by loans (which could be paid in from earnings) required of all of their members, through lending by only willing members, or through borrowing from outside lenders. Members or outsiders may also hold a restricted form of equity in the firm; instruments such as preferred stock or nonvoting common stock would be appropriate. Finally, members might pay in a required amount of equity when starting or joining the firm, and then retain an equity account with the firm as long as they remained a working member of it. That account would be recoverable, it would receive a scarcity rent, and, as in Mondragon, it could be adjusted up or down depending on the firm's performance. Elements of each of these financing options will be discussed further in later chapters on actual case histories.

CONDITIONS 6 THROUGH 8

Conditions 6 through 8 focus on information and skills sharing, individual rights, and settling internal disputes.

According to Condition 6, all members must have open access to information within the firm. Monopolies over information, whether at the shop floor or among those who perform staff or managerial functions, make democratic control impossible. If workers at all levels of the firm are to be actively involved in its control (Condition 1), then they must have control over the firm's information as well. To restrict information would immediately imperil the opportunity for participation by the excluded group, resulting in representative or paternalistic democracies—second best alternatives to fully participative democracy.

The need for industrial secrecy in a market economy is sometimes cited as a fundamental barrier to attainment of this condition. There is no reason to believe that information on new product development, marketing plans, and other matters of strategic importance might be better guarded by individual members of management in a traditional firm than they would by individual members of management (all members) in a self-managed firm. If there is some increased risk of leakage of information because it is known by more people, a firm may decide to accept that risk in order to preserve its democratic environment. Alternatively, in special cases members may decide to limit information on specific issues for specific periods of time. Such a plan should be temporary and agreed to by a large percentage of the membership. To allow any small group within the membership to determine what information will be withheld from the larger membership would severely limit the firm's ability to sustain and expand the practice of democratic management.

The second part of Condition 6 has to do with what members do with the information once it is theirs. It is possible that few workers within a large enterprise will have the technical knowledge to assimilate information on financial performance, investment planning, or very technical aspects of production. The challenge to the working community in control of production is to break that skills oligopoly and broadly disseminate the knowledge, and with it the confidence, to deal effectively with what has been defined as management-level information and decision making in the capitalist firm. Within the individual firm efforts to meet this challenge can take the form of manuals written by and for members; formal training programs and job rotation (*Work In America* 1973); skill sharing through pairing of the skilled with those attempting to learn the skill (Vanek 1977); breaking down stratification through use of small coordinating and learning groups similar to the "triple combination" of management, manual, and technical workers that was employed in China (Andors 1977, pp. 225–240); and other techniques. Labor unions can play a vital role in this educational process (Bernstein 1980, p. 71; Vanek 1976), as they have in providing their members with training for effective collective bargaining. Educators and practitioners interested in the development of workplace democracy have begun to develop institutions (such as the New School for Democratic Management) and materials (Wilson 1974; Brous et al. 1977; Alvarado-Greenwood et al. 1978; Brandow and McDonnell 1981) to respond to this need.

While changes are being made to diminish the separation between manual and mental work, members of self-managed firms must still keep them operating efficiently. If necessary, new members who have managerial skills and a commitment to work in a democratic environment can be recruited to the firm. Members of the working community who already possess managerial skills can be appointed to councils or boards responsible for management decisions. Outside expertise can be hired on a consulting basis. Some or all of these strategies can help until fuller internal development of managerial knowledge and skills can be attained. If workers are to control production fully, that development has to remain a high-priority goal.

Education is treated as a scarce commodity at the macro or social level. Long-run chances for successful implementation of worker-controlled production may be closely tied to changes in the way education is allocated among members of society (Bowles and Gintis 1976) and how it prepares citizens to either accept authority or empowers them to manage and control their own destinies (Freire 1972).

Conditions 7 and 8 have to do with the maintenance of democratic rights and process. Members must be assured that they will not be penalized for participation, particularly when that participation involves taking minority positions on issues (Bernstein 1980, p. 75). Freedom of speech and assembly, secret balloting, an established mechanism for petition of grievances and fair appeals in cases of discipline, and constitutional stability are fundamental elements of a bill of rights in the workplace, as they are in the broader social context (ibid., chs. 7 and 8).

Examples of the explicit recognition of these rights can be found in the U.S. plywood firms (Berman 1967), the Scott Bader Company and John Lewis Partnership in Britain (Bernstein 1980, ch. 2) and in the Yugoslav self-managed firm (Horvat 1976b). The futility of attempting to expand participation without these guarantees can be seen in many corporate participation programs, as in the case of American Cast Iron Pipe Company (Zwerdling 1974; Bernstein 1980, pp. 37–39), in which workers were afraid to say what they really thought. Their participation was therefore circumspect at best. The experience at American Cast Iron Pipe also points up the need for a judiciary that is independent of members in positions of authority. Bernstein's study, which involved cases of workers' participation within otherwise traditional firms, stresses the importance of a judiciary system that is independent from management. In firms with full workers' self-management, the judiciary must also be independent of members who hold, even temporarily, positions of administrative authority. A workers' judiciary committee with rotating membership is one way to achieve that end. An outside arbitrator or tribunal might be developed by a network of firms to provide an additional appeals process.

A judiciary committee could also be charged with one of the most fundamental tasks in sustaining democracy in the firm—safeguarding the constitution and bylaws of the firm, the embodiment of the collective will of the organization. The constitution or bylaws must be adaptable as the organization changes and develops, but at the same time it must be a stable guide to that development—a guarantee of rights, statement of principles, and source of inspiration to members of the firm. Requirement of some minimum vote greater than a simple majority of members to modify the constitution helps assure against its modification as short-term expediency or as a tyranny by a bare majority of members.

CONDITIONS 9 AND 10

Conditions 9 and 10 are concerned with the survival of self-management within the firm and survival and expansion of self-managed firms, both in a nonsupportive environment. Condition 9 stresses the need for cooperative and participatory values within the enterprise and recognizes the need for cooperative education among members to ensure a consciousness based on those values. The need for an enterprise-level development of cooperative values is particularly acute when the enterprise is part of a larger society that reinforces individualistic and competitive values (Ben Ner 1982).

A number of researchers (Freire 1972; Maslow 1954; Argyris 1964) have identified human behavioral characteristics that tend to contribute positively to participatory organizations. These qualities generally fall under the headings of self-reliance, flexibility, and activism. Other characteristics, such as servility, dependency, and rigidity, can undermine participatory process in the collective. Bernstein (1980, pp. 93–97) has assembled in some detail, and with an appropriate caveat concerning generalizations about personality traits, the characteristics that lend themselves to a participatory-democratic consciousness. He summarized these positive characteristics as resistance, which makes people less prone to manipulation, and activism, which is well suited to organizing and creating policy. These positive characteristics, which often include the ability to think critically, receptivity to the needs of others, a facility for compromise, and a sense of humor, are those the organization must seek to foster in order to sustain a democratic, cooperative process. Bernstein divided traits that do not lend themselves to participatory democracy into two categories: compliance, which makes people more prone to manipulation, and passivity and abstention, which imply lack of ability or interest in policy making and organization.

Various groups have worked to develop a decision-making process designed to strengthen behavioral characteristics that reinforce participation. They are frequently based on a belief that traditional parliamentary procedure and majority rule reinforce competitive, individualistic ways of interrelating. Respect for others' insights, a desire to explore issues in decisions rather than simply attempting to win members to a point of view, and a desire to involve all members affected by a decision in its making have led cooperatives, collectives, and social action groups to develop a variety of consensual decison-making procedures (URPE 1979). The procedures have proven effective both in getting decisions made and in encouraging individuals to participate. Feminist groups and organizations such as Movement for a New Society have helped foster this development.

Consensus decision making works best when a group has a high degree of unity, but it can also help develop and sustain that unity. In a two-step process of self-management, a group first arrives at an understanding of the principles that unite its members—principles to which all members can agree. It then works to strengthen those principles, with the understanding that they will be the bonds that hold members together through the disagreements and tensions of planning and accomplishing its objectives (URPE 1979, p. 42).

Educational concepts of Paulo Freire have been utilized to further the development of workers' self-management within Cooperativa Central, an agricultural cooperative in California (Salinas 1977). An external facilitator was invited by the co-op to help increase members' awareness of problems shared by all families in the enterprise and to further the development of cooperative solutions to those problems (ibid., p. 45). The process reinforced members' confidence in their ability to act upon their problems, to analyze those problems despite their minimal formal education, and to realize their potential for controlling and modifying administrative processes to attain their goals. The main thrust of this educational effort was to demystify problems and develop modes of thought within members which would lead to cooperative solutions to the problems of the enterprise. The methods jointly developed by members and the facilitator empowered members to analyze their goals, limitations, and potentials and to proceed from that analysis with a feasible plan of action to resolve immediate administrative problems. These methods later served the ongoing needs of the enterprise without an outside facilitator. An educational process much like that used by Salinas at Cooperativa Central has been advocated by Jaroslav Vanek. Its purpose is education in the broadest Freirian sense—the transformation of human consciousness (Vanek 1976). It is seen as a long-range and ongoing process within the democratically organized enterprise, and it involves both personal and organizational commitment to growth and change.

Recent research on attitudes of owner-members of U.S. plywood co-ops (Greenberg 1981a, 1981b, forthcoming) indicates that democracy practiced among co-op members in day-to-day work relationships may not be enough to support changes in personal values. Co-ops can be successful in providing substantial income to their members, but when income and job security are the members' sole aims, other cooperative principles, such as not exploiting nonmember workers, may be forgotten. Evidence points to the need for continual adherence to and reinforcement of cooperative values, particularly when the environment surrounding the enterprise is not supportive of those values. Paths to reinforcement might include not only the democratic practice of work within the enterprise, but a commitment on the part of the enterprise to expand its democratic environment and process (Rothschild-Whitt 1979) and to develop cooperative and democratic practice in institutions that members are involved in outside their work (Pateman 1970; Bettleheim 1969; Vanek 1976).

Condition 10, the last in this synthesis, refers to the need for development of support organizations to serve as advocates of self-managed firms, provide technical assistance to them, and help generate and broker financial resources for them. Support organizations perform a combination of the functions of what in a capitalist economy would be financial brokerage houses, chambers of commerce, consulting firms, business schools, and economic development authorities, to name just a few.

Any one support organization may not perform all of these functions. Advocacy and general public education concerning workers' self-management are two functions that could easily be combined in one agency. Publication of technical manuals and guides for developing self-managing organizations might be well combined with providing technical assistance to firms or assisting groups interested in launching self-managed firms. Agencies that could accumulate and administer both equity and debt funds for self-managed firms would free them from constraints imposed on them by less than sympathetic traditional brokers of capital. This latter group in particular would understand the special financial characteristics of the firms that they would help to finance. Being established to serve worker-controlled firms, they would have immense strategic importance in extending workers' control to the process of capital accumulation; they could help provide a vital economic base for additional worker-controlled firms. That process could develop a capital stock that would be administered by and for workers (Fusfeld 1979). Attention has been drawn recently to the enormous amount of workers' capital held in union pension funds and the fact that it is frequently invested in firms that are either not unionized or firms that are eliminating their union work force as they move overseas (Rifkin and Barber 1978). The financial arm of support organizations could serve as risk-diversifying brokers for investing union pension funds in enterprises controlled by workers.

The early argument for a support organization took the form of theoretical rationale based on the difficulties historically faced by self-managed firms in inhospitable environments (Vanek 1970, ch. 15). In more recent years researchers have become aware of a remarkable example of such an organization in the Mondragon group and its *Caja Laboral Popular* (CLP) or, literally, "bank of the people's labor." The CLP is a combination of savings institution (as a savings cooperative the CLP has more than 80 credit-union-style branches throughout the four provinces where the Mondragon co-ops operate); lending institution for financing the co-ops; and management consulting service for cooperative member firms.

As Mondragon's financial support organization, the CLP is structured as a second-degree cooperative, meaning that it has two classes of members: individuals who work in it and cooperatives associated with it (Thomas 1982, p. 132). Its control rests with a general assembly made up of representatives of these two classes of members. A contract of association, entered into by the CLP and member co-ops, serves as both a document of understanding and a binding legal contract spelling out the terms of that association. The CLP offers funding and managerial expertise to its member co-ops. Complemented by vital relationships between forms of education and work in the Mondragon group (Thomas and Logan 1982, chs. 2 and 3), it provides a powerful base of support for those co-ops.[3]

Several recently created organizations in the United States demonstrate some of the characteristics of support organizations. One is the Northwest Forest Workers' Association (NWFWA), created by the forest workers' co-ops to serve their needs. It is described in Chapter 3. Two others are the National Consumer Cooperative

---

3. Organizations that serve some support organization functions in other countries include: in Britain, the Industrial Common Ownership Movement (ICOM) (Pateman 1970, pp. 79–88; Oakeshott 1978, pp. 74–107); in France, Sociétés Coopératives Ouvrières de Production (SCOP) (Oakeshott 1978, pp. 121–144); in Israel, the three federations of kibbutzim (Barkai 1977; Melman 1970); and in Italy, three federations of producer cooperatives (Jones and Zevi unpublished, Zevi 1982).

Bank with its main offices in Washington, D.C., and the Industrial Cooperative Association based in Massachusetts.[4]

The National Consumer Cooperative Bank (NCCB or Co-op Bank) is the result of legislative and lobbying efforts throughout the 1970s. A national financial and service organization for cooperatives has for some time been the objective of a diverse coalition of consumer, labor, and cooperative groups. Legislation chartering the Co-op Bank was passed in 1978, and the bank opened its doors in 1980. Initial funding, provided by the federal government, was to be paid back as the bank gradually became owned by the co-ops that it served. It was designed to be a self-supporting public corporation consisting of three main parts: (1) a bank fund to provide loans at market interest rates to eligible co-ops; (2) a self-help fund to provide lower-cost loans to new, low-income, or troubled co-ops; and (3) an office of technical assistance, which was intended as an all-purpose training and consulting arm. Although it was directed at consumer and housing co-ops, ten percent of its funding and assistance was targeted to "producer cooperatives."

The Reagan administration nearly killed the bank in 1981. The White House Office of Management and Budget asked Congress to terminate the bank by rescinding its funding, a request that automatically froze its funding for 45 days. Subsequent maneuvering and appeals to Congress saved funding for much of the bank's activities. Its gradual transfer to a private organization was to have taken thirty years, but in order to save the bank from a hostile administration, the transfer was accomplished in a matter of months. It occurred at the end of 1981, and the Co-op Bank became what is known in Washington jargon as a "mixed ownership government instrumentality," with the U.S. Treasury holding much of its stock in the form of notes. Final legislation did not

---

4. Two other U.S. organizations deserve mention. The Federation for Economic Democracy was formed in the mid-1970s as a support organization for workers' self-management. It did not survive as an organization partly because its members could not agree on which functions it would perform with its very limited resources and partly because it never firmly established its own democratic internal process. The other organization was People for Self-Management, formed at the First International Conference on Self-Management in 1974. It has evolved into the Association for Workplace Democracy, an organization that supports all forms of participation. Its membership is largely academic and professional, and it concentrates on organizing conferences and marketing a newsletter and publications. It thus performs some of the educational functions of a support organization.

fund the bank's self-help fund or the technical assistance branch. A self-help fund is being created as a wholly controlled subsidiary of the Co-op Bank and is being structured so that it can receive tax-deductible private funding. The technical assistance branch has been eliminated.

The Co-op Bank's early years of operation have been discouraging for advocates of workers' co-ops and self-management, and many in the co-op movement in general (Ridgeway 1981a, 1981b, 1982). The Bank's internal operations have been characterized as chaotic, and the management style of its appointed administrators top down, secretive, and far from a model of cooperative management (Kreitner 1982). Staff members at the bank who tried to unionize have reportedly been threatened with loss of their jobs (Nazario 1982), an ironic outcome from an organization created with heavy labor union lobbying support. The technical assistance group may have been "sacrificed" because it was politically the most active in the bank. In short, the bank thus far has not shown itself to be the progressive organization that many of its supporters hoped, and assumed, it would be.

There are other problems in attempting to redirect the Co-op Bank's mission. In theory, it was to act, in part at least, as a development bank. The Co-op Bank has scrapped much of its commitment to helping co-ops develop and acts much like a commercial bank. Part of that change was thrust upon it in its quick transfer to private operation, but the change also seems to suit most of the bank's administrators and the staff they have assembled. This researcher's encounters with several bank lending officers have left the impression that they know little or nothing about workers' co-ops.

The Co-op Bank was capitalized at approximately $200 million for its primary lending function. Ten percent of that, an impressive $20 million, is supposedly available for "producer cooperatives." If that term is interpreted to mean workers' co-ops, those funds could help create and strengthen self-managing work in hundreds of worker-controlled organizations. If the word "producer" is interpreted to mean agricultural producers' processing and marketing co-ops, those funds could quickly be eaten up in loans to traditionally run corporate style co-ops such as Land O' Lakes, Ocean Spray, and Sunkist. The question of which interpretation to use has not been settled.

The Industrial Cooperative Association (ICA) had a far less grandiose beginning. Formed by Boston area researchers and activists who had been members of the Boston chapter of the Federation for Economic Democracy, ICA was organized in the late 1970s to provide technical assistance to industrial cooperatives. The term *industrial cooperative* was chosen to avoid the ambiguity of the *producers' co-op* label and the political overtones of the term *workers' co-op*. Industrial co-ops were defined as democratically controlled and worker-owned organizations of production. ICA now consists of a staff of approximately a dozen skilled people who work together in a more cooperative internal process than that exhibited at NCCB. They have gained valuable experience through providing assistance to a number of groups—some successful, some not so—attempting to create industrial cooperatives. They initiated a revolving loan fund for those firms in 1983. ICA is maturing into an effective organization and one that is probably the best known technical assistance group for democratically structured businesses in the country. It has concentrated its work on the Boston area and New England economy, but because of the paucity of other organizations that can perform the same role in the United States, it has been called upon for work throughout the country.

ICA offers a model for the kind of technical assistance group that could perform vital services for self-managed firms on a regional basis in the United States. It faces the constant battle, as so many similar organizations do, of gaining funding to keep its staff together and meet expenses. One of the advantages of the technical assistance branch that was to be part of the Co-op Bank was that a cadre of staff members there would have been able to carry on technical assistance without devoting large amounts of time to raising operating funds from foundations. The prospect of regionally based teams of technical assistance providers has appeal in that each could develop more thorough knowledge of area conditions, resources, and firms. Gaining resources for groups of that kind is a matter in part of political struggle and in part of having enough successful self-managed firms to financially support and provide experienced people for these organizations. These strategies and both the Co-op Bank and ICA will be discussed in this light in Chapter 6.

Making Use of the Conditions

Vanek's, Bernstein's, and Horvat's separate sets of principles have been incorporated into the ten conditions just presented with the objective of summarizing current knowledge on the successful operation of workers' self-management. The fragmented and limited nature of experience to date with this form of organization clearly means that these conditions cannot be taken as sufficient, and all three authors were careful to make this clear in their separate presentations. These are not rigid rules that, if followed, will guarantee success. But they can serve as guidelines for people studying and attempting to implement workers' self-management.

This set of conditions will serve here as an analytical framework in the evaluation of cases of full or partial workers' control and self-management that follows. Given the diverse nature of self-managed firms in the United States, this framework will facilitate identification of the important features of each case and comparison of these features across cases. Since this framework is based on conditions thought to be necessary for successful implementation of workers' self-management at the level of the firm, it should prove helpful in identifying areas of opportunity for problem solving or constructive change in the cases under evaluation.

In evaluating cases we can also focus on the conditions themselves. These conditions are critically evaluated after the case discussion that follows, and they can be modified or refined in the light of practitioners' ongoing experiences. Recognition of the interrelationships between actual practice, guidelines for successful practice, and theory that contributes to these guidelines is fundamental to this study.

The next three chapters present case studies of contemporary firms, and groups of firms, in the United States. The first is a case study of the forest workers' cooperatives, which are found to meet most of the conditions of workers' self-management. Next the plywood co-ops are studied. Although they constitute the longest lived and industrially most important cluster of workers' co-ops operating in this country, they fall short of meeting several important conditions for self-management. The last of these three chapters draws together two cases from different industries, but with common origins. Both formerly existed as conventional firms, and both are now largely worker controlled because of local labor union initiatives. One has adopted a cooperative structure, and the other has not. Important issues raised in the course of case evaluations will be highlighted and discussed separately in each of these chapters.

PART II

CASES AND ISSUES

CHAPTER 3

The Forest Workers' Cooperatives

The late 1960s and 1970s brought the formation of a new wave of workers' cooperatives and work collectives in the United States. Although these firms were created in disparate industries and locations throughout the country, one significant cluster of workers' co-ops can be identified within that wave. This group consists of twenty-three forest workers' co-ops and several related organizations in Oregon, Washington, Montana, Idaho, and Northern California with a total work force of close to 800 workers (see chart).[1]

These co-ops work on a contract basis, usually on public timberlands of the Coastal, Cascade, and Northern Rocky mountain ranges. They compete with each other, and with a larger number of traditional private firms, for contracts to perform a range of industry services. Originally the co-ops concentrated on planting clear-cut timberland and thinning young forests. As they have developed other forest industry skills, they have expanded their work into surveys of forest acreage, erosion control, seed collection, trail building and maintenance, fencing, manual brush control as an alternative to herbicides, and other activities. Their primary work and source of income remains manual reforestation over steep mountain terrain. After the sale and private harvesting of timber on public lands, the reforestation process is essential to new timber

Research for this study of forest workers' cooperatives involved on-site interviews with members and officers of co-ops in Oregon and Washington during the period 1979 through 1982. That direct contact with co-ops was supplemented by information provided me by the staff members of the Northwest Forest Workers' Association and access to the minutes of Hoedads Co-op's council meetings and many of their quarterly general meetings during the same period.

1. These figures represent the number of co-ops and membership in the summer of 1982, a period of economic depression and contraction for the timber industry. At its peak in the 1979–80 period, this cluster's total membership was close to 1,000 people.

Forest workers' cooperatives and related organizations, with number of members

State	Name of cooperative	Location	Approximate membership[a]
Oregon	Ace Reforestation	Eugene	25
	Cooperative Forest Workers (CFW)	Ruch	50
	Golden Reforestation	Winston	25
	Great Notions	Eugene	25
	Green Side Up	Cave Junction	100
	Hoedads	Eugene	200
	Homegrown Reforestation	Days Creek	35
	McKenzie River	Finn Rock	25
	Mudsharks	Cottage Grove	40
	Northeastern Oregon Worker-Owned Cooperative (NEOWOC)	Imbler	35
	Northern Star	Eugene	15
	Second Growth	Eugene	55
	Siuslaw Workers Co-op	Deadwood	25
	Southwind	Eugene	15
	Tioga Trading Company	Tioga	20
Washington	Central Washington Reforestation	Yakima	25
	Olympic Reforestation	Port Townsend	25
	Marmot Construction[b]	Seattle	30
California	ENT Reforestation	Forks of Salmon	40
	New Growth	Ukiah	20
Montana	Earth Reclamation Project	Jefferson City	25
	Kootenai Reforestation	Eureka	15
Idaho	Idahoes	St. Maries	25

Related co-ops and organizations
Northwest Forest Workers' Association, Oregon and California (support organization)
Groundwork, Eugene, Oregon (forestry research)
Prindle Creek Farm, Tidewater, Oregon (cooperative seedling nursery)
Second Street Mercantile, Eugene, Oregon (cooperative forestry equipment store)
Center for Labor and Natural Resources, Eugene, Oregon (research and consulting firm)
Northwest Coalition Against Pesticides, Eugene, Oregon (research and lobbying on pesticide use)
Plus numerous small partnerships and co-ops performing auto repair, yurt and conventional building, and food distribution

SOURCE: Author's survey, July–August 1982.
[a] August 1982.
[b] Marmot is a conventional corporation with co-op bylaws.

production, and in most clear-cut areas it constitutes the defense of, or restoration of, forest ecology. Workers sometimes refer to themselves as the "custodians of the woods." The co-ops' work is usually done for either the Forest Service of the U.S. Department of Agriculture, or the Bureau of Land Management of the U.S. Department of the Interior.

Generally made up of men and women in their twenties and thirties, these co-ops provide work for people whose values and political views frequently make work in traditional organizations less than appealing. Some members have had previous tree-planting experience with private contractors, but many acquire their work skills after joining the co-ops. Women make up as much as 40 percent of the membership of some of these co-ops—a high percentage for forest work. Reforestation work tends to be seasonal. Dry summer months are not good for planting, and snow in the Cascades makes winter work impossible, while it is possible in the more temperate Coastal Range. Since individuals, or work crews within some co-ops, are free to determine how many contracts they work per year, members' incomes vary over a wide range. Members who work most of the year (eight to ten months) earn $10,000 to $12,000 annually. A few hard-working members, "high rollers," have made more than $20,000 a year during good times in the industry.

The internal structures of the forest workers' co-ops vary. The medium-sized co-ops (40 to 100 members) generally operate as labor pools; members indicate when they are available for work, or how many contracts they want to work in a fall or spring season. The largest of the co-ops, with close to 200 members, has both a labor pool and several semiautonomous crews, each determining its seasonal or annual work load. The smaller co-ops (15 to 40 members) often work as one unit. The small and medium-sized co-ops use a process of direct democracy on policy issues, with elected officers and appointed or voluntary committees carrying on much of the day-to-day administration. Larger co-ops use a mix of direct and representative democratic processes.

The forest workers' co-ops have been financed by membership fees. That fee, set at $2,000 in most of the co-ops, is payable out of a new member's earnings. New members, upon acceptance into these co-ops and recognition of their obligation to pay the membership fee, receive full rights of membership even if the fee will not be paid for months or years. The membership fee is refunded to members who leave the co-ops. These co-ops do not hire non-member workers. All who work in the co-ops are members,[2] and all members are fully enfranchised with an equal vote in the management of the co-op from the time they join. Their right to share control of the organization flows from participation in work, not the amount of capital supplied.

The largest number of forest workers' co-ops are located in Oregon. That state's Cooperative Corporation Act recognizes the workers' (producers') cooperative as a legal entity, making the task of starting these alternate organizations in Oregon much simpler than in most other states. Western Oregon's extensive timberlands also make this a natural location for these co-ops.

Federal tax treatment of workers' co-ops as well as their state-determined legal definition emphasize an "association of individuals" character. Income to a co-op belongs to all its members. It is distributed on the basis of patronage—the work a member does with the co-op (Alvarado-Greenwood et al., 1978). Income that flows through the co-op to the member is taxable only as income to the member. Income that is not distributed, that is retained in the co-op as surplus, and any nonwork income is taxable for the co-op. Figure 1 shows the pattern of income flow through a typical forest workers' co-op. The forest workers' co-ops deliver 75 to 90 percent of the income flowing through the co-op in any accounting period to their members.

Work performed by these co-ops has been highly labor intensive. Although the need for investment in equipment is small, the co-ops need working capital to smooth income flow to their members and to serve as collateral for bonding agents. Most federal contract work requires that a bond be posted against its successful completion. For the forest workers' co-ops, accumulated membership fees have served both purposes.

The forest workers' co-ops perform approximately 10 percent of all forest service work contracted in the Northwest, and approxi-

---

2. One exception to this rule has been Marmot Construction. It is a conventional corporation, even though its internal operation is collective in nature. Marmot hires new workers on a trial basis, and they become members after several months of work. Marmot has extended ongoing employee status to several of its regular workers.

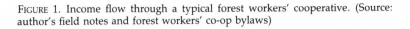

FIGURE 1. Income flow through a typical forest workers' cooperative. (Source: author's field notes and forest workers' co-op bylaws)

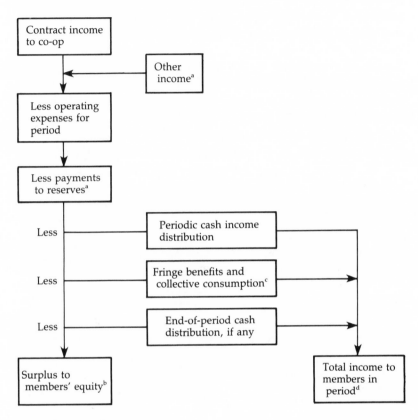

[a] May be taxable for co-op.
[b] Taxable for co-op.
[c] May be taxable for member.
[d] Taxable for member.

mately 25 percent of the work in public timberlands.[3] Many of the large timberland-owning corporations deal exclusively with private contractors, in part because of longstanding relationships with them and in part because of hostility to the activist and countercultural character of the co-ops.

The forest workers' co-ops have become enough of a force in their industry that they have been the target of a lawsuit by the

3. Estimates provided by the Northwest Forest Workers' Association, July 1982.

Association of Reforestation Contractors (ARC), the trade association of private contractors. The ARC contends that the co-ops have an unfair advantage in bidding contracts because they are not required to supply their members with the same level of benefits that private employers are required to provide. The co-ops have defended themselves based on their status as associations of independent contractors. That line of defense has tended to emphasize, within the larger co-ops, an individualist rather than collective consciousness among some members—historically a common characteristic of the co-op movement. At the same time, the lawsuit filed against two of the co-ops by the ARC, aimed at forcing them to pay members workers' compensation insurance, helped the forest workers' co-ops overcome another problem co-ops faced—isolation from each other. The lawsuit helped catalyze the Northwest Forest Workers' Association (NWFWA), an organization that had been discussed among the co-ops for several years before its inception. NWFWA is organized by state offices; the Oregon office, which represents sixteen co-ops with 700 members and combined gross income of $5 million to $6 million, is the most fully developed. It has enabled co-ops that formerly fought individually for survival as alternate organizations to carry on that battle from a more united front. NWFWA exists to serve the material interests of its members (group health insurance, etc.) and to provide its member co-ops with a voice for cooperative, environmentally sound forest practices.

Thirty-five forest workers' co-ops have been created in the Northwest since 1970. The twenty-three listed in the chart continue in operation, and twelve have terminated operations.[4] That record of survival compares very favorably with the routinely high failure rate for traditional small businesses in their early years of operation.[5] Equally significant is that no forest workers' co-ops have

---

4. Data as of August 1982. Co-ops counted as no longer operating are: in Oregon, Pacific Rain, Oregon Happy Trails, Na-wak-wa, Wildroot Co-op, and Side Hill Reforestation; in Washington, Steep Terrain, Happy Trails, and Nogler Tree Farm; and in California, Integrated Forest Management, North Coast Rehabilitation Group, FLATCO, and New Trails.

5. Precise and comparable data on business failure rates for traditional firms is not available. Figures most frequently cited are those compiled by Dun & Bradstreet's *Monthly Failure Record*. The sample for that data is only those firms listed in the *Dun & Bradstreet Reference Book*, which excludes many small businesses. Dun & Bradstreet's definition of failure counts only involuntary and voluntary discon-

ceased operation through bankruptcy. Those that have ended operations have been dissolved, distributing assets to members. Most of the co-ops that have terminated in this cluster have been small, with decreasing membership that left too few active workers for the co-op to continue bidding contracts.

Departure of members from these co-ops takes place for several reasons.[6] First, the co-ops have tended to attract a mobile, young population of workers, many of whom are not looking for a long-term work relationship. Second, most forest work is seasonal, and a paucity of jobs in summer months discourages those members who want year-round work. Third, the work is intensely physical and so best suited to young and healthy workers.[7] Last, much of the work requires members to travel and live in camp near their work for weeks at a time. That outdoor and wilderness experience is appealing to many members. But others, especially members with children or other ties to a co-op's home location, find it difficult to commit to long contracts for distant work.

The co-ops have responded to these problems in a number of ways. Some of the medium-sized co-ops bid some work near their home location specifically for members of their labor pools who cannot be away from home for long. Most of the co-ops try to arrange a mix of work so that not all of it is highly demanding physically. Neither of these solutions fully alleviates problems inherent in the nature of the work and the way it is contracted. The co-ops have urged federal contracting agencies to experiment with a new, stewardship form of contract that would allow a firm to take a site through the entire reforestation process, from prepa-

---

tinuances that involve losses to creditors. During five-year periods between 1946 and 1975, they reported annual industrial and commercial failure rates ranging between 21 and 57 firms per 10,000 in their total sample (Dun & Bradstreet figures are also reported in the U.S. Statistical Abstract; see 1981 ed., pp. 538–539). At the other extreme of estimates of failure is that of the Small Business Administration (U.S. Department of Commerce), which indicates that 80 percent of new businesses fail within their first five years of operation.

6. An indication of the extent of turnover in forest workers' co-ops is provided by Hal Hartzell, longtime Hoedad and chronicler of that co-op's history. He estimates that in 1979 approximately 40 percent of Hoedads' 1974 membership was still active in the co-op.

7. Some observers of the forest workers' co-ops suggest that there is a degree of "self-exploitation" of members' own physical well-being and that it contributes to short-term membership. This thought has been expressed by Katrina Berman in discussions with her.

ration to planting to thinning. That form of contracting, it is argued, would enable workers to gain greater satisfaction from their involvement with the timberland and also provide more successful results for the agencies. A limited number of stewardship contracts were to be let on a pilot basis for the first time in late 1982.

The question of how to provide long-term, stable employment for members of all ages and physical abilities continues to plague these co-ops. Experienced and committed co-op members leave each year because of the limited nature of their work. Diversification to a broader range of work, both within and outside the timber industry, is an important issue both for this reason and because of the depressed condition of the timber industry.

Most of the forest workers' co-ops view themselves as members of a larger group of alternate organizations in the Northwest. One feature that distinguishes these co-ops from earlier workers' co-ops is their willingness to foster other cooperative and progressive community-based organizations. Most of the forest workers' co-ops help support, directly or indirectly, other alternate organizations, including health clinics, food distribution warehouses and co-ops, a community credit union, and an environmental research group.

Perhaps the most significant characteristic of the forest workers' co-ops as a group is that they tend to be activist organizations. Unlike earlier U.S. workers' co-ops that have avoided public notoriety, the forest workers' co-ops devote time and resources to environmental and social causes. Some engage in the mainstream political processes of their cities and states, and others target their energy more to the rural communities in which they are located, but all are committed in some way to working for social change.

Three co-ops from this cluster are profiled in the next section of this chapter. The cluster of co-ops is then evaluated using the conditions of Chapter 2, and two issues affecting all of these co-ops—diversification and the role of NWFWA as a support organization—are explored. The cluster's significance relative to the development of self-management in the United States will also be assessed.

Forest Workers' Co-ops: Three Approaches

The following profiles provide insight into the operation of specific co-ops. There is no representative co-op for the cluster as a whole, and these profiles highlight some of the disparity among the co-ops that make up the cluster.

HOEDADS

Hoedads Co-op, Inc. is located in downtown Eugene, Oregon, in the Growers' Building, across from what was for years the Daily Planet Cafe. Hoedads[8] holds a special place among the forest workers' cooperatives: it was the first, it is the largest, and it has helped to create several others. Hoedads developed from a three-person partnership formed to work a reforestation contract in 1970. After successful completion of its first contract, the partnership gradually expanded. It operated as a crew with the name Hoedads over the next two years and developed a loosely cooperative internal process with just enough structure to function as a team. Further expansion took place, and in February 1974 relationships were formalized through incorporation of Hoedads Co-op under Oregon's Cooperative Corporation Act. Several semiautonomous crews were formed within the co-op, and the original Hoedads crew became Cougar Mountain Crew. The co-op took on a character described by one early member as "tribal." Hoedads grew steadily to a peak membership of 515 in 1978. Many of those members worked only occasional contracts. New membership was then slowed with the intention of decreasing membership to approximately 300, a size that seemed to facilitate democratic process in the co-op. Hoedads further reduced its size to a range of 150 to 200 during the lean 1981–82 period in the industry. Size reduction has been achieved through attrition only; the annual turnover sometimes approaches 50 percent. Many young tree planters have joined with the intention of working only one or two lucrative seasons and then moving on. One longtime member estimates that 1,800 people have been "Hoedads" (as members are called) since the co-op's inception. Hoedads' recent smaller membership consists of fewer people seeking quick, short-term income and more who are committed to developing forestry skills and working in a cooperative organization.

In the early years Hoedads was shaped largely by the founding members of the original crew. With the 1973–74 expansion, the

8. The name *Hoedads* comes from the name of the tool used for manual tree planting. A hoedad resembles a cross between a pickax and a hoe.

structure, process, and politics of the organization changed. Organizational structure designed to assure democratic internal processes began to emerge, and over the course of a year new members increasingly took the place of original members as the co-op leaders. In 1973 a partnership agreement was reached, and by 1974 a formal set of bylaws was established. With it came a clearer role for officers, a representative council to work with them, and bidding, treasury, and other administrative committees. Crew names such as Red Star, Cheap Thrills, and P.F. Flyers reflected a mix of leftist, countercultural, and anarchist tendencies within the organization. Crews retained a great deal of autonomy; they had a voice in contract selection through their representatives to the bidding committee, ran their own internal finances through their own crew treasurer, and chose their new members as they saw fit. Each crew sent a representative to the co-op's council for weekly meetings. The council was the co-op's coordinating board; it set policy that was carried out on a day-to-day basis by three officers and several members who worked in the office and treasury. Officers were elected for one-year staggered terms. During the late 1970s Hoedads had a large membership and was relatively decentralized.[9]

The period of 1980–82 was one of transition for this co-op. First, the co-op departed from its all-crew structure and formed an internal labor pool that members could assign themselves to for work. Initially the labor pool was created for members seeking specific summer work or more work than their regular crew sought. The labor pool has become institutionalized and has evolved into a group containing relatively experienced workers. Its members are frequently involved in working several different contracts at one time, whereas other remaining crews generally work individual contracts.

Second, the co-op reorganized its council into a board of directors. When originally formed it was composed of five members, four of them elected at large by the entire co-op membership for six-month terms and one remaining crew representative to be elected by his or her crew. It was then reduced in size to three at-large representatives. Those changes were designed to give the co-op a

---

9. A more detailed picture of Hoedads in the late 1970s is presented in "Hoedads Co-op: Democracy and Cooperation at Work" (Gunn forthcoming). See also Gunn 1980c; Nagle 1979a; Smith 1981.

more regular nucleus of council members and greater continuity in researching, discussing, and acting upon difficult policy matters.

Third, the role of Hoedads' president changed to focus more on questions of internal reorganization and planning for the future of the organization. That work is done in conjunction with task force committees. In the late 1970s Hoedads' presidents were found to spend considerable time on state legislative and regulatory issues. The emergence of NWFWA as public representative for the forest workers' co-ops has reduced that burden for the Hoedads' president, although he or she still devotes time to representing the co-op in its external relations.

Hoedads' decision-making process and organizational structure have allowed three forms of democracy to operate within the co-op. First, several times a year at general meetings, every member has the opportunity to discuss and vote on issues. Second, face-to-face, direct democracy exists at the crew level. Some crews successfully developed consensual processes, but the norm in crews has become direct majority voting, frequently with two-thirds majorities needed to decide matters relating to money. Third, both some crew representatives and representatives-at-large serve on the co-op board of directors.

Crews continue to provide a means for direct democracy in decision making. With most crews varying in size from ten to thirty members, crew meetings allow for broad and intensive discussion among members. Most crews use a modified parliamentary meeting process, and others work to develop a more consensual meeting process. Crews still control their own work process, their internal finances, pay systems, and camp life when working a contract. Crews alone have traditionally admitted new members to the co-op, and they have been largely responsible for training new members for work and teaching them how the co-op functions. Recent changes have diminished crew autonomy in those areas.

Hoedads' financial structure and operation reflect its legal status as a cooperative. It exists to provide its members with the opportunity and the material conditions for work (Hoedads Co-op, Inc. 1978, Art. I). Hoedads collects contract earnings for its members, deducts a percentage estimated to cover the operating expenses of the co-op, deducts any individual member's payments toward the membership fee, and distributes the remainder to members. Hoedads' gross contract revenue has averaged just under $2 million annually in the early 1980s. Approximately 25 percent of that pays co-op and crew expenses, and the remainder is distributed to members. Crews use various methods of payment for their members, ranging from a piece rate per tree planted, to an hourly rate, to a blend of the two.

Hoedads has been capitalized through membership fees. When a new member is accepted by a crew, and thus into the co-op, he or she becomes liable for that fee. In the early days of the co-op it was $1,000; currently it is $2,000. It is usually paid through an 8 percent deduction from a member's earnings until the full fee is paid. Since it is payable over time with no penalty or interest charge, it does not constitute a barrier for a member's entry into the co-op. Departing members recoup their membership fee within one year of resignation. If an amount of less than $250 is paid in, though, that amount is not refunded; it is paid to the crew as compensation for training costs. The co-op does not pay interest on membership fees. The financial limit of a member's liability in the co-op is the full $2,000 of the membership fee. The co-op normally has a quarter million dollars in paid-in membership fees on hand, which primarily constitutes working capital for the organization. Work in forest services thus far has required little investment in fixed capital; working capital is needed to smooth the seasonal nature of cash flow, to make distributions to members before payments on contracts actually reach Hoedads' treasury, and to repay membership fees to departing members.

Capital investment takes place at several levels within the organization. The co-op has committed investment funds principally to office equipment such as typewriters, a photocopier, and a computer for the treasury operation; it rents office and meeting space. Crew-level capital investment typically involves a small bus for crew transportation and possibly one or two four-wheel-drive vehicles, some chain saws, and a yurt. That nomadic structure serves as common living space for many crews while they are in camp. Crews can equip themselves with minimal used equipment for $3,000 to $4,000, although some have perhaps double that figure invested in commonly held equipment. Individual crew members also make investments; they are responsible for providing their own boots, rain gear, and clothes, a hoedad for planting, and a tree bag for carrying seedlings. Members face minimum expenses of $100 to $150 to begin work at planting, and they must replace boots and rain gear on a regular basis. They can sleep in the yurt or supply their own tent. Experienced planters may own their own four-wheel-drive vehicle or truck camper, which gets them to the camp site and serves as their sleeping quarters while there.

Tree planters' incomes vary depending on how hard they work, how experienced they are, and, of course, the conditions of the contract site. Hourly incomes averaged between $7 and $10 per hour in 1982 for contract work; co-op officers and office staff members are paid an hourly wage set by the general membership. It is generally lower than the average wage for contract work. Members can elect to participate in a group health and accident insurance plan, but otherwise there are no traditional fringe benefits.

Hoedads began as a tree-planting co-op, and that activity still provides most of its income. It has managed to expand into other forest industry work in recent years. For instance, in 1982 crews worked on contracts for trail building, thinning young forest growth, fence building, fire lookout and fire fighting, seed collection, watershed rehabilitation, small woodlot management, and timber stand exams. Much of this work has provided relief from planting; it has helped fill in the lean summer months when little planting is done; and some of it, stand exams in particular, requires new skills in forestry that some members seek to develop.

Hoedads' history has been one of change, but specific periods emerge in that history. The years from 1970 to 1974 can be characterized as start-up years—the period in which the organization's form, structure, and style developed. The period 1974 to 1979 was one of large size, the primacy of crews, and concern that too much central authority might be vested in officers of the organization. It is referred to by some members of the co-op as their period of "ultrademocracy." From 1980 to the present, Hoedads has struggled with more difficult market conditions and changes intended to enable it to face those conditions. Proposals to trim office and administrative costs are under review, as are revisions in new member entry and training procedures. For the first time in the co-op's history, serious consideration is being given to extending the term of the co-op officers to 18 months in order to gain more experienced months of service than the present one-year term allows. A special fund for research and development is intended to spur movement toward diversification out of the forest industry.

Hoedads can be considered the prototype forest workers' co-op.

Many others have been formed by members leaving Hoedads, and each is at least in part a product of knowledge and experience gained there. Before the creation of the Northwest Forest Workers' Association, Hoedads largely carried on the battles to define and defend co-ops in relations with state and federal agencies. Hoedads has devoted time, energy, and resources to developing other co-ops, attempts to develop a Eugene-area federation of co-ops, environmental issues and political campaigns, and the formation of other progressive organizations in the Eugene area. It remains the best known of this cluster of cooperatives.

MARMOT CONSTRUCTION

Marmot Construction Works, Ltd., is a small forestry firm based in Seattle, Washington. It was created in 1976 by four people who had worked together on trail maintenance and others who had worked with a cooperative fire-fighting crew and in tree planting.

Marmot differs from the other forest workers' cooperatives in several ways. First, it is not legally a co-op. Marmot has been a conventional corporation since its inception, even though internally it has functioned as a cooperative. Its size has varied between twenty-five and forty-five members. At times it may use a crew system to work several contracts, but it is not organized into on-going crews.

Marmot's collective decision making involves all members in a monthly meeting, in which each member has one vote. Day-to-day decisions are made by committees designated to deal with specific administrative matters and by crews and "responsible individuals." Major decisions and policies are dealt with at general meetings. When the members are working contracts, specific days are set aside for crew meetings. Crew evaluations of their own work are scheduled on a weekly basis. Although contracts may be allocated to a group within the collective to work as a crew, each project undertaken by Marmot remains a responsibility of the whole collective.

New members are accepted into Marmot after they have successfully served a trial period as employees. The trial period is not fixed, but it generally involves work on at least one full contract. Members of the crew working that contract then must recommend the prospective member to the full collective. Some prospective members have themselves decided to remain in an employee's status with the collective. That has been agreed to in some cases, although it has presented problems for collective process in the organization. The person serving a trial period is treated as a full-fledged member-in-training. He or she serves on committees, attends all meetings, and has full rights, with the exception of a vote on policy matters. Members-in-training receive one dollar less than the base wage received by collective members for their first 200 hours of work. They are then automatically moved to the collective's base wage, which was $6.50 per hour in 1982. There is no piece rate system at Marmot. The base wage is set for all workers, and it is paid for all administrative, logistical, and production ("on-slope") work that a member does. Members who have worked more than 4,000 hours or three calendar years with Marmot earn 50 cents more than the base wage. Both trainees and members working more than 1,000 hours per year receive medical and dental insurance, and all people working with Marmot are covered for unemployment insurance and are given "camp tender" to cover expenses for transportation and food while on a contract. Members share in a collective replacement fund for boots and rain gear.

Marmot overcame the initial hurdle of surety bonds for contracts with the help of a friend of the founding collective members. She put a $200,000 inheritance in escrow to serve as security for the bonding company. The collective acquired equipment as funds came in from its first contracts and eventually built working capital and capital equipment funds that together are maintained at the level of $40,000 to $50,000.

Capitalization has occurred through members' stock purchase and through internal finance from retained earnings. Each member acquires one share of stock in the corporation at a cost of $2,000. The cost of a stock share has remained the same over the life of the organization. It can be paid off through a 50-cent-per-hour assessment against earnings for 4,000 hours. When members depart, they sell their share back to the corporation for whatever they have paid in, or for $2,000 if it was fully paid up. An annual distribution of surplus was instituted to avoid problems associated with a gradual accumulation of value in the corporation. This distribution has helped sidestep questions associated with valuation of stock shares over time. Although members must acquire a share of stock, it is their acceptance into membership in the collective that gives them a vote in managing the organization, not their stock ownership.

More than most of the forest workers' cooperatives, Marmot has placed great emphasis on making prospective new members aware of its unusual nature. That process has two facets. First, members feel that prospective members have to make an informed decision as to whether they want to get involved in a self-managing organization. The information packet that they hand out to prospective members tells of the history of the organization, describes in general terms its internal procedures, and cautions that "working without a boss requires personal time and energy for the sake of the collective." It also stresses the rigors of the physical labor of much of their work. Second, Marmot wants to assess whether prospective members will fit into their particular collective. An application form written in 1979 asks prospective members to describe experiences they have had living or working with groups of people, to assess their own strengths and weaknesses dealing with stress and uncertainty, and to indicate reservations they may have about working with Marmot. In addition, they are asked what aspects of American society they would most like to change and how they would define workers' self-management. The application goes to the labor committee within the collective where it is used as a basis for subsequent interviews with prospective members. New member education begins with a glossary of forest service terms and an outline of tree-planting maneuvers and practices, as well as tips on keeping in good physical shape and avoiding injury.

A Marmot newsletter serves as a forum on collective issues and a way of assuring that all those involved in the collective receive notices of general interest to forest service workers. It is entitled "Slash Struggle," and its masthead indicates that it is "Published in the Center of the Chaos of the Great Feedback Loop."

Marmot members share a strong commitment to gender balance, both in terms of number and power, within their collective. The politics of the organization can best be described as a mix of feminist and socialist principles blended with concerns for making self-management work, gaining forestry skills, and surviving as a business. Women have held a full share of leadership and important committee assignments in the organization, and there has been a continual emphasis on finding and recruiting women who might want to work in a forestry collective. Overcoming patriarchy and male privilege has been a constant objective of the collective. When special training has been required in areas such as timber stand examination or blasting for trail building, women have shared it equally with men. Skills and confidence gained in work with Marmot have helped past members go on to work in skilled trades, study in forestry graduate school, and advance from work they had done before their time with Marmot.

In comparison with the forest workers' cooperatives, Marmot's status as a corporation is somewhat paradoxical. Members feel their corporate legal form and use of employer/employee status have enabled them to avoid some of the pitfalls the co-ops have encountered. Avoiding the independent-contractor status of co-op members, Marmot has provided its employees and members full benefits and forms of collective consumption along with a decent cash income. Marmot has had to spend less time fighting battles with state and federal agencies that do not understand cooperatives. At the same time, they have more easily attained a strong commitment to feminist principles, to collective values and process, and to socialist precepts that separate them from any traditional corporation in the United States.

Marmot faces the future with several unresolved dilemmas. One it shares with the co-ops is that of making a decent living in an industry that is in the throes of a deep recession. Diversification is a topic of discussion and research at Marmot, as it is at many of the co-ops. In addition, Marmot plans to move out of Seattle. The cost of maintaining an office and living there is very high compared with other locations. Plans for that move bring to the surface another issue that has plagued Marmot for years: whether to be an urban or rural based collective. Diversification that could serve the interests of both, such as rural production and an urban distribution system for forest products, could potentially help resolve that problem.

GREEN SIDE UP

Green Side Up is a loosely organized forest workers' cooperative based in a rural area near Cave Junction in southwestern Oregon. Its origins can be traced to the early 1970s, when friends came together in partnerships to work tree-planting contracts. Some early members had planted trees as employees of the U.S. Forest Service

(USFS) in the days before the USFS began contracting out work of that kind. Green Side Up was incorporated as a cooperative in 1975; it had twenty to twenty-five core members and others who worked part-time who counted as members when they were working. Membership had expanded to approximately 140 by the late 1970s, with another sixty to seventy part-time workers. Its regular membership is approximately one hundred today.

Green Side Up began with typical linkages to the other forest workers' co-ops. Hoedads Co-op lent some start-up capital to Green Side Up, and a few early Hoedads were involved in Green Side Up's formation. Some of its founding members describe the process as one involving a diverse group of people who had a strong sense of how they wanted to live—people with good minds working to figure out how to make that life possible while fitting in necessary work for cash income and with patience to work out the appropriate organization. The outcome has been perhaps the most independent of these co-ops. Green Side Up has sought to keep its overhead low; it has minimal office space and no regular office workers. Members savor their rural and communal living, grow much of their own food, build their own shelter either individually or communally, and work at cash income jobs irregularly. Green Side Up was originally active in forming the Northwest Forest Workers' Association, but in recent years it has chosen limited participation in that organization. It contributed capital to the creation of Golden Reforestation, another co-op, and it does become involved in local environmental issues, but in general it maintains a low profile compared to the other forest workers' co-ops.

During fall and spring planting seasons Green Side Up members meet once a month, and a bidding committee meets weekly. Each member is asked to make a work commitment at the beginning of the season as a guide for the bidding committee. Crews are formed from the membership pool for specific contracts, and those crews then set their own meeting and decision-making processes. Officers for the co-op are elected; they are three cochairpeople and a secretary. The officers keep the organization together. They are able to do so largely because they are viewed as people with integrity. They and anyone else who perform administrative work are paid $10 per hour. The mechanic who keeps the co-op's vehicles functioning is paid a similar wage.

New members are taken into the co-op in an informal process

that involves "hanging around, talking to people, and attending a few meetings." Members pay in $1,000 from earnings, and 80 percent of the membership fee is repaid when members leave. New members started at $5 per hour in 1982 and work up a scale to a maximum of $10 depending on experience and ability to produce. Members stressed that when they are on a contract, whether for trail maintenance, planting, or thinning, the work is intense. They want to get the job done quickly and well and get back to their normal lives.

The major objective of Green Side Up is to return as much income to members as possible. The co-op has acquired several vehicles and some other equipment, which it maintains carefully. Aside from that there has been no capital investment. Administrative expenses other than wages are kept as low as possible, with approximately 90 percent of gross income to the co-op flowing directly to members as wages or end-of-year surplus distributions.

Much of the energy of the co-op members goes not into building the co-op, but into developing the community where most members live. Community projects have included creating a food co-op and building both a free school and a combined community center, health clinic, and co-op office. Members have a reputation for being ardent environmentalists who strongly oppose the use of herbicides and are willing to take direct action against their use.

Green Side Up is unique in its rural and very community-based character. Many of the forest workers' co-ops exhibit some elements of anarchist thinking among their members, but in Green Side Up that tendency is more fully developed than in the other co-ops. The co-op's very loose organization is made possible largely because strong ties outside of the co-op hold members together. Such ties are much less common in more urban-based forest workers' co-ops.[10] Green Side Up may be thought of as a minimalist cooperative. The co-op is an appropriate vehicle for gaining work, but work in the traditional sense is not a high priority for members. The co-op, then, operates with a minimum investment of time, energy, and resources on the part of its members. The processes of the cooperative strongly emphasize individual rights within a larger community, rather than the development of a collective work

10. I am indebted to Greg Nagle of Hoedads for clarifying this point.

organization. The results reflect unusual ways of living and working in this Oregon co-op.

The Ten Conditions

The defining and facilitating conditions from Chapter 2 serve as a framework for the evaluation of the forest workers' co-ops in the chart on pages 87–89. These firms have enough features in common to allow for evaluation as a group, and exceptions will be noted when necessary.

Two issues that emerge from this evaluation of the forest workers' co-ops are their vulnerable location within one industry and the related question of the potential for further development of their support organization. These two issues are explored next, and then the significance of this group of cooperatives is assessed.

Issue: Diversification

Forest workers' co-ops share with several other twentieth-century clusters of U.S. workers' co-ops—including the cooperative shingle mills, plywood cooperatives, and refuse-collection co-ops—the attribute of common work within one industry. These clusters have typically developed from a prototype that has paved the way for the rest, no doubt contributing to the development of industry-related groupings of co-ops. But because of their ties to one industry they have remained vulnerable to the changing conditions of their industry and the market for their product or service. Decline of an industry is largely a function of factors that no small firm can affect. Firms caught in a declining industry face the choice of staying with that industry and declining with it or attempting to produce new goods or services for new markets. Diversification offers a means of escaping the decline of an industry or of attenuating cyclical or seasonal ups and downs. Few workers' cooperatives or other self-managing organizations have diversified.[11] Can these organizations expand into new work while retaining their democratic, self-managing character?

11. Workers' cooperatives are formed by people who come together with specific skills or to perform specific tasks. Conglomerates in the business world are a product of units of capital (corporations) that hire skills (workers).

Summary evaluation of the forest workers' cooperatives

Condition (see page 35)	Evaluation
Condition 1	Control and management of all of these firms lies in the hands of their members. Several forms of direct democracy are evident in these firms, supplemented in many cases by delegation and representative democracy. Members of all these firms have equal voting power, although Hoedads' period of council governance with one representative from each different-sized crew did not amount to equal representation. Marmot is the only one of the group that employs labor, and Marmot's few employees are encouraged to take an active role in managing the work and camp life of each contract. They have the opportunity to discuss and voice their opinion on policy issues within the organization, but they do not vote on those issues, in violation of this condition. Co-op members agree to pay a membership fee as they join their organization, and in Marmot they buy a stock share. However, with the exception noted for Marmot, neither stipulation serves as a barrier to the full participation of those involved based on work.
Condition 2	Income of all the co-ops in this cluster belongs to the co-ops' members. Because of its status as a corporation with shareholders and employees, Marmot is again the exception. Even though its employees receive essentially the same benefits and pay as members, that is a matter of policy rather than a result of the structure of the firm. Income distribution is determined democratically, with varying levels of individual and collective forms of income assignment and distribution among the firms. The widest wage spread within a firm is a ratio from highest to lowest wages of 2:1; most of the firms reflect more nearly equal wage rates than that.
Condition 3	The forest workers' co-ops have been funded by members' contributions and some debt financing. Members retain individual claim on their membership fees, and they recover those fees when they leave the co-ops. Collectively held assets have been acquired largely from earned surplus. Marmot generally meets this condition as well, in that departing members must sell their stock shares back to the firm.
Condition 4	Capital does not impart any form of control to capital suppliers either within or outside the co-ops. All co-op members agree to supply capital in the form of the membership fee. At Marmot, internal stock ownership carries with it a voice in policy making, but ownership is available to any worker there. The amount of capital supplied does not, in any of these firms, determine the amount of voting power the supplier has in the organization. None of the forest workers' firms pays a scarcity-reflecting rent on funds supplied by members. They all pay interest to outside lenders.
Condition 5	Since rents are not paid to member capital suppliers, they are essentially reinvested in each of the firms. Members of several of the co-ops have argued that they in fact receive a nonmonetary return on their capital in the form of work in a liberating environment that they have helped to create (Gunn forthcoming).
Condition 6	Internal information is widely disseminated in all of these firms, most notably through published meeting agendas and minutes, budgetary projections and reports, and newspapers and newsletters. Some co-ops depend more heavily than others on word-of-mouth communication among their members, but that is, of course,

Condition (see page 35)	Evaluation
	a more uncertain method of information dissemination. All of the firms actively encourage members to learn managerial skills through work on bidding, treasury, or other committees. Firms that use a crew structure provide opportunities for members to gain managerial skills and experience at that organizational level as well.
Condition 7	No formal statements of individual liberties exist in these firms' bylaws. However, a strongly rooted countercultural/libertarian tradition in most of them does serve as some common assurance of individual liberties. Minority and individual positions on issues are given hearings in meetings and publications. A fine line between individual rights and common bonds seems to exist in all of the firms.
Condition 8	None of the forest workers' co-ops have provisions in their bylaws for an independent judiciary. For Hoedads that function was carried out first by the co-op council, then by the board of directors. Since both have also been the co-op's major policy-making body, they have not been ideally suited to the task. Hoedads is considering creation of a formal grievance committee. Conflicts in many of the co-ops are frequently resolved, especially at the level of the work groups or crews, by informal group conflict resolution techniques on a case-by-case basis. More routinely, use of criticism/self-criticism processes helps to resolve conflict. The lack of an independent judiciary means that all of these firms rely on the general membership, officers, and representatives to their boards or councils to safeguard the organizations' bylaws.
Condition 9	Participatory and democratic consciousness takes different forms in the forest worker's co-ops. All exhibit high degrees of that consciousness compared to the norm for any traditional firm. Most of the co-ops go through periods in which members with high levels of participatory consciousness, skills, and energy work on a regular basis to maintain much of the organization's momentum; times when greater involvement and participation on the part of members are called for; and times when those in positions of authority are called to task for not adhering to broadly participatory principles. Education for worker's self-management in these firms remains largely a matter of gaining experience with an organization's structure and processes. This can perhaps be described as on-the-job development of participatory and democratic consciousness. Hoedads in particular has found that wanting. Its size, turnover of members, and lack of co-op-wide membership criteria has left it in need of an educational program for new and ongoing members. That task has been addressed by sporadic articles written for the quarterly newspaper, occasional use of orientation booklets or training sessions, and educational efforts of the co-op's officers and long-term members. More politically committed crews, especially feminist crews, have also played important roles in that effort. It is anticipated that the final product of Hoedads' history project will contribute to members' understanding of the co-op's evolving structure and processes. Little progress has been made in accomplishing educational objectives in a more structured or formal way. In this regard, Marmot Construction offers the clearest contrast to Hoedads. By providing potential candidates for membership with a statement of the firm's unifying political and philosophical basis

Condition (see page 35)	Evaluation
	and its management processes, it assures some self-screening of new members from the start. As a much smaller and more homogeneous group than Hoedads, it is more able to maintain a high level of democratic and participatory consciousness.
Condition 10	The Northwest Forest Workers' Association performs many of the functions outlined in Condition 10. It has thus far performed those functions, understandably, in industry-specific service of its member firms. Its basis of action is the support of democratically managed forest workers' firms. Since the organization's first few years of full operation were years of recession for the industry, it did not play the developmental role that this condition suggests. It has managed to create one firm outside the industry, and that has been structured much like a service co-op for the member firms. There are indications that NWFWA could serve as a catalyst for a broader-based support group for democratically run firms and work collectives in the Northwest.

The answer to that question is yes, but diversification involves both problems and opportunities. Making decisions in a large, democratic organization is complex and time-consuming. New ventures are frequently launched by a small, tightly knit group of people. It would be a heavy burden for a small group within a self-managing organization to take most of their decisions to the larger organization for ratification. They would expend much of their energy and possibly lose crucial time educating and persuading members of the larger group. In addition, new ventures may create few jobs at first and thus they may cause resentment in the larger group, particularly if the venture is perceived as taking scarce management time from existing co-op activities. New operations may also diminish the original group's cohesiveness, particularly in terms of differing interests among short- and long-term members. But opportunities also exist. A subgroup attempting to create new productive work within the organization would have the benefit of an established base for their work, diverse skills among the existing co-op membership that could be taught to other members, sympathetic and experienced colleagues who could offer advice and assistance, financial resources in several possible forms, and eventually a pool of colleagues for the new venture who are well versed in cooperative work.

On balance, diversification is surely not impossible for a self-managed firm. Several facets of diversification will be explored here: diversification within an industry; diversification outside the industry; planning, skill, and capital needs for either form of diversification; and an organizational structure that might facilitate them. We will also consider creation of new firms as spin-offs from existing firms and institutional support for such spin-offs. Since the forest workers' co-ops' survival in the 1980s may depend on the question of diversification, reference to them will serve to focus this inquiry.

Broadening the range of work performed, or products made, within an industry is a limited form of diversification. Knowledge of the industry and its markets already exists within the organization, and members have skills that are applicable to a broad range of industry activities. More income or work for its members naturally is one incentive an organization may have for diversification. It may be combined with a desire for more interesting, pleasant, or safe work. The forest workers' co-ops cite all these reasons. Most of them have expanded into a broader range of forest activities. Income generated from non-tree-planting work has grown from providing less than 10 percent of NWFWA's members' income in the 1970s to close to 40 percent of that income today.[12] This diversification within the industry has been made relatively simple by similarities in contracting and bonding procedures, similar work life in the forest, and some continuity in skills necessary for the work.

Diversification outside of the firm's industry presents a greater challenge. The self-managing organization must find a fit between the skills, desires, and knowledge of at least some of its current members and a new activity. A new activity must show promise of providing acceptable work for enough members to make it worthy of the drain on resources and added risk it will impose on the firm. Criteria for acceptable new activities can be outlined by members. Such criteria as labor process characteristics, capital-labor ratios, and the fit between the new activity and the local or regional resource base will then guide further efforts.

Organizationally, a new venture may require partially and temporarily separating a team from the larger organization. For example, after preliminary guidelines and desired characteristics for new work are agreed to by members of the entire organization, groups may be encouraged to develop ideas for new ventures,

12. Estimates provided by the Northwest Forest Workers' Association, July 1982.

gather preliminary information on their feasibility, and present them to a research and development or diversification committee of the larger organization. If the ideas and preliminary analysis make sense to that group, further market and production research can take place, with the assistance of outside consultants if necessary. Plans that appear feasible can then be presented to the organization's board or council, along with detailed proposals concerning how much autonomy those attempting to launch the new project would have and for what length of time, what obligations would exist between the parent co-op and subgroup, and other details. The organization and the subgroup can then negotiate and decide whether to go ahead with a project. A final written agreement between an initiating team and the organization would be essential.

Some of the most difficult issues in negotiating new ventures within a self-managing organization have to do with financial resources and obligations for the project. For instance, would the venture be a separate income center within the organization? Chances are it will generate losses at first, but later it may generate higher income per person for those involved in it than the average for the organization as a whole. A system for dealing with those variations would have to be agreed upon. Presumably the parent organization would provide some start-up capital, and so any limit to the amount to be borrowed and any arrangements for external borrowing would need to be spelled out. Obligations would have to be clear, with provisions for expected developments and contingencies.

The organization as a whole would probably benefit from providing the new project with a general coordinator, possibly one of its current or former officers or managers. New ventures are by nature egocentric, and at least one person who can represent the interests of all members should have full knowledge of the project. The relationship between the organization and the new subgroup will depend on the size and structure of the organization and its commitment to diversification. There are few models of collective entrepreneurship to follow.

A more common form of diversification is the formation of a spin-off from an existing self-managed firm. Although this kind of new venture can drain resources, particularly in the form of skilled members, from the organization, it has the advantage of organizational simplicity. The forest workers' co-ops have a history of this kind of development. Members of Hoedads have left to form not only other forest workers' co-ops, but also cooperative ventures as diverse as an auto repair shop, mime and theater company, computer consulting firm, taxi co-op, and woodsworkers' supply and equipment business. Members have learned how to work and manage cooperatively while at Hoedads and have then used those skills in new ventures separate from Hoedads. Sometimes their departure has caused resentment among members. Other spin-offs have been regarded more favorably. Hoedads has in some cases lent money to these new co-ops. Many of the more than 200 alternate organizations in the Eugene, Oregon, vicinity have benefited from skills and consciousness developed in the forest workers' co-ops in that area. The new organizations have frequently provided new kinds of work for former forest workers' co-op members, even though they have not provided the benefits of diversification to the original organizations involved.

In facing questions of diversification, self-managing organizations in the United States directly confront their market environment. The creation of new productive activity is traditionally an individual and isolated activity in that environment. It is supposedly an activity motivated by self-aggrandizement. For the self-managing firm, creating new productive activity for members while maintaining cohesion as a cooperative community of producers is a clear challenge. Perhaps the best way to meet that challenge lies in the formation of linkages with other democratically managed firms; in overcoming some of the isolation of the marketplace. That strategy is addressed in the next issue.

Issue: The Support Organization

The development of workers' self-management in an unsupportive macroeconomic, social, and political environment can be assisted by a viable support organization. As described in Chapter 2, that organization would exist to fund and promote the creation of new self-managed firms. The forest workers' cooperatives have created an organization to serve their needs in the form of the Northwest Forest Workers' Association. It provides its member co-ops with several important services, but thus far it falls short of being a fully developed support organization as outlined in Condition 10. NWFWA helps clarify an important distinction to be made between an organization created to serve extant co-ops and one that would have a clearer charge to help develop new self-managing organizations. That distinction will be developed more fully later in this section.

The Northwest Forest Workers' Association grew slowly out of a conference organized by and for forest workers in 1976. That gathering provided a forum in which representatives from several co-ops and other groups planning to form co-ops brainstormed about the nature, role, and scope of an association that would serve forest workers. Participants began by summarizing the goals of each organization represented at the meeting. The list included advancement of co-ops, creation of a nonsexist and nonhierarchical culture, promotion of good forest management practices, and "making bucks," among others (Slentz 1979). They then narrowed the discussion to the desired goals of an association, which resulted in a more manageable list, which included unified lobbying on issues affecting co-ops, shared legal work on common problems, developing solidarity among "high quality worker owners," and creating more work opportunities for others (ibid.). After further discussion, consensus emerged on an association for cooperative forest workers, and a statement of purpose was written for it. That statement read:

> The Northwest Forest Workers' Association joins together for mutual cooperation, survival, unity, and communication among worker owned and managed forestry enterprises. We share a dedication to promote the creation and growth of organizations in which women and men of all races share fully and equally the controls and responsibilities affecting their chosen work, and in which all profits from labor are distributed among the workers. We are personally committed to performing high quality forestry work. We support and practice environmentally sound forest practices which enrich rather than deplete the forest. We seek to develop a locally controlled forestry which serves the people. We believe workers have the right to negotiate with contracting agencies as equals to determine the conditions of their labor. [Ibid.]

The period 1976 to 1979 was one of further regional meetings and discussion and work that slowly fleshed out an organization.

93

Regional dues were assessed, erratically, on individuals as members. By 1979, those dues were $2 per quarter per person. Funds were collected, and some money was dispersed to specific projects or committees. A continual debate of the period was whether members should provide dues before seeing what the new organization could do or whether an organization could do anything before it had funds. Early funding for NWFWA came from a co-op work day in which all income ($16,000) was pooled for antiherbicide projects and legislative lobbying. The Association of Reforestation Contractors' lawsuit against two of the NWFWA member co-ops helped to galvanize the organization in 1979. In addition, by then enough NWFWA advocates were in leadership positions in key co-ops that they were able to develop and sell to their members a plan to establish an active, staffed, and ongoing umbrella organization. A half-time paid staff member was selected for the Oregon chapter of NWFWA in 1979; its office was opened in Eugene in January 1980.

By the summer of 1980, Oregon NWFWA represented thirteen forest workers' co-ops, with a membership of approximately 700 forest workers. By mid-1982 the Eugene office served sixteen co-ops in Oregon, Washington, Idaho, and Montana. NWFWA co-ops in northern California have maintained their own state organization, representing several other co-ops.

NWFWA was developed on the basis of co-op membership, rather than individual membership. Member co-ops support the organization financially through co-op dues of one half of one percent of the gross income of each co-op. That allowed the NWFWA staff to expand to two coordinators jointly working sixty hours per week.

NWFWA is governed by a council of one elected representative from each of its member co-ops. At monthly meetings member co-ops and the NWFWA staff present reports, decide pending issues, and make policy. The council attempts to operate by consensus, although it often resorts to majority vote. If a decision is needed on a controversial issue, a weighted voting system that helps account for the different size of member co-ops is used. The council has used a weighted system rarely, and primarily for election of officers.

Four major areas of concern dominated NWFWA's early work: (1) maintaining communication and coordination among the forest workers' co-ops, (2) providing tangible services to members of these co-ops, (3) representing the co-ops' interests in state and federal legislative activity, (4) and funding research on forest ecology issues of concern to members, particularly in the area of regulation of the use of herbicides. As the organization matured and the timber industry experienced hard times, NWFWA has broadened its work to include increasing the effectiveness of members' bidding on contracts and working against federal budget cutbacks for forest services. The early 1980s have been a period in which NWFWA has become essentially a public representative of its member co-ops. Prior to its creation, much of that task fell to the one or two largest co-ops.

The most concrete service that NWFWA provides for its co-ops' members is health insurance, which it established in the form of a self-funding trust. It began as the Northwest Forest Workers' Association Health Trust and was expanded in 1981 under the new name of the Workers' Insurance Trust. It serves not only workers' co-op members, but partnerships, associations, and nonprofit organizations as well. The Trust is tailored to pay for a broad range of mainstream and alternate forms of health care, and it covers both on- and off-the-job accidents and illness. The Trust is a founding member of Co-op America, a group designed to provide consumer services for members of co-ops, socially responsible businesses, and nonprofit organizations.

Two systems have been developed to foster cooperation among NWFWA member co-ops. One is a guest worker system, which allows a member or members of one co-op to work temporarily with another. The other is coordination of joint venture contracting operations, a system that has helped member co-ops, especially the smaller ones, join with other member co-ops to bid large contracts.

Is NWFWA an example of the kind of support or shelter organization described in the defining conditions? The answer is yes and no. NWFWA's function has been to provide services to its member workers' co-ops and their members. It has performed that function well, relieving a few co-op officers of an enormous burden, while providing more comprehensive, balanced, and professional services to all its members.

NWFWA represents workers' co-ops of one industry. That has been an advantage in keeping its energies focused and in developing the expertise to be effective in its work. NWFWA meetings, especially in the days before the organization was fully developed, provided an environment in which people wanting to form new tree-planting co-ops could get advice and encouragement. NWFWA's member co-ops have been beleaguered by state and federal agencies and attacked through suits, rumors, and other forms of alleged harassment by the Association of Reforestation Contractors. NWFWA provides for a common line of defense. In short, NWFWA is a progressive and effective association for its member co-ops. It is democratically managed by a representative council, and it sees part of its mission as the promotion of democratic and cooperative activities.

Yet NWFWA is also a captive of its industry-specific co-ops. It was not conceived to perform, and does not have the resources to perform, several functions envisioned for a support organization for workers' self-management. It does not provide technical assistance or debt or equity funding for workers' co-ops or other self-managed organizations. Since it is funded by co-ops struggling to survive, its scope, mandate, and mission are clearly delineated by that struggle.

The depressed condition of the timber industry might have several effects on NWFWA. NWFWA may be constrained in a role of trade association, serving to protect the material interests of its member co-ops. That could take the form of discouraging the formation of new forest workers' co-ops to forestall increased competition for shrinking numbers of contracts. The fact that 80 to 90 percent of service workers in the industry still work for private contractors, many for very low pay and all without any form of organized protection, makes that unlikely. So does a continuing missionary zeal for more co-op formation on the part of many members. Conditions in the industry could, alternatively, lead NWFWA to help develop new workers' co-ops as it served member co-ops seeking to create new jobs outside of their highly cyclical industry. NWFWA staff members are concerned about diversification by member co-ops; they have planned at least one regional workshop on that topic. Further work in that area might lead to a broader mandate for NWFWA to become more involved in helping to reproduce the organizational form, rather than simply helping to maintain existing forest workers' co-ops.

The seeds of a full support organization may lie in NWFWA and other cooperatives in the Northwest. An affiliation of democrati-

cally managed organizations across industries is possible there because of their numbers and the resources they now command in
the region. Some feel it is essential—that the advocacy work for
co-ops that such an organization could perform is crucial to surviving a backlash against co-ops orchestrated by organizations of
small-scale capitalists in the region. Initially a support organization
would be heavily linked to food distribution and forestry firms,
but it could serve the cause of further expansion and diversification
for all co-ops and self-managed firms in the region.

Evaluation

The forest workers' co-ops constitute the first major cluster of
workers' cooperatives in the United States since the last of the
plywood co-ops were formed in the 1950s. By generally avoiding
the use of hired labor, acquisition of capital stock as a means of
entry into the firm, and linkages between levels of ownership and
levels of voting power, these co-ops come closer to fitting the conditions for workers' self-management than any previous cluster of
co-ops formed in this country.

The success of the forest workers' co-ops can be assessed in more
traditional terms as well. Their survival rate in a troubled industry
and their avoidance of bankruptcy have been remarkable. They are
a small part of their industry, but they have become a far larger
force within it than their numbers would suggest and have done
so in a relatively short period of time.

Hoedads is the best known of these co-ops, and for good reason.
It was the prototype for the cluster, it has been the largest, and it
carried much of the weight of the political battles for the cluster
through the 1970s. Hoedads probably extended open, democratic
internal processes further than any other large workers' co-op has
done in the United States. Its use of a crew structure for work
groups provides an interesting parallel to efforts to decentralize
the Yugoslav self-managed firm and to attempts to overcome problems of large firms in the Mondragon group. The early 1980s finds
Hoedads working to develop more efficient management processes
while at the same time retaining members' democratic control of
the organization. The co-op is going through a period of maturation

as it seeks to respond to a changing industry while remaining faithful to its co-op ideals.

Marmot Construction is also significant in this cluster. It stands apart from the others in its traditional corporate legal framework. That has saved it many of the energy-draining battles required to fit the square peg of workers' co-ops into the round hole of the capitalist economy. Marmot's energy was expended more on internal political issues and developing internal solidarity than on fighting external battles. Marmot can offer important lessons for the creation of democratic firms based on a mixture of concerns for democracy and progressive labor issues. It can also serve as a useful example in the formation of self-managed firms in states where co-op incorporation statutes are defective or nonexistent.

This cluster of co-ops has also extended cooperation *among* firms in the cluster further than any previous grouping. Although these firms regularly compete with each other for the same contracts, they have created a support organization to serve their common needs and goals. The Northwest Forest Workers' Association has made significant contributions to the well-being of the cluster, and at the same time it has given the forest workers' co-ops a voice in their regional industry. That voice allows their concern for sustained-yield, ecologically sound forest management techniques, for woods-workers' rights, and for democratic management to be heard in an industry better known for exploiting people and resources for profit.

The forest workers' co-ops offer evidence that self-managing work organizations can be created in the United States and important lessons for the further development of workers' self-management. They also offer evidence for the ability of those firms to carry out their work while contributing to progressive social and political causes at the local and regional level.

CHAPTER 4

The Plywood Manufacturing Cooperatives

The plywood cooperatives of the Pacific Northwest are the longest lived cluster of workers' co-ops in the United States. They are also the largest, measured in terms of number of co-op members and the amount of production they account for in their industry. A sizable literature exists on these firms.[1] This chapter will briefly summarize their history and their general performance. It will then focus on critical aspects of their organizational, decision-making, and financial structures. The plywood co-ops will be evaluated in light of the conditions developed in Chapter 2, and three issues specific to these firms and historically problematical for workers' co-ops will be investigated: the use of hired, nonmember workers to augment the member work force; the dilemmas of stock ownership as the vehicle for financing these firms; and the use of retained earnings for capitalization. The chapter concludes with an assessment of the significance of the co-ops' 60-year history.

The plywood co-ops are distinguished from the conventional, outside investor-owned counterparts in their industry by the fact that their owners also work in them. Co-op owner-members adhere to cooperative principles such as equality of vote in decision making, and they practice equality of pay based on hours of work. They own a share, or a block of shares, in their firm. Members are

Research for this case study involved on-site visits to plywood cooperatives in 1979 and 1982, interviews with co-op managers, owner-members, and hired workers, and the author's survey of operating and staffing levels of firms in July 1982. Additional information was gained from secondary sources, discussion with other researchers, and an interview with an attorney for several of the plywood co-ops.

1. See Bellas 1972; Berman 1967, 1982a, 1982b; Berman and Berman 1978; Bernstein 1974, 1980; Greenberg forthcoming, 1979, 1981a, 1981b; Gunn 1980a; Rhodes 1978; Zwerdling 1978.

generally required to work in the co-op, and their remuneration is based on their work, which in legal terms is their business done with the co-op.[2] Dividends are rarely paid, and so there is little incentive for ownership by nonworking owners even in firms whose bylaws allow it.

Owner-members elect their board of directors, and the firm's general manager is appointed by that board. The board and the manager administer the routine operations of the co-op; policy decisions are made on a one-person, one-vote basis by all owner-members in semiannual or quarterly general meetings. Major decisions are discussed extensively by owner-members, who have full access to information concerning the co-op's operation. The core of production workers in these co-ops essentially hires and fires its manager. The plywood co-ops represent an unusual and important example of democracy at work in U.S. manufacturing firms.

The first of the plywood co-ops was Olympia Veneer Company, which was formed in 1921 by 125 workers. Each member contributed $1,000; then members secured a bank loan and built the plant and installed its equipment themselves. Their first year of building and then operation brought them minimal incomes, but within a short time they were earning one and a half times the pay of employees in conventional plants (Berman 1982a). Olympia Veneer was one of the first eight plywood plants in the United States. It helped to develop the manufacturing technology of the industry, and it served as a prototype that other plywood co-ops followed (ibid.).

The plywood co-ops' history is naturally intertwined with the development of the industry and historical events during that development. When demand for plywood was high during World War II, four co-ops operated six plants, producing 20 to 25 percent of the industry's output. As the industry grew into the 1950s, a rising number of co-ops maintained that share. In the 1960s and 1970s the share of industry output supplied by the co-ops dimin-

---

2. Legally the owners of a cooperative must be its patrons. Cooperative ownership is defined in terms of participation in the business, which in workers' (producers') co-ops means participation in the work (production). A workers' co-op is jointly owned by a group of workers who patronize the business and who are classified as its members (Alvarado-Greenwood et al. 1978, pp. 78–79).

Plywood cooperatives, with number of members and employees

State	Name of Cooperative	Location	Working owner-members	Employees at full capacity
Oregon	Astoria Plywood	Astoria	170	71
	Linnton Plywood	Portland	180	35
	Multnomah Plywood[a]	St. Helens	152	50
Washington	Buffelen Woodworking[b]	Tacoma	200	12
	Ft. Vancouver Plywood	Vancouver	300	10
	Hardel Mutual[c]	Olympia	150	250
	Hoquiam Plywood	Hoquiam	100	30
	Mt. Baker Plywood	Bellingham	182	30
	North Pacific Plywood	Tacoma	160	70
	Puget Sound Plywood	Tacoma	125	20
	Stevenson Co-Ply	Stevenson	160	140

SOURCE: Author's survey, July 1982.
[a]Multnomah's primary product is texture 1–11 siding.
[b]Buffelen's primary products are hardwood plywood and doors.
[c]Hardel acquired and operates a large building supply outlet, which accounts in part for its high number of employees.

ished to approximately 10 percent (Berman 1982b). No new co-ops have been formed since the early 1950s.

There are eleven plywood cooperatives operating in the United States today (see chart), all in Washington and Oregon. One of them is legally a cooperative corporation; the rest are conventional corporations with co-op bylaws and tax treatment. Their combined co-op membership totals approximately 2,000. Seven co-ops terminated their operations in the 1970s; four were sold to private investors, and three others were liquidated, one of them through bankruptcy proceedings.[3]

Paradoxically, even though the number of plywood co-ops has dropped in the past decade, in the early 1980s they again account for possibly as much as 20 percent of softwood plywood production in the U.S. There are several reasons for this phenomenon, but principal among them is that the industry itself is severely depressed. In mid-1982 36 percent of U.S. plywood manufacturing capacity was shut down; the figure for the Northwest was estimated at over 40 percent. Those plants still open were operating

3. Co-ops that were sold in the 1970s were Lacey, Elma, Anacortes, and Peninsula. Brookings Plywood was sold in 1980. Those that were liquidated were Everett and Western States Plywood. The only co-op that underwent bankruptcy proceedings was Medford Veneer & Plywood.

at 70 percent of capacity.[4] As one seasoned co-op manager put it, "It's a hell of a time to be in a housing-related industry." Despite their problems, the co-ops were weathering the 1982 economic crisis (depression in their industry) more successfully than the conventional firms have done. As of the summer of 1982 none of the co-ops had shut down in that period. The co-ops' concentration in high-quality sanded plywood, one of the most stable portions of the market, is one of the reasons for their ability to survive. The other is that they are independent firms that exist to support their members, even at reduced incomes. They cannot afford to shut down.

The plywood co-ops have proven themselves to be a viable form of business organization. Data indicate that twenty-seven co-ops were formed between 1921 and the early 1950s.[5] To date, seven of that total have been sold by their members to conglomerates and private investors. Some of the seven can be considered business successes in traditional terms, as their sales resulted in significant capital gains for owner-members. From a co-op perspective, these sales are perhaps best labeled "failure by success," since they no longer exist as co-ops. The remaining nine co-ops that are no longer in business failed for a variety of reasons, including losses due to fire, unscrupulous activity by business promoters, lack of timber supply in an oligopsonistic industry, and bankruptcy during cyclical downturns. Excluding co-ops that have been sold, the co-ops' failure rate of 9/27 or 33 percent after operating periods of eight to forty years compares favorably with national business failure rates.[6] In their region and industry, American Plywood Association (APA) data indicate that West Coast softwood plywood mills reached a peak of 141 in 1963 (American Plywood Assn. 1982a). In July 1982, 35 units were operating in that region (American Plywood Assn. 1982b). Although APA data do not separate conventional and co-op production units, it is clear that the co-ops listed here account for almost a third of active West Coast region production units in 1982. It can be assumed that some conventional firms will reopen if and when market conditions are more favorable and that the co-

4. Data is from American Plywood Association 1982a, 1982b, and from an unpublished estimate of APA's staff economist, July 1982.
5. Estimated by author from APA census data and secondary sources.
6. See note 5, Chapter 3.

ops' share of a then larger national market will be smaller than it has been during this depressed period.

The co-ops have repeatedly demonstrated the ability to survive the severe downturns experienced by their industry. In addition to the quality of their product, there are two other reasons for this ability. The first is that in bad times the entire membership takes a cut in income to keep the mill in production. A second survival technique, used in unusually difficult periods, is the same as that of their conventional counterparts in the industry: laying off their nonmember workers. Each of these techniques will be discussed more fully below.

The ability to survive is only one possible measure of how the co-ops have performed. Other measures of the plywood co-ops' performance include the following:

(*a*) The hourly return to co-op members has generally been above the union average wage for plywood workers. In some of the co-ops, it has been consistently 50 percent or more above union averages (Berman 1982b).

(*b*) The ability to provide continuous employment to owner-members, along with frequent work in excess of 40 hours per week, has meant that annual incomes of members have been higher than for plywood workers in general. In a few of the co-ops, members' annual incomes reached $40,000 before the downturn of the early 1980s.

(*c*) Several of the plywood co-ops were created when their original, privately owned mills were about to close. Some of those co-ops eventually closed, but they provided jobs in their communities for periods of fifteen to twenty-five years (ibid.). Others have continued to operate, providing jobs for even longer periods.

(*d*) The co-ops have repeatedly demonstrated higher labor productivity than comparable traditional mills. Measures employed have been physical volume of output per hour, quality (value) of product, and economy of material input use. Measures of 30 percent to 50 percent higher co-op productivity have withstood the test of tax court challenges (see below at note 8) (ibid.).

(*e*) The co-ops have been efficient users of raw materials, and they have tended to require less capital per worker than traditional plywood mills, while still showing greater productivity (ibid.).

In sum, they have provided their members with secure and well-paid employment over an extended period of time, and in doing so they have used natural and capital resources efficiently.

It can be argued that an almost unique combination of factors accounts for the plywood co-op experience in the United States. First, the need to create employment in the states of Washington and Oregon was met by people who were used to hard work and self-reliance, people who could also count on long-term work based on the area's timber resources. Second, the Pacific Northwest has a heavy concentration of people of Scandinavian origin, people who may have been culturally more inclined to seek cooperative solutions to common problems than some other ethnic groups have traditionally been.[7] That factor might have been particularly significant in the early years of the co-ops. Third, the co-ops were formed in the growth period of a major new industry. These early positive factors have given way to dramatic cyclical fluctuations in the industry, rising capital costs, resource scarcity, and the development of a diverse array of work opportunities in the Northwest— factors that have made the industry a less favorable one for new co-op formation in the past 25 years.

An unusual feature of several co-ops in the 1950s involved the role of promoters in their development. Promoters established themselves as brokers of co-op stock shares and also occasionally as sales agents for their product. Speculation and eventually fraud developed in the sale of co-op shares, and criminal charges were brought against promoters (Berman 1982a, p. 163). The publicity of their trials, according to Berman, cast suspicion on worker-ownership proposals of any kind and worked against the formation of additional co-ops in the industry.

The plywood co-ops have ranged in size from 60 to 500 workers, and their average plant size has been close to that of the industry (Berman 1982a). Within the co-ops, the work force is made up of both owner-members and employees of the co-op. Employees have historically made up between 10 and 50 percent of the total work force of these mills. Recent data (see chart) indicate that employees currently make up between 3 and 63 percent of co-op work forces. Employees have traditionally received pay and fringe benefits that

7. For an indication of the influences of Scandinavian culture in the Northwest, see O'Connor 1964. The role of cooperatives in the Swedish economy today is assessed in Schaaf 1977, ch. 4.

equaled or slightly exceeded those received by workers in traditionally owned mills (ibid., p. 164; Bernstein 1980, p. 22).

Co-op owner-members are predominantly male, and there is little representation of minority groups in the population. In one sample of approximately 250 members from four co-ops, males accounted for 97.1 percent of membership. Whites were the same percentage. Median age of respondents in that sample was 43.5 years (Greenberg 1979, p. 20). When owner-members were asked why they had joined the co-ops, the most important factors cited were the appeal of the financial investment, potential for good income, and job security (Greenberg forthcoming). More recent research has substantiated earlier findings that owner-members enter the plywood co-ops with individualistic, property-holding motivations and that their experience with the cooperative relations of production in these firms does not alter those motivations (Greenberg 1981b). The degree to which relations of production in the plywood co-ops are cooperative and the impact of those relations on people working in these firms are issues addressed below.

The plywood firms have been members and supporters of the American Plywood Association, the industry-wide trade association that they share with independent, privately owned mills as well as with the industry giants such as Weyerhauser and Georgia-Pacific. This association has served as a promotional organization, and it has undertaken research and development and quality grading tasks, thus providing the smaller, independent producers, including the plywood co-ops, with services they might not have been able to duplicate individually. In recent years five plywood co-ops formed the Plywood Marketing Association (PMA), a cooperative organization designed to provide them with some of the benefits that their more vertically integrated competitors enjoy. One of those original five co-ops is now a traditional firm. The PMA has ventured into railroad car ownership by establishing a Plywood Marketing Transportation Corporation (PMTC), which is owned by the five PMA members. During busy periods it has owned or held purchase agreements for as many as 1,000 cars that were used solely for shipment of PMA plywood. The PMTC was described to this researcher by a co-op manager as both a means of assuring that the co-ops involved could deliver their high-quality product with a minimum of transit damage and as a good source of depreciation for its co-op owners.

The plywood co-ops have formed few linkages beyond those mentioned above. There is some evidence that they have lent funds among themselves, and they have occasionally shared management personnel. They also formed a Worker-Owned Plywood Association to study their tax situation and lobby on their behalf. Although they have the potential to share other administrative, marketing, and financial services, they have not developed further linkages for several reasons, as follows:

(*a*) Many of the co-ops do not see themselves as advocates of a cooperative form of organization. Some seem to view themselves as accidents of history, as firms that adhered to a co-op model out of necessity rather than any strong commitment to it.

(*b*) They have sought to avoid publicity, particularly in light of the attention paid to them by the U.S. Internal Revenue Service. The plywood co-ops won the landmark tax court battles that enabled workers' co-ops to treat members' earnings as patronage, and they also won the right to pay their members at higher rates than industry norms owing to their greater productivity.[8] Those higher payments reduce the co-ops' (but not individual members') tax liability. Believing that the regional IRS office would still like to win reversal of those rulings and that anything that calls attention to them could stir up expensive new litigation, they are publicity shy. Recent Department of Justice—Antitrust Division investigation of price fixing in the timber industry has also made the co-ops cautious of any further linkages or attention-generating activities. At least one attorney who has represented the co-ops has advised them to keep out of the news, avoid researchers (the IRS has reportedly offered to subsidize the work of at least one researcher), and be very cautious about any form of joint undertakings.[9]

(*c*) The realities of the competitive marketplace work against linkages. Plywood co-op members have been found to think of their individual co-op as "one big family," united against a hostile outside world (Greenberg forthcoming).

---

8. The cases were, respectively, *Linnton Plywood Association v. U.S.*, 236 F. Supp. 227 (D. Oregon 1964) and *Puget Sound Plywood, Inc. v. Commissioner*, 44 T.C. 305 (1965); and *Linnton Plywood Association v. U.S.* and *Multnomah Plywood Corporation v. U.S.*, 410 F. Supp. 1100 (D. Oregon 1976).

9. From interview with Robert M. Kerr, attorney and senior partner of Tooze, Kerr, Marshall & Shenker, Portland, Oregon, June 19, 1979.

Informal oral communication between co-op managers does roun-tinely take place. Five co-ops exchange their periodic financial state-ments among themselves. Whether the difficult times in the industry will stimulate interest in new forms of interaction remains to be seen.

The plywood production process is similar in the co-ops and traditional mills. Logs come to a mill by road, rail, or water trans-port. They are peeled into veneer, and the veneer is trimmed and fed through a drier to achieve a specific moisture content. The veneer is then glued and "laid up" into plywood panels, which are cured under heat and pressure. Defects in a panel are patched, and the panel is sanded if it is to have a finished side. Inventories are kept low in a well-run plant. One co-op this researcher visited was particularly proud to point out that only three days generally lapse between entry of logs to their holding pond on the Columbia River and shipment of their finished product from their railroad siding. Some plywood firms are increasingly buying veneer from independent veneer suppliers and cutting down or diminishing their "green end," veneer-peeling operations.

The plywood co-ops are located near the region's supply of their raw materials: Douglas fir, spruce, and pine. In outward appear-ance nothing except perhaps a word or two on a sign differentiates the co-op mills from their conventional counterparts. A small, wood frame building typically set apart from the plant houses the office staff; some of the mills have a retail sales shop adjacent to the mill. Inside the plant itself production goes on for two or three shifts a day, five to six days a week. The shop floor is a world of machine and manual work, of ear protectors and hard hats, and of the constant aroma of softwood. As the manager passes through the plant, members want to know, "How' we doing this month?"

The plywood co-ops are part of an industry in transition. Re-sources are not as readily available in the Northwest as they once were; much of the prime growth on privately owned land has been cut, and publicly owned land is now cut on a sustained-yield basis. Technological advances in log peeling make it possible to use smaller and lower-quality logs in plywood production. That change has sped up new development of the industry in the southern United States, where smaller-diameter pine can be grown more rapidly than the high-quality fir and spruce of the Northwest. Big pro-ducers have invested heavily in the "coniferous corn rows" of their southern plantations. With them have come new, more mechanized harvesting techniques and more automated plants located in Louisiana, Alabama, and other southern states.[10] To date, those plants cannot produce quality sanded plywood more competitively than the co-ops of the Northwest.

Organizational and Decision-Making Structure

The plywood co-ops share remarkably similar organizational structures, a result of adherence to the original organizational form of Olympia Veneer and, later, the need to meet legal requirements for tax treatment as cooperatives. In all of these firms, the general membership has final authority over and responsibility for all matters. Members of the co-op are those who own a "working share" or a "working unit" of shares in it. Shares are transferable, although most co-ops specify that before a share is sold, it must be offered to the co-op for purchase, and that if the co-op does not purchase the share, it must approve the new individual purchaser. Thus members have control over who is to become a member of their co-op. A share carries with it the right to work in the plant and to share in its proceeds.

Co-op members have universally agreed to delegate the day-to-day responsibility for running their firm to their board of directors and manager. A typical co-op will elect all seven or nine of its directors at its annual meeting. Candidates for the board must be nominated at the quarterly meeting that precedes the annual meeting, and the nominees' statements of qualification are distributed to members in advance of the election. Incumbent board members must be renominated each year if they are to be reelected. Some bylaws specifically exclude co-op members who are already in positions of some power, such as the superintendent, foreman, or log buyer, from serving on the board. Board members can be removed by majority vote of the membership.

Directors generally meet biweekly. Minutes of all board meetings must be posted within a few days of meetings. Those minutes include detailed information on motions made and how directors

10. The majority of plywood production units in the South were built in the late 1960s and mid-1970s. APA data list no mills in the South prior to 1964 (American Plywood Association 1982a).

voted on motions. The board has authority to make capital expenditures, although sometimes a maximum figure, $20,000 in one co-op, is stipulated. Beyond that figure, a majority of the general membership must approve the expenditure. Directors generally elect officers of the co-op from among elected directors for one-year terms. They also choose a manager and superintendent(s), subject to ratification by members in some of the co-ops.

Plant committees, typically chosen by the board, play an important role in the operation of these co-ops. Staffing of many of the jobs in the plant is generally the function of the elected bid committee. It determines the mix of seniority and skill necessary to place a member in a particular job, and it runs the system whereby members bid for jobs. This form of self-determination helps assure equality of assignments and procedures for job rotation. A plant committee may serve as the co-ops' judiciary, hearing complaints, conducting hearings, and imposing a limited range of penalties or recommending action to the board of directors. In some co-ops a separate grievance committee serves similar functions.

The organizational structure of one of the plywood co-ops is represented in Figure 2. Notes indicate some of the variations found in other co-ops. As the figure shows, authority flows from the co-op's owner-members, and the board and management administer the co-op on a routine basis. This organizational chart differs from other representations (Bernstein 1980, p. 16; Greenberg forthcoming) by showing the duality in the work force: owner-members control the co-op, but another sometimes sizable portion of the work force exists outside of the organization's governance structure.

Organizational charts do not convey the actual human interaction and process of decision making within the co-op. At general membership meetings there are discussions about everything from the manager's performance to capital investment decisions. All major decisions are put to a vote. Information that forms a basis for policy decisions is widely available to members. Monthly reports on performance are mailed to members, and minutes of all meetings are posted in the mills. Members have (and practice) the right to ask to see any documents or data that might interest them. Board members continue to hold their regular jobs in the mill, so they are constantly available to discuss policy matters with owner-members. Greenberg (forthcoming) found that approximately two-thirds of a sample of 280 co-op owner-members answered "always" or

FIGURE 2. Organization of a typical plywood cooperative. (Source: author's field notes and plywood co-op bylaws)

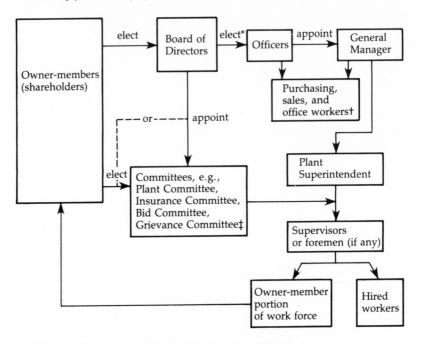

* Officers may be elected within the board or elected directly by members.
† May be appointed through Bid Committee.
‡ Generally elected directly by owner-members.

"very often" when asked if there was much discussion in the plant concerning production, investment, and other policies. Levels of participation vary, but policy issues are widely debated, information is available, and none of the writings on these co-ops points to a situation in which a small group of owner-members actually controls a firm.

Decision making on the shop floor offers some contrast to the level of participation and involvement evident in policy decision making. The work process of the co-op is similar to that in traditional firms, and shop floor participation in decision making is not the norm. Workers do have more freedom to perform jobs as they see fit in the co-ops, but they are subject to a hierarchical job structure and a pace and flow of work largely determined by the production technology. The co-ops use significantly fewer supervisors than their conventional counterparts; the average in the co-ops is one or two per shift of 60 to 70 people as opposed to five to seven in conventional firms. Some co-ops simply place the "lead operator" in charge of a particular operation in the production process. Owner-members are willing to take direct action to solve production problems, and they also perform some of the policing function that supervisors and foremen perform in traditional mills. There is considerable peer pressure among owner-members to perform a job well.

Bylaws of the co-ops usually specify in detail how a job is to be carried out. Jobs such as master mechanic, sales manager, head electrician, and office manager are awarded on critieria of skill and seniority. Duties and responsibilities of each job are determined by the board of directors, and a hierarchy of supervision for normal operations is clearly spelled out in bylaws. Disciplinary action, including provisions for appeals, suspension, and discharge, are also generally enumerated. A two-thirds membership vote is required for discharge, which takes the form of elimination of work and voting rights and leads to sale of the working share.

Many of the co-ops have had or now have subsidiary operations. These have been primarily veneer plants that operate near forest sites. Subsidiary operations of the co-ops are not themselves cooperatives. They operate with a hired work force and one or several co-op owner-members as supervisors (Bernstein 1980, p. 21). The Plywood Marketing Association and its Plywood Marketing Transportation Corporation are also structured as traditional firms, not co-ops.

Plywood co-op members control their co-op with a combination of representative democracy in the election and in the operation of the board of directors and direct democracy practiced at general meetings. The organizational form and decision-making process that are common to the co-ops reflect a pragmatic, income-oriented motivation on the part of members. Members seem satisfied that they have adequate opportunity to direct their organization through participation in major decisions and policy formulation. They take their work process as given, and they explicitly affirm a need for hierarchy in shop-floor relations of production. The organizational and decision-making structures of these firms contain a combination of both traditional and nontraditional structures and methods. This same mixing of the familiar with the unusual is apparent in their financial structures and methods, which are discussed next.

Capitalization, Financial Structure, and Income

The plywood co-ops were financed originally by workers contributing equal amounts to capitalize their firms. Their working share or unit entitled them to employment, to one vote in general membership meetings, and to the income and risks associated with ownership.

Members in the co-ops own their shares individually. When they decide to sell their shares, they must locate a buyer who can pay their asking price and be approved for membership by the co-op. Information about shares for sale is made available through word of mouth and by newspaper classified advertisements. Shares in the most successful co-ops have occasionally sold for as much as $100,000. Shares of that value generally require $20,000 to $25,000 down payment to the selling member, and payments of $500 to $600 per month until the balance is paid off. Interest on the unpaid balance has recently varied between 7 and 10 percent (1979–82). In some cases a percentage of the new owner's patronage dividend (earnings distributed periodically from accumulated earnings above the payment of monthly advances) is also paid to the seller for several years. In less financially successful co-ops, shares have sold in the range of $10,000 to $25,000. Some firms are involved directly in the repurchase and sale of the shares of their departing members, and some of those firms do not charge interest on the unpaid balance of the share purchase price.

The co-ops do not generally create new shares. To do so would diminish each owner-member's annual income (Bernstein 1980, p. 21), and for those organized as corporations creation of new shares would also involve expensive compliance with state and federal securities regulations. Firms that have sought expansion have been able simply to hire more workers, avoiding the less readily reversible commitment to additional members. Firms have occasionally retired shares by exercising their option to repurchase when a share comes up for sale. Through that process, at least one co-op has recently reduced its number of owner-members.

FIGURE 3. Flow of revenue and sources of equity in a typical plywood cooperative. (Source: author's field notes and plywood co-op bylaws)

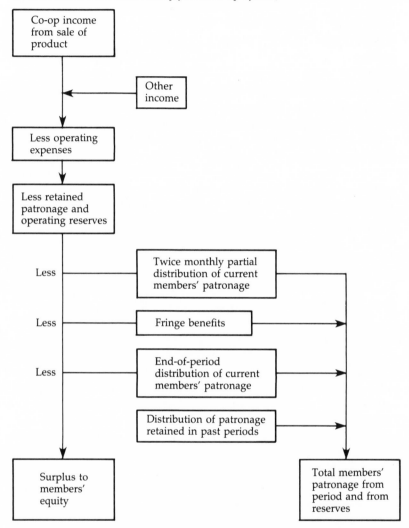

Figure 3 shows the flow of revenue to a co-op's members in a typical plywood co-op. Net proceeds remaining from operations after all co-op expenses are paid are considered members' patronage. From these earnings, board members determine the amount to be held as retained patronage, and the amount to be paid as routine bimonthly advancements. One important function of retained patronage accounts is to accumulate funds for payment of the co-op's taxes. Determination of tax liability with the Internal Revenue Service is a slow process, and a year's tax bill frequently is not known until late the following year.[11] Patronage retained for this and other specific purposes is often classified as restricted reserves and patronage for general business purposes as unrestricted reserves. One co-op divides unrestricted reserves into accounts called contingency reserves and capital reserves. Contingency reserves represent the equivalent of short-term working capital to the co-op. The capital reserve fund is the primary source of new investment capital for the co-op. The members' share of each of these funds is credited to their patronage accounts according to the hours they have worked in the period of the income. No interest is paid on this capital contribution. It is not considered a debt of the co-op to any of its members, and members' claim on this patronage contribution is subordinate to all debt and liabilities of the co-op. If at any time the board determines that it has an excess of retained patronage, it is paid out against members' income credits in the order that the credits were earned. If income for a period is insufficient to cover advances that have been made, reserve accounts of members during that period will be adjusted to reflect the "loss." Such a situation of insufficient reserves generally results from a period of fast-falling prices.

The plywood co-ops rely heavily on member financing and debt for new capital investment. They venture into capital markets for short- and medium-term debt, but they rarely issue bonds, preferred stock, or nonworking equity shares. Their use of debt was, for some time, limited. Reasons commonly cited were, first, that they are an unconventional organizational form, one in which lenders could not easily identify "the person in charge." Second, given the co-ops' complex accounting system, the lending officer in a commercial bank was unable to assess easily the magnitude and legal status of owners' equity to be used to provide security for major loans. The co-ops' record over the years has helped diminish those problems. Co-ops that are major employers in a small city or town tend now to have close working relationships with local lenders. A recent example is Astoria Plywood, which was able to

11. I am indebted to Katrina Berman for pointing this out and for clarifying some details of the plywood co-ops' financial structure reported here.

work through a local bank and a port development authority to finance a major capital improvement.

Co-op income is distributed to members on a basis of their hours of work during an accounting period. Opportunity for capital appreciation is not likely to attract outside ownership, since stock prices in part reflect the relatively high earnings to be realized through work by owner-members.

All owner-members punch a time clock, and a strict accounting of work time is maintained. Work performed by owner-members is paid equally, no matter what the skill involved or the seniority of the owner-member. Most of the co-ops not only pay their members equally on an hourly basis, but also seek to equalize members' annual incomes by equalizing the hours worked during the year. Many of the co-ops hire skilled workers for a few special positions, such as plant electrician, and those workers are paid regular salaries.

Co-op members' incomes vary considerably with fluctuations in market conditions for their products. In the relatively strong markets of 1979 and early 1981, many of the co-ops used a base wage rate of $12 per hour. Members' incomes were augmented by their ability to work more than 40 hours per week, by time-and-a-half pay for that overtime, and by distributions of excess retained patronage from previous accounting periods. In those good times, members' annual incomes reached $40,000 in the more successful firms and more than $20,000 in the less successful. By the summer of 1982, the impact of high interest rates in the economy and a depressed housing market had produced 10 to 25 percent reductions in the base wage, loss of overtime opportunities and some fringe benefits, and, for some firms, the threat of end-of-year losses. Data gathered by this researcher indicate that in the three years 1979–82, owner-members' incomes dropped approximately 25 percent in unadjusted dollars and perhaps as much as 50 percent in real dollar terms.

Despite their reduced incomes, co-op owner-members are still working. Their employees in many cases have been less fortunate. By mid-1982 most of the co-ops had laid off some or all of their production employees, and they had reduced the pay and benefit package of the remaining hired work force by an average of 10 percent.

The plywood co-ops vary their labor input in two ways. First, members may decide to work more or fewer hours, according to market conditions. Many of the co-ops have operated for long periods of time with extended work weeks. With time-and-a-half rules in effect, these are periods when members can greatly increase their annual incomes. If market and cost considerations dictate, members can also cut back their hours, and sometimes they take on other jobs in addition to their co-op work. The second and more traditional way the labor force is adjusted involves nonmember workers. Some of these employees are relatives or close friends of owner-members. Other nonmember workers are prospective owner-members who are saving money to buy a share. All employees can be laid off if poor market conditions dictate production at less than full capacity. Only one of the eleven co-ops has a unionized work force; approximately 25 percent of its total work force is made up of employees, and they are represented by the International Wood-workers of America.

Financial pressures of the plywood industry have accelerated in recent years, taking their toll on the co-ops. These pressures include need for substantial new capital investment to meet environmental requirements and, most important, a spectacular rise in the price of timber, the co-ops' raw material. One estimate of the price increase is a 400 percent rise in the past seven years, including a 90 percent rise in the worst of those seven years (Berman 1982b). Other figures indicate a 1000 percent increase in the stumpage price for Douglas fir in the ten years between 1971 and 1981 (Alaska Consulting Group, Inc., 1981, p. 5). Some co-ops have experienced severe difficulty in maintaining the supply of logs to their mills at any price. Financing log inventories has also become very expensive in periods of high interest rates. None of the presently operating co-ops has had the capital to invest in timberland at a level that would assure their own source of supply, as the industry giants have done. Federal government programs to set aside timber from national forests for small businesses have proven inadequate (Nagle 1979b).

With the co-ops heavily dependent on capital reserves built from members' withholdings from earnings, and many of them starting from failing traditional firms that were badly in need of recapitalization, their history has been one of capital shortage. Some have managed to sell nonvoting equity shares in their communities; an example is Astoria Plywood's sale of $250,000 in preferred stock in 1952. Those funds were needed to meet a financial crisis not long after the co-op was formed. All shares have since been retired. Recent changes in industry technology and shortages in timber supply have left the co-ops with increased need for capital, but that need, as has traditionally been true of co-ops, comes at a time when incomes are not increasing and members are least able or willing to reinvest. Past research has recorded the tendency of co-op owner-members to seek to maximize their take-home income at the expense of future investment and income (Berman 1982b). One manager interviewed by this researcher estimated that 50 percent of his time was spent identifying potential areas for, and especially *encouraging*, capital reinvestment. He was both a manager and an owner-member, and his predecessor had been as well. Berman points to the willingness, or lack of it, on the part of the plywood co-op members to undertake long-run capital investment as possibly "the crucial difference between successful and unsuccessful cooperatives" (ibid.). Principles of business finance indicate that the price of shares should reflect the present value of the future stream of income they represent. One of the principal determinants of the magnitude of that income is a firm's level of capital investment. Berman suggests that if members would think more like owners and less like workers, they would invest at higher levels (ibid.). Another co-op manager concurred. He argued that there has been a change in the attitudes of owner-members he has worked for, with young owner-members today desiring more present income for consumption (homes, pickup trucks, boats) than younger owner-members did twenty years ago. No matter how much members choose to invest, it is unlikely they will be able to buy enough timberland to assure their firm a steady and more competitively priced flow of logs. Thus their access to timber sold from both private and public lands is crucial to their survival.

In terms of their industry, these co-ops are small, independent, and locally based. Their industry is increasingly dominated by vertically integrated multinationals, and the market for softwood plywood will be affected by new substitute products that can be made more cheaply in the South or in another country. The co-ops have been able to survive because of the superior quality veneer available in their region and because of the high quality of their finished product. As the price of that product climbs, greater room for substitutes is created. Whether any of the plywood co-ops acting alone will have the continued financial strength to operate successfully under that kind of multinational market pressure remains a vexing question.

The Ten Conditions

In the chart on page 119 the plywood co-ops are evaluated in light of the ten defining and facilitating conditions for workers' self-management. Three issues raised by that evaluation are discussed below.

Issue: Self-Management with Hired Labor

In organizational terms, the most obvious difference between the practices of the plywood co-ops and the defining and facilitating conditions for self-management is that these co-ops hire workers.[12] The issue of hired labor has been a long-standing problem for workers' co-ops, one that has historically been linked to their degeneration.

The owner-members of the plywood co-ops are their core work force. The co-op can adjust the size of that core upward by selling more shares or downward by exercising the option to buy shares of retiring members. Historically membership has been adjusted downward as labor-saving technology has been adopted (Berman 1982b). In general, a workers' co-op might adjust membership downward if it does not foresee an opportunity to expand its production by adding new capital and holding constant or increasing its membership, if it chooses to use a higher proportion of hired labor, or if it chooses not to expand.

The plywood co-ops use hired labor for two purposes. One is to fill a limited number of positions that require specific skills, such as the plant electrician. People in those positions generally receive a wage or salary that is higher, on average, and more stable, than the income of owner-members. The second purpose is of greater concern in this discussion.The plywood co-ops hire labor to make up as much as 47 percent (63 percent in the unusual case of Hardel) of their overall work force. Their long-term membership levels generally are based on the number of members who can be kept

12. The term *hired labor* is used here to refer to regular or seasonal employment relationships between co-op members (the co-op) and workers. Some self-managed firms use a trial membership period in which prospective members must legally be employees. If so, that trial period should ideally be of a specific length (e.g., three to six months), and it should end in either membership or termination of the relationship.

Summary evaluation of the plywood cooperatives

Conditions (see page 35)	Evaluation
Condition 1	Control and management is not the right of all who work in these firms. The right to participate has to be purchased through share ownership, rather than being based on work. Both of these issues are discussed in the next section of this chapter. Owner-members do share equality of voting power, and these firms use mostly representative and some direct democratic processes.
Condition 2	Income earned by these firms belongs to their owner-members. Employees who are not owners earn a wage, rather than sharing in income. Owner-members determine income distribution; it is highly egalitarian among themselves, and it takes a largely individual, cash form.
Condition 3	Originally these firms were funded through stock sale. Ongoing capital needs are met by retained earnings that are individually accounted for and by debt financing.
Condition 4	This condition is violated by the linkage between member's ownership of a share and the right to participate in control of the co-ops. Members' allocation of reserve funds do not receive interest. Debt from external sources receives market interest rates, and some loans from members have been paid interest.
Condition 5	Rents to capital in these firms are not accounted for separately, so there is no clear way to set them aside for accumulation. See the next section for a discussion of the use of retained earnings for capital investment.
Condition 6	Information is readily available to owner-members and partially available to employees. Shop floor task skills are shared by owner-members, and managerial skills are shared through committee and board service. Sharing of some skills is limited because a few highly skilled jobs are not generally filled by owner-members.
Condition 7	Bylaws spell out provisions for voting by secret ballot on important issues, redress of grievances, and due process in disciplinary cases. Other rights, such as freedom of speech, are generally practiced but not formally guaranteed.
Condition 8	Most of these co-ops have some form of elected plant committee to serve as an independent judiciary. Appeals go to the board of directors and are not part of a fully independent process. The board is also charged with upholding the bylaws of the firm.
Condition 9	A participatory consciousness is evident only in limited ways in these firms. There is little or no education for self-management.
Condition 10	Shelter or support organizations that exist to serve the needs of the co-ops are few in number and limited in function. The Plywood Marketing Association is the one linkage among several of the co-ops, and a Worker-Owned Plywood Association has sporadically served some of their common interests.

working during periods of low demand for their product. Labor needs for periods of higher demand and for seasonal periods such as popular vacation times are met with hired production workers. Employment security does not exist in the U.S. economy as a whole, and it is one of the members' leading objectives in joining the co-ops. They largely meet that objective, but they do so while providing minimal security for nonmember workers.

Another aspect of this relationship also deserves attention. The plywood co-ops provide their owner-members with higher incomes than other mills provide for similar work. That higher income is no doubt the result of the firms' higher productivity and lower supervisory costs, but it may also be partly attributable to members' collective exploitation of hired labor. If employees are contributing to surplus, then owner-members have the same incentive a traditional employer has to use hired labor to augment their own income. Since the co-ops with the highest numbers of hired workers are not necessarily those returning the highest incomes to their owner-members, confirmation of a hypothesis of exploitation will have to await careful analysis.

A third important aspect of hired labor in the plywood co-ops is that employees do not have the right to participate in decision making. Both in this sense and in their job vulnerability, they are truly second-class citizens of these co-ops.

Are plywood co-op members better off because they use hired labor in production? The answer is clearly yes, because they are able to vary the output of their mills considerably while varying their own labor time over a relatively smaller range. Of course, they also feel they are providing jobs that pay well to people who want them and thus helping their communities. But there are probably costs in this process for owner-members. They are less readily apparent than the benefits, but worthy of investigation.

Earlier in this chapter it was noted that the internal work process and organization of production is similar in the co-ops and traditional plywood mills. This similarity is surprising given that the co-ops have had sixty years to modify their production process to suit their own goals and needs. In other situations with high levels of workers' control, research has reported rapid changes in the way work was carried out, and cases of technological innovations based on significant participation by workers in shop floor decision making (Espinosa and Zimbalist 1978, pp. 148–151). It can be argued that unique changes in technology have not taken place in the plywood co-ops because of the dual status of workers on the shop floor and because the technology and traditional work process constitute for owner-members a form of technical control over hired labor (Edwards 1979, ch. 7). Technical control serves to mask potentially antagonistic interests between these two groups of production workers.

Having two classes of workers in these firms also impedes an organizational culture of cooperation. Education for cooperation and self-management would be hypocritical in this setting; it would emphasize the lack of equality among people performing the same tasks but not having equal voice in the management of the firm. Any progress toward an all-inclusive form of self-management would be shattered when a downturn occurred and one part of the total working community was laid off while the other kept working. In sum, the dual citizenship structure of these co-ops raises the specter of exploitation, it may be responsible for limiting innovation on the shop floor, and it stunts the development of a fully cooperative work organization. Could it be overcome?

There are several alternatives to hiring labor for these and other co-ops. The most obvious for the plywood co-ops is for the members to absorb the impact of cyclical fluctuations more fully themselves. That would mean expanding membership to higher than core levels and then cutting back hours among all members during downturns. Members' income would rise and fall over a wider range from good to bad times in the economy, although reserve funds could be used to smooth some of that variation. Co-ops could also seek members who, for whatever reason, did not want full-time or year-round work. Those members' rights to participate could be based on their degree of involvement. For example, they could have partial votes in policy decisions based on the number of hours that they work. The co-ops' method of income distribution according to hours of work would lend itself to such an arrangement.

If enacted, these changes would essentially transfer the burden of the economy's instability onto all of an organization's members. By doing so, and at the same time allowing the organization to function as a full-fledged cooperative body, they would create incentives and organizational means by which the co-op could seek more imaginative solutions for problems of cyclical fluctuation. One such solution might be diversification into other industries; capital contributed by incoming members could help finance that diversification. Another solution might be linkages with other co-ops to develop marketing programs aimed at both increasing and smoothing product demand. Confronting market instability might even involve the co-ops in developing and working toward nonmarket forms of distribution for the firms' product through a local or regional planning process. Facing the full impact of fluctuations could weaken these firms, but on the other hand it could help mold them into more cohesive, innovative, and forward-thinking organizations.

Hiring labor is a clear violation of the most fundamental condition of workers' self-management. It blocks the development of an effective self-managing internal organization, and it re-establishes the employee-employer relationship that self-management should overcome. It constitutes the clearest path by which workers' co-ops have historically slid backward into capitalism.

Issue: Financing through Stock Ownership

The plywood co-ops illustrate some of the problems inherent in attempting to establish a cooperative form of production in an economy in which private ownership of productive assets is the rule. Financing these organizations through stock ownership creates fundamental barriers to establishing and maintaining workers' self-management. These barriers include the property rights rationale that is fundamental to stock ownership, problems of placing a value on stock in a cooperative venture, the tendency of stock shares to bring about future distortion in power within the organization, and the barriers that shares create to member entry and exit.

Stock ownership carries with it a bundle of property rights. One way to create a firm that can be controlled by the people who work in it is to allow only people working in the firm to own its stock. That leaves control, one of the property rights, in the hands of the producers in the firm. The plywood firms were not created under such a rigid rule, but they have created much the same outcome by eliminating most incentives to nonworker stock ownership. But workers' self-management is based on the principle that the right to control is based on work, not on capital ownership. That right should remain with those who work; it is not property to be bought or sold. In a political and philosophical sense, property rights of stock ownership are part of a capitalist rationale of control over property and accumulation, and they do not mix well with an organizational form based on other principles.

In more pragmatic terms, how to value stock in a cooperative venture is a serious problem. According to conventional investor logic, the value of stock shares is based on their potential future income stream, including both periodic distributions and a projection of any gain (or loss) in value of the share itself. Most stock transactions for publicly traded companies are highly impersonal; people and institutions buy and sell millions of shares daily based on a wide range of public information and analysis. Investors' individual strategies might differ, but investors are fundamentally seeking monetary gain. A prospective investor in a workers' co-op, though, is doing much more than simply investing funds. He or she is purchasing a claim of a firm's assets and income as is the traditional stock purchaser, but is also buying a right to a job and membership in a cooperative organization. How is a value calculated for those acquisitions, even if one claims that they should be rights to be acquired? For members buying into the plywood co-ops, there are indications that prices of shares are arrived at on the basis of expectations of relative job security and of income that, though variable, is often higher than the share purchaser might expect for other similar work. The rights and responsibilities of a voice in the management of the firm are viewed simply as flowing from the fact of stock ownership.

Although not the case in the plywood co-ops, stock ownership that links the right to participate in decision making to the fact of ownership has historically led to violation of the one-worker, one-vote principle for cooperatives. Under traditional property rights, votes are allocated by shares, and those investors who have more financial investment in the firm are thereby afforded a greater voice (more votes) in making decisions. Stock-linked voting rights in co-ops have historically led to members buying other members' shares and gaining a greater voice in management, or they have led to the sale of shares to people outside the co-op and a gradual loss of control by those working in the organization. Co-ops seeking to raise more capital have issued new shares and allowed members to acquire multiple shares, multiple votes, and multiple claims on income paid to capital.

The plywood co-ops have avoided some of these problems by

use of their working shares or working units. Their share or block of stock carries with it only one vote, and members can hold only one share or unit. But these co-ops have had other problems inherent in linkage between membership and stock ownership. Most notable is the barrier to entry created by rising share prices. This problem becomes more acute as a firm becomes more successful. Few prospective members have $10,000 to $20,000 for a down payment on shares, even if their future income as owner-members will enable them to make payments of hundreds of dollars a month. The problem also affects members who want to retire or leave the firm; they encounter difficulty in finding buyers for the expensive shares of the firms they helped to make successful.

Given these problems, some of the successful plywood co-ops have chosen to sell out to investors, effectively terminating the co-op. The sale has allowed owner-members who wanted to retire to do so and others to work for their new boss while investing elsewhere their receipt from the share sale. One co-op that recently had financial difficulties is being sold in another way. Shut down for six months and near failure in 1980, Puget Sound Plywood brought in a new manager and gave him a contract allowing him wide discretion in developing a strategy to "save" the co-op. With the backing of a majority of members, he exercised the firm's option to buy back shares, acquiring them from approximately 35 percent of the membership who were not put back to work after the shut down. Some members attempted to mount a legal challenge, but were unable to do so because of a first-offer clause that gave the co-op the right of first refusal in any stock transfer. Members whose shares were to be retired were offered $10,000 each for them, and they were encouraged to sell by the argument that their shares would be worth far less if the co-op closed. Members to be retained were selected by the manager and board of directors on the basis of "ability to produce." The firm continues to employ twenty non-members. The manager's strategy is to prepare the firm for sale. It is generating surpluses now and it is apt to be most saleable when the plywood market revives. Owner-members who remain at that time will receive substantially more for their shares than the $10,000 received by those who were first bought out. A number of complicated issues are involved in this transition, but at the heart of it is the idea that membership in a co-op is somehow a property right, to be marketed for one's best advantage.

Problems of stock ownership can be avoided. A financial structure and capitalization plan that reflects the defining and facilitating conditions for self-management is consistent with a full-fledged workers' cooperative, rather than one that is an amalgam of co-op and corporate structures. Such a plan involves payment by members of a membership or capitalization fee. For a firm already in operation that fee can be paid over time from earnings; if a firm is being created, then an initial payment toward the fee may be necessary. The fees are kept in individual equity accounts, and future payments toward capitalization are credited to those same accounts. When the member retires or leaves, the amount in the account and its accrued interest are payable to the departing member. Although all of the individual account is due a member on departure, some co-ops have found that delaying repayment helps discourage members from resigning because of immediate cash need. Repayment can also be spread out over several years to help insure against rapid decapitalization in the case of multiple retirements or departures.

An equity account specifies a member's claim on a well-defined portion of a firm's assets, but unlike a stock share it carries with it no "property right" of control. Members share in decision making and income (or loss) based on their work. They retain a claim on their invested funds, on any portion of surplus credited to their account, and on interest that it has earned. The problem of stock valuation is eliminated, and appreciating stock share prices do not constitute a barrier to entry of members or to their departure.

This arrangement essentially eliminates use of an equity (stock) market for the most basic financing of self-managed firms. All members do contribute funds, but under different rights and conditions than with stock ownership. The firm retains the ability to vary the amount of assets available to it by changes in membership fees, adjustments in the amount of income assigned to reserves, and creation of funds for special purposes. It can create a limited amount of collectively held equity from its income. It also has the ability to use its assets as a basis from which to contract for external debt financing if it so chooses.

Issue: Using Retained Earnings for Reinvestment

Among the difficult decisions to be made by members of a self-managed firm, few are as important to the life of the firm as how to renew capital through investment. Some portion of the funds for new investment typically has to be derived from retained earnings. If the firm is structured to avoid underinvestment (see Chapter 2), earnings retained in a firm can be an effective means of capitalization. But if the firm is generating income at a level considered by its members to be less than adequate, reaching agreement to channel some of that potential cash income into new investment is not easy. Yet the firm's chances of generating higher incomes in the future are apt to be directly affected by the level of investment in the present.

This dilemma is not a new one. Workers' cooperatives have been heavily influenced by consumer co-op models, which have not emphasized the importance of capital accumulation. In addition, workers' cooperatives are not typically created by people with significant wealth or sources of nonwork income. Their original capitalization process frequently takes most of their members' savings, and possibly personal debt on their part. When a new co-op begins to generate income, it is apt to be needed on a daily basis by its members. Co-op members' natural tendency has been to opt for the payout of most income. Add to this the fact that most new workers' co-ops are relatively labor intensive, with little opportunity for income tax protection generated from depreciation of plant and equipment, and there are powerful forces operating against increasing ratios of capital to labor through retained earnings.

U.S. tax law for co-ops allows an advantageous method by which they can accumulate capital through retained earnings. Subchapter T of the Internal Revenue Code allows co-ops to retain a portion of members' patronage dividends and "evidence" them to members by written notice of allocation. The member remains liable for paying tax on those retained funds, but they are held in the member's name in the co-op. Evidenced retained patronage dividends can take two forms: qualified and unqualified. Under qualified written notice of retention, the co-op does not pay tax on the retained earnings, and the individual member does. Tax law requires the co-op to distribute to members at least 20 percent of the amount tagged for retention so that members can meet their tax liability on retained earnings. With nonqualified written notice of patronage allocation, the co-op pays the tax on the total amount retained, but when the funds are distributed, the co-op's tax payment is reimbursed by the IRS, and the members incur the tax liability at time of distribution. Under both of these plans, the individual eventually pays the tax on patronage income. Both allow for accumulation of funds and for retaining individual claim on members' invested capital.

It is worth recalling here that it is the members who decide the level of regular periodic distributions of income ("wages"), and thus their decisions, along with the firm's overall performance, determine the amount left as surplus at the end of an accounting period. Assuming that workers' co-ops have an astute enough tax lawyer to provide them with good advice on the use of Subchapter T, they still must decide how much of that surplus to set aside. When they do decide, they may make it mandatory for that amount of the surplus to be "evidenced" and used for new investment or they may set a lower mandatory amount and give members the option of adding an additional amount. That kind of choice might help satisfy members who need immediate income, while encouraging reinvestment for those who do not. It would require accurate co-op accounting practices, which would already be in place if co-ops are maintaining members' accounts. A base of retained earnings would be available for new investment, and it could be used to leverage additional debt financing if the new project and financial health of the co-op allowed.

The plywood co-op that makes most complete use of retained earnings specifies in its bylaws what they call a "revolving patronage capital fund." The co-op's board decides each year what portion of surplus should go to this account in order to capitalize the organization continually. The fund revolves on a five- to seven-year basis. Amounts contributed are distributed to members (or departed members) after they have been in the fund for the specified period. In the case of this plywood co-op, no interest is paid on the funds, and they do not constitute debt of the co-op to its members but, rather, its patronage capital. In the early 1980s, when many of these co-ops are feeling heavily burdened with high-interest debt, the co-op with this fund is recognized (and envied) as financially the most secure in the cluster. Its relatively modern plant and equipment have helped it achieve consistently high earnings per member relative to most other co-ops in the cluster.

A consumer cooperative in Nanaimo, British Columbia, uses an unusual form of financing that could be applied to workers' co-ops. Its net effect is similar to the plywood co-op revolving patronage account, but in this case the financing takes the form of debt, rather than equity. The Hub Co-op in Nanaimo is a direct-charge consumer cooperative. The aspect of its capitalization relevant to this discussion is a system of mandatory saving through a 2 percent service charge levied on consumer purchases of goods that are otherwise priced at a break-even level. This service charge is converted to debt owed by the co-op to the member. A loan certificate is issued when a member's account balance reaches a specific amount; the certificate stipulates the term of the loan (three years in 1982) and the amount of interest to be paid. It is redeemable at the end of the period, when the member receives the principal and accrued interest. This system allows the co-op to plan ahead for and vary the amount of capital it has on hand, and consumers contribute debt funding to their co-op in proportion to their patronage with it. Applying the same principle to a workers' co-op, some portion of retained surplus would be converted to debt. Members would pay taxes on it as distributed patronage in any tax year, and they would receive interest payments on their debt, holding their certificates until maturity and then receiving the principal. As the certificates matured, they would have, in addition to the interest income regularly received, payments of the principal from each certificate they held. The interest paid to members would be a tax deductible expense to the co-op. Members who worked more with a co-op would both earn more and loan proportionately more to their firm.

Financing through retained earnings is most necessary in an economy in which income distribution makes it difficult for potential members to save funds or in which financial institutions such as Mondragon's *Caja Laboral* are nonexistent. Funding through retained earnings has led to fundamental problems for co-ops, but even when many of them are solved through appropriate financial structures, the challenge to set aside enough from earnings to increase capitalization remains. Some of the plywood co-ops have managed to do this, especially in years when the market favors them. Many other self-managed firms, including the reforestation co-ops, still face the problem of, on the one hand, getting their income levels up enough to retain and invest more and, on the other hand, achieving higher levels of capitalization to generate higher incomes. When society leaves the provision of funds for co-op development to private sources, and members do not themselves have much savings to invest initially, then some form of retained earnings provides a difficult but necessary route to eventual financial strength.

Evaluation

At least two authors have recently argued that the plywood cooperatives fully meet their criteria for workers' cooperatives or self-managed firms. Berman states, "The worker-managed plywood enterprises conform to the principles of cooperative organization" (1982b, p. 77). That statement is technically correct, since traditional (consumer) co-op principles allow "nonmembers" to do business with them. Greenberg states, "It can be said without hesitation, then, that the producer cooperatives in plywood are genuinely self-managed enterprises, being institutions in which all policies are subject to the control of the workforce" (1981b, p. 33). While claiming that the plywood co-ops are the "only large-scale industrial enterprises in the United States where the people who work in them are in complete control" (Greenberg 1981a, p. 969) and that they are "truly self-governing institutions" (ibid., p. 970), Greenberg does not mention that not all of the people who work in them take part in the governance process. The defining and facilitating conditions used in this study inform a different understanding of these firms. Because of the plywood co-ops' use of hired labor and their linking of membership rights to stock ownership, these firms resemble egalitarian (for owner-members) capitalist partnerships, rather than fully cooperative or fully self-managed firms. Owner-members share control and a material incentive system that give the plywood co-ops the characteristics of a conventional partnership among equals. Like a conventional partnership, the owner-members employ second-class citizens who, even if they are paid the full value of what they produce, still work only when their employment serves the material interest of the controlling partners.

The use of hired labor and the vesting of control in owners of stock are closely linked and major shortcomings of these co-ops relative to conditions for full self-management. They result from basing the rights of members on the fact of ownership, not on cooperative production and work in common. These co-ops are controlled by capital. Owner-members provide funding for the co-op, and they are thereby entitled to control the firm. From the perspective of nonmember workers, there can be only marginal differences between working for a co-op with many owner-members, and working for a conventional plywood firm owned by traditional investors.

It surprises some observers of the plywood co-ops that organizations that are democratic and egalitarian at their management levels do not demonstrate those same characteristics at the shop floor level. Observers do note the need for less supervision on the shop floor, in part because all owner-members tend to act as supervisors. They also note the relatively greater autonomy of shop floor workers in the co-ops. But the pace of work, the technical relations of production, and the actual technology observed in the co-ops are very similar to those in the traditional mills. Greenberg has observed that:

> the actual day-to-day governance of the work process does *not* demonstrate a great degree of variation between the plywood cooperatives and the conventional firms. This is especially the case with respect to the pace and manner by which raw logs are transformed into finished plywood panels. The similarities can be traced to the simple fact that the technical processes, the composition of the machinery, the optimal level of operation of the machinery, and the division of labor are virtually identical in all of the plywood plants, cooperative and conventional. That is to say, unless one were especially knowledgeable and blessed with a discerning eye, one could not easily tell the difference in the actual production process between cooperative and conventional firms. [Greenberg 1979, p. 25, emphasis in original]

That this degree of similarity exists in the labor process and production technology of these two types of firms is remarkable. The co-ops have had decades to modify a frequently noisy, dirty, and sometimes dangerous production process to suit the interests of the owner-members who work with and control it. But in this instance the owner-members do seem to act more like owners than workers. It appears that their interests are well served by allowing a particular technology and a traditional hierarchy largely to determine work relationships.

The shop floor is the arena where the co-ops' organizational contradiction is most apparent. There two classes of workers come together, and an attempt to apply the egalitarian processes of co-op management in this setting would surely raise traditional tensions between employer and employee, between capital and labor. Members have made a decision, consciously or subconsciously, to leave conventional technology and work process unchanged in their co-ops so that they provide a rationale for how work is carried out. In capitalist firms that same technology and process have been derived from specific organizational objectives that are closely related to the goal of private accumulation of capital (Braverman 1974; Marglin 1974; Edwards 1979). The labor process in conventional firms expresses a specific work relationship: that between decision maker and subordinate. The same relationship exists in the plywood co-ops, where the potential for self-management within the firm has been severely diminished because of adherence to traditional concepts and prerogatives of ownership.

This critical evaluation of the plywood co-ops must at least note the fact that they are located in a capitalist environment and that most of their members have joined them based on desires for a sound financial investment, good wages, and assurance of a job. The reality of competing in a market economy, weathering its ups and downs, and remaining solvent has obviously helped shape these firms. Although the impact of a firm's macro environment on it will be addressed in Part III, it could be argued here that in many respects these firms have managed to remain remarkably egalitarian and cooperative *despite* their environment.

Although they cannot be considered fully self-managed, the plywood cooperatives are unique among workers' co-ops in their numbers, their presence in their industry, and their longevity. In the best of cases, they do offer further evidence that workers *can* operate their own firms, and in doing so achieve the income, output, efficient use of resources, and quality of product that are at least on a par with traditional firms, and in some cases superior to them. They offer important lessons about organizational and decision-making structure and about some of the special financial problems in the United States for which workers' co-ops must seek solutions. They most certainly provide encouragement for the further development and refinement of production that is fully controlled by all of its workers.

CHAPTER 5

Worker Takeovers of Established Firms

Over the past decade, there have been numerous attempts by workers and communities to buy established firms. These attempts have frequently involved firms that were going to be shut down, either because they were losing money or because they were not making enough profit to satisfy their owners. The impetus for these efforts has generally been saving jobs.

Most attempts to save failing firms are only marginally related to the subject of this study. Whether they lead to viable firms or not, few involve a shift in control over the firm to the people working in it. Even in cases where control is shifted to workers, it may lie with a few managers who own most of the capital, with a small percentage of employees, or with a trust that is not under workers' control. None of these situations establishes a very sound basis for development of workers' self-management.

This chapter deals with two firms in which forms of workers' control have been established. Neither firm was shut down before its takeover, although one, the Rath Packing Company, had been losing money for years. It has continued to dance on the edge of bankruptcy after its bailout by its workers. The other case is one of workers buying out their former owner. Denver Yellow Cab

Research on the Rath Packing Company involved on-site investigation and interviews with union, company, city, and county officials in July and August 1979, February 1980, and August 1982. Other sources have included company quarterly and annual financial reports, drafts of various stages of the agreement between Local 46 and the company, and public agency planning documents. Research on Denver Yellow Cab Cooperative Association involved on-site interviews with union and co-op leaders in 1979 and 1982. Other sources included early drafts of co-op bylaws, debates over the transition as represented in union and co-op newspapers, and current co-op bylaws.

Company was purchased in its entirety by its workers. Yellow Cab was a profitable company, and it has prospered and grown in the years that it has been a co-op.

Rath Packing Company is a nationally known meat processor. The worker takeover there has kept the firm alive for four years, protecting more than 2,000 jobs. The union local that initiated the takeover was able to achieve a substantial amount of worker and community control through its bold action, but movement at Rath toward workers' self-management has been slow. The union local that initiated the Denver Yellow Cab takeover had prepared a plan to restructure the firm into an organization that could be controlled by its work force. More rapid progress toward workers' self-management has been made there.

Both of these takeovers were the product of union action. The role of unions in planning and initiating takeovers and their role once workers' control is established will be explored as one issue emerging from these cases. Another issue to be explored is control itself—how it has been won, its particular significance in these cases, and its importance for workers' self-management.

Rath Packing Company

Rath Black Hawk hams, bacon, and sausage are known throughout the country. Less well known is the fact that Rath workers own a controlling interest in their firm. The story of the Rath takeover begins in 1979, at the end of a dismal ten-year period for that company. The history of Rath and events surrounding the takeover will be summarized here; they have been reported elsewhere.[1] This study will focus on the changes that have taken place inside the firm, and Rath's efforts to survive after the takeover was accomplished.

Rath started doing business in 1891. Its primary production facility is in Waterloo, Iowa. A smaller production plant is leased in

1. The literature on Rath includes Gunn 1980c, ch. 3, 1980b, 1981a, 1981b; Foote 1981; Minsky 1981; "An Acid Test For Worker-Owners" 1982. Material from Gunn 1981a © and reprinted by permission of The Trusteeship Institute, Inc., Cambridge, Mass. Gunn 1981a was erroneously retitled "The Fruits of Rath: A New Model of Self-Management" by editors of the journal in which it appeared. Its more pedestrian but also more accurate original title was "Rath Packing Company: Issues of Workers' Ownership and Control."

TABLE 1. Rath Packing Company sales and profit or loss, 1970–82

Year	Sales in dollars	Profit or (loss)
1970	$280,131,000	$ 804,000
1971	280,986,000	3,787,000
1972	277,436,000	(4,616,000)
1973	363,308,000	106,000
1974	389,183,000	323,000
1975	399,365,000	(6,066,000)
1976	388,887,000	(7,187,000)
1977	365,197,000	(999,000)
1978	330,688,000	(6,441,000)
1979	316,895,000	(1,485,000)
1980	424,705,000	2,388,000
1981	465,434,000	(9,582,000)
1982	434,700,000	(6,492,000)*
Net results from thirteen years of operations		$(35,460,000)

SOURCE: Rath Packing Company annual reports, 1970–82
NOTE: Figures are rounded to nearest $1,000.
*Does not reflect extraordinary credit from termination of retirement and pension plan.

Indianapolis, Indiana, and the company owns a second slaughter plant in Columbus Junction, Iowa. The Waterloo plant was once the nation's largest meat-packing plant; years ago it employed more than 5,000 workers. From hog pens to shipping dock the six-story plant sprawls over two urban blocks beside the Cedar River. Across the street are Rath corporate headquarters, the L & M Tap ("open for breakfast at 5 A.M."), and the Union Hall of Local 46, United Food and Commercial Workers International Union, AFL-CIO (formerly Amalgamated Meat Cutters and Butcher Workmen).

Few attempts to save a firm provide such a graphic example of the uphill battle involved. Rath's problems have a long history. Their annual sales and profit or loss are summarized in Table 1. A lack of capital investment in the 1960s was heavily responsible for the disastrous decade of the 1970s. By the end of that decade Rath operated under the multiple burdens of old plant and equipment, declining market share, and a shortage of working capital. The company was paying very high interest rates for essential short-term funds and had little chance of raising capital for plant renewal. Rath's working community has been locked in a struggle for survival. Rath workers are on average over 50 years old, and most of them harbor few hopes of other decent work if Rath closes. The largest employer in Waterloo, a John Deere manufacturing facility, has been operating at less than capacity for several years. There are few other alternatives that pay anywhere near the Rath wage average of $10 per hour.

The effort to save Rath has been both a private and a public one. Rath is the second largest employer in Black Hawk County; it accounts for 2,200 jobs in the local economy, a local annual payroll of approximately $35 million, and a market of $30–40 million for local hogs. A shutdown at Rath would give the county's economy a severe jolt.[2] Concerned for Rath's future in 1978, the Black Hawk County Economic Development Committee landed a U.S. Department of Commerce–Economic Development Administration (EDA) grant to hire consultants to work with the firm to determine how to make it competitive again. The consultants concluded that $4.5 million in improvements to plant and equipment were needed if Rath was ever to be profitable again. Since funding at that level was not readily available to a firm with losses of over $20 million in its previous four years of operation, the Economic Development Committee sought funding for Rath through the Urban Development Action Grant (UDAG) program of the U.S. Department of Housing and Urban Development (HUD). HUD-UDAG officials indicated that a grant could be provided for Rath if new equity capital was also invested in the company.

Finding a supplier of major new equity capital to a firm in deep financial trouble seemed unlikely, except for a special enticement. Rath had authorized, but not issued, a block of stock that was larger than the amount already issued. A new investor could acquire that stock and effectively control the firm. At least one investor was seriously interested, and he presented a plan to make the company profitable again. As so many plans do, his plan required the company's meat packers to take substantial pay and benefit cuts. Since very little new investment had taken place in the firm over the previous decade, it was argued that the only way it could be competitive was for members of Local 46 to give up

2. In 1978 Black Hawk County's labor force was 67,000; its unemployment rate would have taken an immediate jump of over 3 percent if Rath had shut down. Planners estimated that secondary-effect unemployment caused by loss of consumer and company purchases would have pushed the rate from 4.9 percent at that time to 15 percent. For additional information on the economy of Black Hawk County, Iowa, see Gunn 1980c, ch. 3.

their nationally negotiated contract wage and benefit levels. For the workers involved, that meant giving up years of important gains, with no assurance that more sacrifices would not be called for in the future to assure profits for some owner. Workers were likely to reject those concessions.

In March of 1979, Local 46 officials presented their own plan for gaining the needed equity. The employees of the firm would provide equity capital by taking temporary pay and benefit cuts, and the foregone wages and benefits would be used to purchase the treasury stock shares for the employees. The workers' contributions would leverage the HUD loan, and workers would retain their contract. At the end of the two- to three-year period of this plan, employees would own a majority of stock shares. They could, by voting those shares as a block, control the company.

Other employees' funds were also involved in this plan. When negotiations over Local 46's plans got under way, employees began to deposit the equivalent of the proposed wage and benefit cuts into an escrow account. If the plan was approved, those funds would be released to the company, to be paid back without interest through future profit sharing. If the plan was not approved, the funds were to be distributed to employees. If those funds looked appealing to stockholders, another crucial part of the plan did not. With approval of the plan Local 46 would have the immediate right to name the majority of members of an enlarged Rath board of directors. Employees would thereby have majority representation on the board well before they would own a majority of shares.

Stockholders had little choice, and in June 1980 they and employees approved the plan (by then officially called the Employee Stock Wage Payment Plan). Over $5 million was released to the company from the employees' contributions to the escrow account. The employees' nominees for the board of directors were approved by stockholders, as the plan prescribed. Late in 1980 HUD gave final approval for its $4.6 million loan to the City of Waterloo, which would then loan $4.5 million of those funds to Rath for capital improvements to the Waterloo plant.

The Employee Stock Wage Payment Plan had won solid support from all quarters, but it had not yet cleared all of its hurdles. From the beginning of their initiative, leaders of Local 46 had intended to establish a democratically controlled trust to hold employees' stock. They were committed to a trust in which all members would have one vote, rather than one in which the number of votes would be based on the number of shares that each owned. They also sought to assure that employee-owned stock would be voted as a controlling block. Union officials were advised by their own attorneys and by the company's counsel to have the plan reviewed by several federal agencies, including the Employee Retirement Income Security Act (ERISA) section of the U.S. Department of Labor (DOL). That step seemed necessary because the trust would hold stock that employees could use for retirement income. The union anticipated a waiver on the ERISA regulation that limits to 10 percent the amount of a related company's stock that a pension fund type of trust can hold. Obviously, this plan's trust was of a special sort; it was not the primary pension vehicle for employees, and it was specifically designed eventually to hold 60 percent of Rath stock. In the final months of the Carter administration, the ERISA section of DOL refused what seemed like a routine waiver, and provided no reason for doing so other than "that is the rule."

That decision set union officials to work again redesigning the trust so that it would win necessary approval, while retaining the key features of democratic control and block voting. They turned to an attorney who specializes in designing employee stock ownership plans (ESOPs).[3] After considerable work and legal expense to gain what they wanted within the ESOP framework, union officials went back to Rath's new board with what is called the Rath Packing Company Employee Stock Bonus Plan and Trust. This plan provides employee stock ownership trust (ESOT) tax benefits to both the company and to employees participating in the trust. Those benefits are: (a) employee contributions to the trust need not be counted as current taxable income to them and (b) Rath can claim federal income tax deductions for its contributions to the trust. The trust should assure employees ultimate control over the company until the mid-1980s. After that time retired employees' stock will be removed from the trust, eventually diminishing its majority position unless equal or greater amounts of stock are lodged

3. Employee stock ownership plans (ESOPs) are stock purchase or stock bonus plans designed to encourage employers to sell or give a firm's stock to its employees in return for federal tax advantages. The stock is held in an employee stock ownership trust (ESOT). Employers have used ESOPs as a source of investment capital, to shift control to some or all employees, and to limit or modify pension obligations. A thorough summary of legal, tax, and organizational characteristics can be found in Olson 1982.

with it. The revised plan was approved by the Rath board, and then by Rath employees and stockholders in a December 1980 vote. The Internal Revenue Service also approved the plan. Beginning in early 1981, Rath was a company fighting for survival while experimenting with a substantial amount of workers' control.

ORGANIZATIONAL AND DECISION-MAKING STRUCTURE

A number of important changes took place in the months following ratification of the Rath deal. After a lengthy search, board members and union leaders chose Herbert Epstein as president. His past business experience, interest in the challenge facing Rath, and general sympathy with Rath employee involvement in the company made him acceptable to all parties with a voice in his hiring. In addition, his past experience in the brewing industry made him aware of the problems of industries undergoing rapid change. With his arrival several other changes were made in management personnel. On the shop floor, the union and management began attempts to involve workers in decision making.

Several new committees and a score of teams were designed to bridge the gap between what had been distinct camps of management and labor. Ideas for these committees took shape with the help of two consultants who were well versed in worker participation programs. Two top-level committees were established. The first is a Labor-Management Steering Committee composed of six top managers and six labor representatives. Its work focuses on the plant operations, and it coordinates the formation of action research teams in specific departments of the plant. These teams consist of several "natural leaders" in a department and its supervisory personnel; together they attempt to smooth production and cut costs of the departments. By mid-1982, fifteen teams were operating. They involved approximately 100 production employees in committee work on their own time, including twice-monthly meetings with the Steering Committee. Their tangible successes varied by department, but they served to diminish hostility and encourage cooperative action in problem solving.

The second major committee shares some personnel with the Steering Committee, but its focus is more forward looking and policy oriented. Called the Corporate Planning Committee, it is a policy-making group that is just subordinate to the board of directors. The Corporate Planning Committee includes the president, vice presidents for sales, finance, and production, the plant manager, and the union president and chief steward. Consultants who work with the Steering Committee and action research teams also meet with this committee.

The newly constituted and enlarged Rath board began to meet in 1981. Local 46 had selected several Rath employees for board positions, as well as a local high school principal, a former U.S. senator from Iowa, a past president of the Amalgamated Meat Cutters, and a university professor known for her research on employee ownership. Their first year was largely one of learning to work together, learning about the industry, and about the special economic conditions facing Rath.

Distinct from the company and outside stockholders is the group responsible for administering the Employee Stock Ownership Trust. Five trustees attend to the fiduciary and actuarial needs of the trust and organize meetings of its members in order to reach agreement on how to vote the trust's stock at corporate stockholders' meetings. All five trustees are Rath employees. They were originally named by the union to serve one-year terms, with subsequent trustees elected by participants. No union officials can serve as trustees. This group is quite distant from day-to-day operations of the firm, but it is potentially a powerful group should the management hierarchy not perform to its satisfaction.

Lastly, there is Local 46. It continues to perform the functions that it did before the takeover, in particular serving as intermediary between employees and their employer on issues of rights, seniority, work assignments, grievances, and other routine matters. The local works to uphold the contract that exists between it and the company. Grievances have diminished by approximately a third since the more traditional relationship existed at Rath, and they have also changed in character. Employees are increasingly filing grievances for what the union calls "bad process"—problems on production lines caused by what are perceived to be poor managerial decisions or job performances on the part of foremen and supervisors. This is one way that union members have come to demand better management of "their company."

Union officers continue to work together, but the fact that two of them were closely involved in management has occasionally strained relations among them. Lyle Taylor, then President of Local

FIGURE 4. Organization of the Rath Packing Company. (Source: author's field notes)

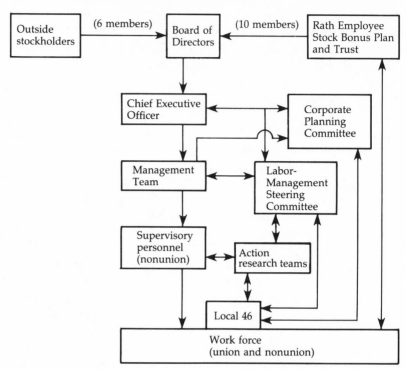

46, and Charles (Chuck) Mueller, its chief steward, served on both management committees. Union officers who are not involved in management sometimes thought that Taylor and Mueller did not always tell them all they know about the company. Taylor and Mueller contended that they withheld nothing other than personal information about management personnel. Both were directly involved in the round of contract negotiations that followed the takeover.

The hybrid corporate organizational structure that has emerged at Rath is illustrated in Figure 4. A conventional corporation would consist of the stockholders, board of directors, chief executive officer, management team, supervisory personnel, and work force, with all stockholders electing the board of directors. The union would serve as a buffer between supervisory personnel and the union work force, and it would negotiate contracts with management representatives, most typically senior personnel and financial officers. What makes Rath unique is the trust, committees, and teams on the right side of the figure. Since employees control a majority of Rath stock, there is a loop between the work force and the board of directors that most clearly distinguishes this from conventional corporations, even corporations with committee structures that allow substantial worker participation in management.

Do Rath workers control their company, and if so, how? They do have control, but they exercise it cautiously and without much direct involvement. For example:

1. The two key workers' representatives in management decisions in the company are their union local's president and its chief steward. The president is labor's direct representative on the Rath board, and both officers also serve that function on the two management committees. The members of Local 46 seem content to let two people carry much of the burden of their representation with respect to routine operations.

2. Action research team members serve as workers' representatives in departments. They work with and sometimes confront supervisory personnel, and they have contact with top management through routine meetings of the Steering Committee. Workers who serve on action research teams are volunteers. The union approved all who wanted to serve on them when they were first formed. Action research team participants constituted approximately five percent of Rath Waterloo employees by late 1982.

3. Workers are very indirectly represented by "their people" on Rath's board of directors. In exercising its negotiated right to name a majority of board members at the time of the takeover, union leaders chose a mix of people they felt they could trust and count on to do a good job. They seem satisfied that "their board" has evolved into a hard-working and capable team. Its primary task for the present is to help save the company.

Rath management is put in place by the board, and the workers' ESOT will determine the future shape of that board. Workers who choose to participate in the trust have effective but indirect control over the firm through it.

Changes took place gradually as various participants in the Rath drama felt out their new roles. Epstein worked hard to gain the trust of Rath workers and at the same time to convince them of the need for changes he felt were essential for their well-being as both workers and owners. He held regular meetings with employees to listen to their suggestions, answer questions, and sell his program. He felt that the workers should "have more say in how the company is run, but not actually run it." He argued for continuation of foremen's ability to discipline workers, but supported workers' right to a voice in getting competent foremen. In his view a small percentage of workers still needed policing, but he felt that the percentage would diminish both as workers identified their interests more closely with the company's survival and as they became more effective in policing each other.[4]

Rath's first extensive experience with changes in the management structure of production involved a seven-person meat-processing group. In setting up this experiment, the union leaders, workers, and management agreed to a common wage rate for these seven people. No job description or pay scale was established for a foreman, as plans called for the group to rotate the coordinating and disciplinary tasks that normally would fall to that person. The first year of the operation was a difficult one. One of the seven workers involved was thought not to be working as hard as the others, but the six would not confront him directly with their complaints. No one person wanted that responsibility, and there was no procedure for dealing with the issue. The problem worker eventually became aware of his colleagues' unhappiness with him, but only after months of tension among team members. Several of the group's workers slowly took over some of the coordinating tasks normally performed by a foreman or supervisor, rather than having them rotate among the group. For management, the slow development of effective team work and reemergence of a traditional hierarchy in this early experiment was embraced as evidence for the necessity of conventional authority structures.

Perhaps the most noticeable change on production lines has been the willingness by workers to cross job categories to contribute to overall production. For instance, problems with machinery now sometimes get straightened out without the delay of waiting for a mechanic. This is a change that management had sought for years at Rath.

The relationship between the union leadership and Rath's top

4. From personal interview of August 19, 1982.

management after the takeover was generally one of cooperation. Differences that arose were "pounded out." In what was a startling change at the time, Taylor ended up with two offices: one in his union hall and one in corporate headquarters on the far side of the board room from the president's office. The relationship between the union local and its parent United Food and Commercial Workers International continued to be an uneasy one. What the International views as concessions to save Rath also appear as ammunition for other packers to use in negotiations. In addition, Lewie Anderson, vice president of the UFCW's meat-packing division, has stated flatly, "It is impossible for a union official to serve a dual role in management" ("An Acid Test for Worker-Owners" 1982). The International seems willing to tolerate, but distance itself from, this local special case. More concessions would call further into question the relationship between the local and its parent union.

After the uncertainty of the two previous years at Rath, 1982 seemed to be one of some progress on internal matters, even though it was not a good year financially. Absenteeism was cut from 8 to 3.5 percent. New equipment funded by the HUD-UDAG loan cut the finished cost of smoked ham by twenty cents per pound and improved its quality. Overall productivity was up an estimated 10 to 15 percent, exclusive of the impact of new equipment.[5] Personnel changes were perhaps most dramatic: 67 management jobs, including 15 of 68 department supervisors' positions, 3 division superintendents, a shift superintendent, and a foreman, plus numerous staff positions, were eliminated. People in those positions either retired, returned to production work, or were terminated. Savings from that change totaled $2 million annually, and most union people argued that the changes should have been made earlier. Management people who remained with the firm concurred, indicating that the long wait for the inevitable shakeout had been debilitating.

Management people were not the only former employees out of work in 1982. Two hundred people in the union work force who had joined the company in the last round of hiring in 1980 were

5. Estimates of productivity increases are the average of estimates provided in August 1982 by President Herbert Epstein, Plant Manager Leroy Grittmann, and Local 46 officials Lyle Taylor and Charles Mueller.

laid off. They were primarily people working the "second kill," an additional slaughter operation that could not be run profitably at the prevailing hog prices. Although many of the workers were participants in the trust and might have attempted to fight the layoff decision through it, most seemed to accept the economic logic of that decision.

In 1982, Rath management became publicity shy. A December 1981 *Wall Street Journal* article (Minsky 1981) focused on problems of low morale, lack of direct participation, and uncertainty about the future among workers. Its title stated "Workers Who Bought Iowa Slaughterhouse Regret They Did." The article prompted a quick letter of denial, signed by 1,100 of 1,400 union members. Complaining to a reporter was one thing, but unemployment was a bleak alternative to things as they were. An August 1982 *Business Week* article ("An Acid Test for Worker-Owners") was even more disturbing to people in Waterloo because it implied that Rath's chances of survival were slim. For a company attempting to boost confidence in its credit worthiness and its ability to deliver on long-term marketing relationships, that kind of publicity was unwelcome.

In November 1982 a dramatic personnel change took place at Rath. Lyle Taylor, President of Local 46 and principal figure in the worker takeover, was made the company's executive vice president for plant operations. He had declined to run again for the union presidency that fall, and it had been clear that he was increasingly involved in management and that the board counted on his advice and sound judgment in its work. A new local union president was elected, and he took over the tasks and committee assignments that Taylor had performed for the union. Union members grumbled about the transition and about Taylor's executive salary, but they also counted on him to work from inside to help turn their company around.[6]

FINANCIAL STRUCTURE AND INDUSTRY AND MARKET CONSIDERATIONS

Rath's financial structure remains generally that of a traditional corporation. It is owned by stockholders who have provided equity

6. Further important changes took place at Rath in 1983. Herbert Epstein resigned as president of the company, as its financial problems continued. Lyle Taylor, former president of Local 46 of the United Food and Commercial Workers and then executive vice president for plant operations at Rath, was elected president on March 23, 1983.

funding. Those who owned stock before the takeover have seen their power in the corporation and their share of any future earnings diluted by the sale of additional shares. Rath uses debt as any corporation does, but with a stockholders' deficit at the end of fiscal 1982, its balance sheet did not look like those of most other operating corporations.

The major anomaly in Rath's financial situation lies not in the use of common stock, but in the two distinct groups that constitute equity holders. They are outside investors, who seek dividends and capital gains on their investment, and employees, whose desire for income from their investment in the company is mitigated by their desire for higher wages and fringe benefits. The management team serves stockholders both outside and inside the corporation, and chances are that the quest for profit at Rath will be tempered by demands by workers for traditional wage and benefit compensation. The linkage of workers' wages to a nationally negotiated labor contract was designed to guard against possible attempts to establish an employees' compensation program that would be more closely tied to the firm's market performance. How the objectives of these two fundamentally different types of stockholders will be dealt with is a question that is sure to challenge the current cooperative spirit at this firm.

When the takeover plan was originated in 1979, Rath stock was selling in a range of $4 to $6 per share on the American and Midwest Stock Exchanges. The plan called for a paper reduction in the par value of Rath common from $10 to $1 and sale of the existing treasury stock to the employees' trust at $2 per share. Trading of Rath stock on the American Exchange was discontinued in mid-1981, although it continues to be traded on the Midwest Exchange and over-the-counter market. It trades at a very limited volume, and on the Midwest Exchange it came under a temporary exemption from securities dealers' requirements because of the company's negative net worth.

People at Rath exhibited a certain amount of pride that the company continued to exist at all in 1982. If there was one goal that united workers and management, it was survival until market conditions changed for the better. Hog prices were high, but sales were off enough from the previous year that price increases to pass along high raw materials' costs were thought to be too risky. Given an industry whose finished product price and sales are closely tied to the price of substitute meats, 1982 was simply not going to be a profitable year for Rath. After losing close to $10 million in 1981, Rath seemed on the road to topping that record in 1982. That predicament forced yet another tough financial decision for Rath workers.

When workers moved to bail out Rath, one of their hopes had been that a mounting Rath debt to their pension program could be paid off by a rejuvenated company. As operating losses of 1981 continued into 1982, further savings in the company's annual expenses became essential if it was to continue operating. The wage and benefit package was assessed for ways to trim its roughly $17 per hour total by as much as $3 per hour. The place to cut was determined by management and union representatives: it was the pension program. The decision to eliminate it was a difficult one for the union, although its loss was deemed less of a disaster than a pay cut would have been. For the company, eliminating the pension fund cut $10 million from annual expenses. In addition, unfunded retirement and pension obligations of $26 million (as of October 1981) were removed from the balance sheet. Workers with ten years or more of service will lose a small percentage of their vested funds; the rest of their contributions were protected by the Pension Benefit Guarantee Corporation (PBGC). Approximately 400 union employees with less than ten years of service will lose all of their benefits, as will 200 other Rath employees. Rath has entered into a ten-year agreement with the PBGC according to which it will pay its pension liabilities to PBGC and refrain from creating new pension plans for that ten-year period (Olson 1982, p. 760). When all of the legal details of termination of the pension program are completed, union leaders plan an independent and optional worker-funded retirement plan using Individual Retirement Accounts (IRAs).

Elimination of the annual pension obligations was intended to create the possibility of a return to profitability at Rath. Particularly since the firm is dependent on a commercial credit corporation for a revolving loan for working capital, profitability remains crucial. For workers who have provided funds to keep Rath alive, profitability has several implications. First, it would mean that financial contributions to the company could be ended. They have essentially kept the company afloat after its net worth was eaten up by the past decade of losses. It also creates the potential for some retrieval of those funds. Most directly, the funds put up by workers in the original escrow accumulation would be returned to them from half of any profits until all are paid back. During that time the other half of any profits would be reinvested, strengthening the company. Lastly, profitability would increase the value of the stock shares held by the Employee Stock Bonus Plan and Trust. Higher prices would yield monetary gains to workers only if they began to sell the shares publicly, which would diminish their majority ownership position. If Rath were ever financially strong enough to consider creation and sale of more common stock, then profitability would help assure a higher sale price for these shares. If the trust then sought to retain its majority position, the price it would pay for new shares would be determined through a combination of market forces and negotiations.

From the creation of the escrow account to completion of acquisition of Rath shares by the trust, Rath employees committed $8.72 million to the firm through wages and benefits foregone (Table 2). That amounted to approximately $4,000 per contributing employee over the three-year period, or approximately 4.5 percent of annual average wages and benefits (based on an annual total of wages and benefits per employee of $30,000/year) over the period. In much of the rest of the industry, wages and benefits have been frozen during that time. Contributors stand to recoup over half of that individual investment if the firm is sufficiently profitable again and the remainder if the firm survives and there are enough younger employees to continue the actuarial turnover of the trust. Profitability will surely be a source of future conflicts within the firm, as it is closely related to the level of future wages and benefits on the one hand and outside assessment of the firm's success on the other.[7]

In addition to workers' funds invested in Rath, public funds also count heavily in the quest for survival. The grant for the original consultant's study was $50,000. The two major loans from the Department of Commerce and HUD total $7.51 million. If the firm

---

7. Rath's future remained precarious because of losses from operations of over $3 million per quarter in late 1982 and early 1983. Salaries of management personnel were adjusted downward in March 1983. Union members voted to accept a $2.50 per hour temporary wage deferral beginning that same month. Deferral wages will be repaid, given any future profits, through existing profit-sharing agreements. The wage deferral caused the International Union of the United Food and Commercial Workers to file an unfair labor practices action against Rath.

TABLE 2. Sources of funding for Rath Packing Company, 1978–82

Time	Source and terms	Purpose	Amount
1978	Grant from U.S. Dept. of Commerce Economic Development Administration via Black Hawk County Economic Development Committee.	Rath assistance study	$ 50,000
10/78	Loan from U.S. Dept. of Commerce Economic Development Administration via Black Hawk County Economic Development Committee: 6% per annum, 90-day renewable; later extended, secured.	Working capital	3,000,000
4/79–8/80	Contribution according to Employee Stock Wage Payment Plan escrow accumulation from wages and benefits foregone. Released to company in 8/80. Repayable through profit sharing to contributors.	Working capital	5,120,000
1/81–5/82	Equity capital from Employee Stock Bonus Plan and Trust contributions to acquire 60% of authorized common stock through wages and benefits foregone.	Working capital	3,600,000
10/81	Loan from U.S. Dept. of Housing and Urban Development via City of Waterloo: 3% per annum, 10 years, interest payable quarterly and principal repayments beginning 9/83.	Waterloo plant improvements	4,510,000

SOURCE: Compiled by author from Rath Packing Company annual reports, and public records.

can regain enough strength to repay those loans successfully, then their cost to taxpayers will have been the difference between their low interest rates and market rates over the terms of the loans. If the firm fails, the amount of principal the government will recoup is unknown. By helping to keep Rath alive, public funds have served the workers involved and have helped maintain the county's and region's economy. The government has also taken on some of the risk associated with this bailout effort. In addition to those loans, recent termination of the retirement and pension program constitutes a direct cost to the Pension Benefit Guarantee Corporation. It is one of many pension terminations whose cost has been borne by that agency in recent years.

Powerful market forces affect Rath's future. Its battle for survival takes place in an industry that has experienced two major changes in as many decades. Rath remained an independent producer as its industry became increasingly concentrated. The advertising budgets of Swift, Oscar Mayer, and Armour, and their access to capital through their conglomerate parent firms (Esmark, General Foods, and Greyhound, respectively), left Rath an orphan by comparison. A more recent change is quite different, but equally threatening. The beef industry has seen the rapid growth of relatively young companies such as Iowa Beef Processors and Missouri Beef, each now also owned by the larger parent firms Occidental Petroleum and Cargill. Iowa Beef and Missouri Beef are "boxed-beef" producers, that is, they ship wholesale and more finished cuts rather than carcasses. They represent the fundamental shift in beef processing to more rurally based, frequently nonunion plants, with the cost advantage of shipping more fully processed meat. Their nonunion operations pay wages of $6 to $7 per hour in highly automated plants; their cost of wages and benefits are reported to be two-thirds those of the most efficient big-name, unionized packers. Their product allows retail merchants to cut their payroll for skilled butchers. They have managed to drive the big-name packers into difficult financial straits. These beef processors have also driven big-name packers increasingly away from beef packing into pork, so that the big-name packers are competing harder for the same sales dollars that Rath needs. Meanwhile, both of the maverick beef producers are cautiously gaining experience in pork processing, waiting for market conditions to favor their full-scale entry into that side of the business.

Despite these developments, people at Rath feel they have a fighting chance if they can weather the worst of the "hog cycle." They anxiously watch statistics on how many female hogs are held back from market, a leading indicator for larger hog supply and lower prices in the coming year. Other market forces are vital as well; the abundant supply and low cost of grain in 1982 is a favorable sign for a larger hog supply, but high interest rates and high market prices for hogs could continue to hold production down. Survival at Rath involves a crap shoot against a host of market forces that Rath cannot influence.

In addition to the will to survive, workers' contributions, the loans, and relief from pension obligation at Rath, people there feel

149

that it has one major asset that could help bring it to profitability. Pork processing, unlike beef processing, is a business in which a large portion of the product is sold under a brand name. Optimists feel that a turnaround is possible at Rath because of its well-known name. It has enabled Rath to rank third in the country now in bacon sales despite its relatively small size and advertising budget. Part of Rath's strategy over the past few years has been to shift its production to more processed meats. They carry more value added in manufacturing, and they carry the recognized and marketable brand name. The strategy also represents a good defense against boxed producers' entry into pork, where their strength will lie in unbranded fresh cuts. At Rath, workers have nominal control of their company, but market forces and industry developments are also powerful controlling factors.

THE TEN CONDITIONS AND EVALUATION

In the following chart the Rath Packing Company is evaluated in light of the ten conditions for self-management. The Rath take-over is highly unusual. Leaders of Local 46 gained the right to name a majority of corporate board members before workers had a controlling interest in the company. Now, with workers holding a majority of stock shares, their representatives have an unprecedented level of involvement in the attempt to save the firm. If successful, workers will have saved their jobs, largely maintained their pay levels if not previous benefit levels, and recouped the funds that they have invested in the firm. They will also have maintained an important component of the economic fabric of their community.

The significance of the Rath takeover also results from opportunities not yet seized there. Workers at Rath could have an enormous impact because of the power resulting from their central role in production and now because of their power as collective stockholders. But for that power to be translated into meaningful change in the organization and control of production the company must survive, and the battle to survive may overwhelm all others. The need to survive may work against development of more complete self-management. Management can use it as justification for their actions, claiming that only management knows how to bring about a turnaround. The need to survive could also be used by the union

Summary Evaluation of the Rath Packing Company

Conditions (see page 35)	Evaluation
Condition 1	Control at Rath is based solely on stock ownership, rather than the work of people in the firm. Management is responsible to a board of directors that is elected by stockholders. A workers' trust holds a majority of stock shares, and participants in the trust do share equality of vote regardless of the amount of stock they hold.
Condition 2	Income at Rath belongs to stockholders. Workers are paid a salary or a wage; the wage and related compensation are based on a nationally negotiated union contract.
Condition 3	Rath uses multiple sources of equity and debt funding. Contributed funds do generally retain individual claim on them; some portion of any future profits are earmarked for collective reinvestment.
Condition 4	Private stockholders are in control at Rath. A majority of stock is currently held institutionally by a workers' trust. Interest is paid on debt financing, with the rate on some loans subsidized by government assistance.
Condition 5	Under the workers' takeover plan, half of any future profits at Rath are earmarked for reinvestment. Half will be used to repay funds advanced by workers.
Condition 6	Management information at Rath is available to stockholders and to workers' representatives. There is little effort to disseminate managerial and task skills beyond those representatives.
Condition 7	Basic liberties are not assured for people working in the firm. Workers' rights are protected through a traditional union contract.
Condition 8	Rath's judiciary system is the grievance process spelled out in the contract between the company and its organized workers. The corporation's board of directors is responsible for adherence to the bylaws of the organization.
Condition 9	Effort toward development of a participatory consciousness at Rath has been directed toward people serving on action research teams and the two labor-management committees. People involved in those groups make up approximately 5 percent of Waterloo employees. No broader effort to develop values and attitudes conducive to self-management has been made.
Condition 10	Rath is not part of a specific support organization for development of self-management. Union leaders have maintained close contacts with consultants and researchers in areas of employee ownership and participation.

hierarchy as justification for a form of centralized shared power: one that would limit development of a self-managed work force.

The proposal to bail out Rath was the work of a few union leaders who sought advice from a diverse group of outside consultants and supporters. It was not an effort that has actively involved the Rath work force. The union leaders acted in good faith, they put together a dynamic proposal quickly, and they have worked in a style that they were accustomed to. Their proposals won heavy endorsement from their membership, but they have moved cautiously in creating new structures that would stimulate active participation on the part of that membership. The plan was a good one in the protection it afforded workers and in the added power it gave them. It has primarily served to spread that power among elected union representatives, trustees of the Trust, and the Trust's new corporate board members. Local 46, like most union locals, has operated on a basis of representative democracy and traditional hierarchy. The Rath Packing Company board has reflected stockholders' interests, and, of course, it too has operated hierarchically. Opening this firm to a more fully participative governance process will require a conscious and sustained effort on the part of those who are living this bailout gamble.

What is going on at Rath is a struggle for survival in combination with an unusual amount of workers' control over their firm. So far the element of workers' control has served primarily to protect workers' material interests. In terms of their participation in decision making, it has enabled experimentation with labor management committees and shop floor problem-solving teams and the significant involvement of union representatives in management decisions. It has also enabled the appointment of a majority of board members who are friendly toward labor. These changes represent a possible foundation for development of workers' self-management if Rath survives. In the first years of this takeover no collective voice seems to exist inside or outside the union for expanded shop floor participation, a workers' council form of governance, or even significant expansion of representation through the union. It remains to be seen whether this period of substantial workers' control at Rath will lead to development of their more direct democratic participation in management.

Denver Yellow Cab Cooperative Association

Denver Yellow Cab Cooperative Association (DYCCA) was begun in 1979. It is the product of a worker takeover of an ongoing and profitable firm. The initiative to launch it and the cooperative structure that was created for it came largely from local union leadership.

The Yellow Cab Cooperative Association is the fourth largest taxi company in the country and the largest in Denver. With 400 cabs and more than 900 drivers, it is a large organization in an industry where small firms are the rule. It has expanded and operated successfully throughout its early years as a co-op.

The cab business is an unusual one. Drivers tend to be very independent people from diverse backgrounds. Most like the idea of the relative autonomy of their work while they are behind the wheel. Some drivers see their work as temporary; for others it is a longtime occupation that allows them a flexible work schedule. Some are happy to drive company equipment; others prefer to own their own cab and do so under a company license.

Full-time drivers work shifts. At Denver Yellow Cab they are typically eight to ten hours long, three to five days per week. Drivers pick up a car from the co-op ("the motor") and seek fares for the duration of the shift. Expenses are assigned on a per shift basis, and what remains in the drivers' pockets after they have paid shift leasing costs, union dues, gasoline, and other expenses is take-home pay, as follows:

Income from fares and tips
>   *less* DYCCA leasing fees for drivers or DYCCA service and maintenance fee for owner-drivers
>   *less* shift expenses for gas, tolls, etc.
>   *less* IDA dues (including benefit programs)
>   *plus* DYCCA patronage refund

equals net taxable income
>   *less* personal income tax including any tax liability on co-op surplus
>   *less* DYCCA membership fee, first five years as member (represents capital investment)

Equals drivers' disposable income.

One of the keys to making money lies in the ability to figure correctly the odds of getting a fare at a hotel, airport, or downtown cab stand as opposed to cruising likely streets. The other is quick response to radio dispatch calls for cabs.

With the help of people who were involved, it was possible to piece together the events that led to the transformation of Denver Yellow Cab into a co-op.[8] They began in 1969. In that year the

8. I am indebted to Steve Johnson for clarifying several important elements of this history. A brief description of the takeover is available in Gascoyne 1978.

drivers of Denver Yellow Cab parted company with the Teamsters. They were convinced that the Teamster hierarchy was not responsive enough to the particular needs of cabbies, who are independent contractors with their employer. Drivers left the Teamsters with the intention of forming a strong, local, nonaffiliated union to bargain with Denver Yellow Cab. The newly formed Independent Drivers Association (IDA) proved to be just that.

The idea of workers operating Yellow Cab as a cooperative has a substantial history. As early as 1973 drivers investigated the possibility of buying it and running it themselves, but financing was not available. In 1976 Yellow Cab was sold to three Houston businessmen. Their plans for restructuring the company involved the sale of all cabs to drivers. IDA members feared that as soon as enough drivers volunteered to buy a cab under this plan, remaining drivers would be fired. As the relationship between the new owners and the IDA deteriorated, IDA leaders proposed and won strong endorsement for a dollar-per-shift strike fund. That fund was set up in individual, interest-bearing savings accounts. It was begun none too soon. Problems continued in the form of a refusal by management to withhold union dues on daily trip sheets. Although contractually obligated to collect dues in a union shop, Yellow Cab stopped doing so for six weeks in mid-1977 when they claimed that Yellow Cab was an open shop. During that period union members paid their dues on a direct basis; more than 90 percent of dues were paid despite the company's actions. An IDA vote subsequently ratified Yellow Cab as a union shop under the Colorado Labor Peace Act.

In the fall of 1977 IDA members began their longest strike. It was touched off not by a direct confrontation between the IDA and the company, but by the company's lockout of all nondriving employees during a separate dispute with them. Over 900 IDA cabbies honored their picket lines. They then voted down Yellow Cab's contract offer to them. That five-week strike demonstrated the strength and solidarity of the IDA. During the strike, IDA members ran what was termed a "courtesy car operation." It amounted to an alternate cab company. Drivers did not have Colorado Public Utilities Commission authority to charge fares; they could only suggest an appropriate payment for the service they provided. They set up a dispatching operation at the union hall, and when that attracted too much attention, dispatching was done through telephones in a rented truck trailer set up in a vacant lot. Some drivers used their own personal vehicles, while others drove cabs that members owned. The strike ended when the company improved its offer to both the IDA and the bargaining units for other employees. The IDA had shown that it had power, solidarity, and competent leadership.

In early 1978 Stanley Danburg, president of Metropolitan Transportation Company, the holding company for Denver Yellow Cab and its affiliates, bought the other investors' interests in the firm. Later that year Danburg was looking for a buyer. Steve Johnson, the IDA's president, working with Tom Hanlon, Ed Cassidy, John Clingan, others at IDA, and their attorney, Ike Kaiser, set to work thinking out how their members could purchase the organization and how it could then be run as a cooperative. Not only were they able to formulate plans quickly, but this time they had potential equity funds as well; the union's strike fund was over $100,000 and growing.

Negotiations in the fall of 1978 confirmed union leaders' belief that Yellow Cab was a profitable operation and that it could be operated successfully as a co-op. In November, IDA members voted overwhelmingly to buy the company. Attorneys worked out a complicated transaction according to which workers would actually take over Yellow Cab in April 1979. The union upped its strike fund payments to $1.50 per shift in order to have $200,000 by that time. The date also allowed Danburg the tax advantage of holding Metropolitan Transportation for a year. In April the upstart cooperative was financed by a $200,000 loan from the drivers' strike fund and a $300,000 bank loan that together constituted a down payment to Danburg. The balance of the $2 million purchase price was payable to him over a ten-year period, at 10 percent interest. In addition, the co-op assumed close to a million dollars of the debt of the former organization. The drivers purchased the Metropolitan Transportation Company, which included the Yellow Cab fleet and equipment ranging from the radio dispatch system to rows of cab fenders and doors at the company's location on the industrial north side of Denver. It also included a Boulder, Colorado, Yellow Cab subsidiary and an airport limousine company. Denver Yellow Cab's building and the land on which it is situated was still owned by earlier owners of the company, and the co-op assumed the long-term lease on it.

The transition went smoothly, and in April over 900 cab drivers and approximately 150 other workers at Denver Yellow Cab began to run their own company. The organizational and financial structures that they have operated under are summarized in the following two sections.

ORGANIZATIONAL AND DECISION-MAKING STRUCTURE

With the purchase of Yellow Cab arranged and approved by IDA members, a temporary board of directors for the new cooperative association was elected. The board developed a draft of co-op bylaws that were presented to members for "consideration, discussion, amendment, and adoption" (*IDA News*, Feb. 9, 1979). Two votes were taken, as the union offices and bar were alive with discussion of alternatives. The first vote was to decide on controversial items in the bylaws; two or three choices on each item were presented to voters. Proposals that received majority support then constituted bylaw language, and the vote for ratification took place in a second twelve-hour balloting period in early March. The new governance structure was discussed through union meetings, through use of a Co-op Committee table set up in the drivers' room before the two voting dates, and through meetings between drivers and inside employees of Yellow Cab. All drivers and employees of Denver Yellow Cab, Airport Limo, and Boulder Yellow Cab were considered temporary members of the co-op, and all were eligible to vote. The new bylaws for the co-op were approved by a wide margin. Among other things, they specified the conditions of membership in the co-op and the means by which a regularly elected board of directors would be put in place.

All drivers for DYCCA must be members of the Independent Drivers Association and of the co-op.[9] Other people who work for the co-op or its subsidiaries are eligible for membership in the co-op. Including IDA there were then five bargaining units at the co-op. There are now six, and all but two of them have voted to make co-op membership mandatory for their members.

Prospective members in DYCCA sign an application agreeing to comply with the terms of the articles of incorporation and bylaws

9. Organizational and financial summaries are based on *Bylaws of Yellow Cab Cooperative Association*, revised November 30, 1981.

of the organization and agreeing to acquire a membership interest in the cooperative. The initiation fee, membership fees, and co-op capitalization will be discussed in the following section on the financial structure of the co-op. Membership in the co-op is non-transferable, and it is held only during a person's employment or driver relationship with the co-op. If members leave or are expelled, their membership reverts to the co-op. All members are entitled to one vote in co-op decision making.

Membership meetings are held twice a year. Special meetings may be called by a majority of board members or by a written request of 10 percent of the co-op membership. Communication in this co-op takes place through notices and messages posted in the drivers' room of its building. All co-op members receive the monthly *Co-op Post*, a tabloid newspaper. It has a regular staff and an editorial column that is open to members. The *IDA News* is another monthly tabloid that addresses co-op issues. It carries several regular editorial columns and an open letters section.

DYCCA's organizational structure is summarized in Figure 5. The membership elects a nine-member board of directors, which is responsible for managing the co-op. Candidates for the board must have worked at least 200 shifts, or their equivalent in hours if they are not drivers, prior to their nomination. A further restriction forbids any officer of a bargaining unit at the co-op, or any department head at the co-op or its subsidiaries, from being nominated for a board position.

Terms of office are three years; a third of the board is elected each year. Members can be reelected to the board. In 1982 board members were paid $6.00 per hour for preauthorized time devoted to running the co-op. Payment to all nine directors in any one month could not exceed $2,000.

A special provision designed to assure nondriving employees representation on the board was added in a 1981 revision of the bylaws. It guaranteed that once three bargaining units for inside workers required their members to join the co-op, at least one inside employee (the top vote getter) would be on the co-op board. That provision guarded against a co-op board made up entirely of the numerically dominant drivers. It also, of course, served as incentive to bargaining units to have their members become part of the co-op.

Meetings of Yellow Cab Co-op's board of directors take place

FIGURE 5. Organization of the Denver Yellow Cab Cooperative Association. (Source: author's field notes and DYCCA bylaws)

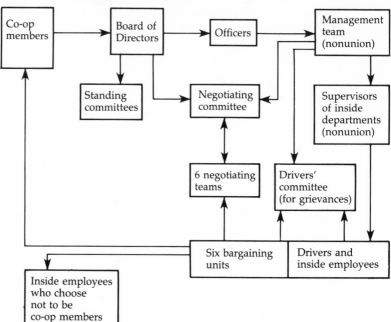

monthly. Board members elect officers of the co-op, who serve one-year terms in office. The co-op officers are president, vice president, secretary-treasurer, and assistant secretary-treasurer. The board appoints the general manager of the co-op and any assistant managers, who together constitute the management team. It has general supervision over the property and affairs of the co-op subject to the direction and control of the board of directors. In the summer of 1982 both the co-op manager and the one assistant manager were former IDA officers and had been involved in forming the co-op. All people in management or department head positions within the co-op were former drivers with the exception of the shop supervisor, who had previously been a mechanic in that shop. A new director of paratransit operations, hired from outside, also did a stint behind the wheel while assuming her new duties.

There are several committees in the co-op's structure, and two are of particular importance. One is the negotiating committee, composed of several board members and co-op managers. It represents co-op members in bargaining with its six unions. Another important committee is the five-member drivers' committee for grievances. It is made up of one co-op board member, one union officer, and three drivers who are selected randomly for any day of grievance hearings. Using a system of violation points, it can suspend drivers for repeated or serious violations of work rules. Its record to date has given it a reputation for relative lenience, although it has terminated members and it is taken seriously as part of the internal governance process.

There is a clear distinction made among two major groups of workers at Denver Yellow Cab. One consists of "outside" lease basis drivers and owner-drivers, who were independent contractors for tax purposes before the takeover and still operate largely that way. Their work is highly individualized. They compete with each other, drivers from other cab companies, and other forms of transportation to make their shift income. This work is largely self-managed in the singular sense. The other major group of workers at Denver Yellow Cab is "inside" workers. They operate the communications network, repair and maintain cabs, do accounting and secretarial work, and generally do work in support of the fleet of cabs and limousines and their drivers. Inside workers work in traditional job structures. Creation of the co-op has not drastically changed the day-to-day work routine of either group. Although both groups can be co-op members, it was the Denver Yellow Cab drivers who initiated the co-op. All members elect a board that hires and fires management, but inside workers continue to have a relatively traditional on-the-job supervisory hierarchy. Other groups in the organization are the Boulder Yellow Cab employees and the limousine drivers.

The six National Labor Relations Board bargaining units at DYCCA are: telephone operators and clerical workers represented by the Office and Professional Employees International Union; three separate units of limousine drivers, dispatchers, and some shop maintenance personnel represented by the Teamsters; skilled mechanics and body shop workers represented by the International Association of Machinists; and the taxi drivers represented by the Independent Drivers Association. All people working at DYCCA except the supervisory and management staff are union members. Over 90 percent of them are also automatically co-op members. The IDA is the dominant union voice at DYCCA. When IDA representatives negotiate a new contract with the co-op, they are, of course, negotiating with several drivers and some former IDA leaders. In general the full co-op board keeps out of actual negotiations, leaving them to its members and managers on the negotiating committee. There is considerable understanding and shared interest among the bargainers, but there is plenty of room for disagreement as well.

Negotiations naturally take place in a different climate than before formation of the co-op. Management wants drivers to make money, and drivers want the co-op to be financially capable of making improvements that will serve their work as drivers. The first contract negotiated between the co-op management and the IDA negotiators was voted down by IDA members. That vote did not result in a strike or lockout. As one former union officer who is now a co-op manager put it, the drivers were telling us "to see if we could do better; they had nothing to lose." Minor changes were made in that contract proposal, and it was ratified the second time it was presented to IDA members. Gone is the background of overt hostility and bitterness that used to color negotiations. They now involve complex bargaining over allocation of costs and division of income among various categories of drivers. Negotiations in 1981–82 produced agreement that there would be no immediate increase in shift leasing rates to drivers and that the co-op and IDA would work together in an attempt to win drivers a rate increase with the Public Utilities Commission. That appeal was successful, leading to a 25 percent increase in fares, the first granted Colorado cabs in over two years. It was agreed that proceeds from the increase would be split so that approximately 60 percent would go to drivers and the remaining 40 percent to the co-op. As the largest cab operation in the state, DYCCA and IDA working together constitute a strong voice before the industry's regulatory body.

The principal task of the IDA has always been to work in the best interest of its members. With the former traditional ownership at Denver Yellow Cab, that meant not only bargaining collectively for IDA members, but providing forms of security that independent contractors normally did not enjoy. For example, the IDA set up group life and disability insurance plans for its members. It also pioneered the first group pension plan in the United States for independent contractors—one that had to win the approval of both the Internal Revenue Service and the Department of Labor. It was created under the umbrella of the IDA's general fund and administered on the basis of seniority according to shifts worked. That program provided a basis for collective responsibility among union members who compete with each other on the streets of Denver. It preceded and strengthened collective action in building a strike fund, and, eventually, in creating the cooperative.

Much of the IDA officers' work consists now, as it did before, of negotiating on-the-job disputes between drivers and management, including department heads. These involve issues such as violations of safety rules and customer complaints. The number and content of these cases has remained roughly the same as before formation of the co-op. Now cases that cannot be resolved by representatives of the co-op and the IDA go to a drivers' committee within the co-op structure.

Do drivers need the IDA now that their numerical strength gives them effective control of the co-op? Answers to that question vary. One manager and former IDA officer argued that the tasks performed by the union could now be handled by appropriately structured committees of the co-op. A board member disagreed, arguing that the union provides a necessary balance, that it protects drivers against the natural tendency of managers and the board to think of the co-op first, at the possible expense of individual drivers. When questioned further, these and other people interviewed by this researcher agreed that a fairly natural division of interests had emerged between DYCCA and the IDA, with leaders of the former attending to the ongoing health of the co-op and leaders of the latter concerning themselves with the material well-being of their members and the protection of their individual rights through the grievance process. Although that sounds like the traditional spread of interests between management and labor, it must be remembered that the mix of common interests in this co-op is far greater than in the traditional firm. In addition, management works for labor at DYCCA.

FINANCIAL STRUCTURE

Financing DYCCA involved extensive use of debt. A portion of it, the portion that represented the workers' front money, was the $200,000 loaned by the drivers' union to their own co-op. By the summer of 1982 approximately two-thirds of that loan was paid off. The rest of the down payment, a $300,000 loan from the First National Bank of Dallas to the co-op, has since been refinanced at more favorable terms with the National Consumer Cooperative Bank. The terms of both obligations have been fully met by the co-op. The balance of the purchase price that had been financed by the seller is being paid off on schedule; it is due to be fully paid in 1989. The debt that was assumed by the co-op in the acquisition has proven an expensive burden, as the interest rate on it varies with the prime rate. It, too, is being paid off on a regular basis.

The financial aspects of DYCCA are typical of a cooperative corporation. Its initiation fee for members is $40 and is non-refundable. It is purposely low to keep it from being an economic barrier for prospective members. The initiation fee does little to capitalize the co-op. In fact, the fee was set originally at a level that would enable the co-op to pay off the approximately $40,000 in legal fees incurred in the formation of the co-op and negotiations for purchase of Metropolitan Transportation.

A membership fee of $1.50 per shift is paid over the first five years of a member's work with the co-op. It was purposely set at the same level as the former IDA strike fund, now deemed unnecessary. The typical full-time driver may work four shifts per week for fifty weeks per year, paying in $300 in that period. By the end of five years, he or she has paid in $1,500 in membership fees, assuming the rate is not adjusted during the period. The total amount of membership fees is repaid, without interest, to departing members within ninety days of their withdrawal from the co-op. Membership fees collected by the co-op serve to capitalize it and, at this point in its development, to pay off its indebtedness. DYCCA borrows operating funds from the First National Bank of Denver. That bank is urging the co-op to double its membership fee in order to pay off debt from the acquisition at a more rapid rate, even though the co-op's debt-to-equity ratio has improved substantially in its first few years of operation.

Operating income flows into the co-op largely in the form of cab leasing fees paid by drivers. The fee represents an estimate of the value of services from the co-op to each driver. The co-op has more than 100 owner-drivers, and the remaining 800-plus drivers lease cabs for each shift they work. Driver-owned cars are leased to an "opposite driver" at the owner's discretion. Owners pay a service and maintenance fee to the co-op for upkeep of their equipment.

All of these leasing fees are negotiated between the co-op and the IDA. As co-op income, leasing fees serve to meet such co-op expenses as equipment replacement, depreciation, interest, and insurance, as well as new leasehold or capital expenditures that the board deems appropriate. Any remainder is available for distribution, at the discretion of the board, as patronage refunds. If the board pays a patronage refund from surplus, it can distribute it either in cash or as retained surplus certificates (see Chapter 4, under Issue: Using Retained Earnings for Reinvestment). Certificates are payable at the end of a specific period, with interest; the period and the interest rate are determined by the board. Patronage refund payments to members are based on the number of shifts a member has worked during an accounting period. Surplus can be used for other purposes by the board, but only with the consent of a majority of members. Figure 6 summarizes DYCCA's income flow.

The past three years of operation of DYCCA have been lean years because of substantial debt service obligations, but the co-op has managed to carry out a limited program of new investment. It faces the cost of an aging cab fleet and increasing cab maintenance costs. The co-op increased its number of Public Utilities Commission taxi permits from 323 to 400 not long after it began operating. It has since acquired additional cabs for its fleet and made progress in converting its existing cabs to propane fuel rather than gasoline. The communications department of the co-op, its connection with its customers, is being moved to expanded quarters that will house new, more sophisticated equipment. The co-op purchased its own computer for financial record keeping at a cost of more than $200,000 in equipment and software. The co-op management and the board felt that the computer would help the co-op serve its drivers better and compete more effectively with Denver's other cab companies. In planning ahead for a major new investment, the board is putting aside funds in a reserve for acquisition of the industrial land and building that the co-op now leases. Board members are building toward a fund of $200,000 as a down payment on what they think will be a $1 million acquisition price. They expect that financing for the deal will come from the current landowners, the First National Bank of Denver, or the National Consumer Cooperative Bank. Board members argue that the down payment and payments on borrowed funds will compare favorably with current lease costs.

FIGURE 6. Flow of revenue and sources of equity in the Denver Yellow Cab Cooperative Association (Source: author's field notes and DYCCA bylaws)

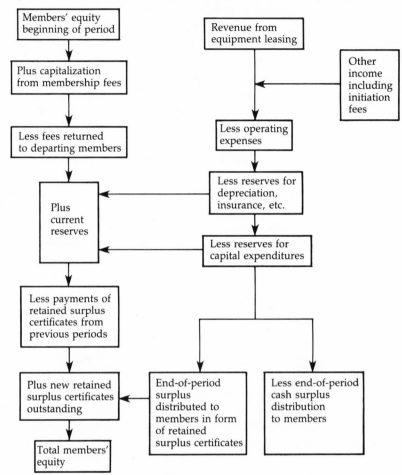

In addition, they can then more easily make badly needed improvements in the condition of the fleet parking areas, thereby eliminating one of their drivers' major complaints.

Co-op managers at DYCCA have devoted considerable time to investigating, and in some cases implementing, new ventures. A significant example is the modification of fleet cabs to run on propane fuel. Propane costs approximately half what gasoline costs per mile in the same vehicle. Converting cabs to run on propane costs $700 to $1,000 per vehicle. Payback per vehicle takes less than a year. After drivers became convinced that propane is, if anything, less dangerous in use than gasoline, and after a pilot project evaluation of both various methods of equipment modification and driver experience with the fuel, work on conversion began. Enlarged propane storage facilities and a pumping station must be constructed to make fuller use of the fuel. Benefits of the conversion are reduced direct cost to the drivers for fuel, lower maintenance costs on the cabs for the co-op as a whole, and, for the Denver environment, a growing fleet of cleaner-running vehicles. When the company was privately owned, there was no incentive to undertake the conversion; the company sold fuel at cost to drivers and could see no gain in the $300,000 to $400,000 modification cost for the fleet and more than $100,000 investment in a pumping station. DYCCA is now the second largest purchaser of propane in Colorado. When its fleet conversion is complete, it will be the largest. It has already been approached by at least one energy company for direct purchase, and when the planned new storage tank and pumping station are in place, cost savings from direct purchase can be realized.

Market growth for the co-op has been opened on two fronts. One is a more aggressive move into parcel delivery in the Denver area. In 1982 large billboards with the outline of a Yellow Cab and the co-op's dispatch telephone number stated simply "Deliverance." Another market has been expanded by the co-op's bidding successfully for Denver-area social service transportation contracts. DYCCA now has a number of vans equipped to carry physically handicapped passengers. It is also expanding its paratransit (shared transportation) operations.

Co-op management is conducting preliminary feasibility studies on other new ventures. One involves its cabs. The bulk of its fleet is made up of Checker A-11s manufactured by Checker Motors in Kalamazoo, Michigan. Checker ceased operations in the summer of 1982, and it is uncertain whether they will ever produce cars again. That could present the problem of a slow conversion to different (and, according to some drivers, less desirable) cars in coming years. DYCCA has considerable expertise in rebuilding Checkers, and it will continue to rebuild its own fleet for as long as doing so makes economic sense. Co-op management is investigating whether the rebuilding could be carried out on a larger scale, for cabs from other companies as well as its own cabs. That would take DYCCA out of the realm of a service co-op toward that of manufacturing. It is too early to know if this development will take place; launching it could take far higher levels of equity and cash flow than the co-op can generate. Its investigation does indicate a willingness on the part of co-op management to look beyond a narrow definition of members' work in planning for the future.

THE TEN CONDITIONS AND EVALUATION

In the following chart the Denver Yellow Cab Co-op Association is evaluated in light of the ten conditions for workers' self-management. Denver Yellow Cab Co-op Association is an important example of what workers can do when they are organized and when they decide to overcome their dependence on capital owners at the level of the firm. This cooperative resulted from an independent union's willingness to move beyond the bounds of collective bargaining. The union accumulated resources that were to be used as a strike fund if collective bargaining broke down and then used those resources to catapult its members into a position of control of the company. It was able to do so because it was prepared for direct confrontation if it had been necessary and because it had thought out how the company could be restructured if its workers were in control. It bought complete control of the firm and simultaneously placed its management in the hands of those who work in it. The union objective of acting in its members' best interest was met, and it continues to act in that role under new conditions today.

Throughout the history of workers' cooperatives in the United States, the first co-op in an industry has frequently served as a model for others that followed it. DYCCA may be such a prototype for other cab co-ops in this country. It has provided advice, copies of its bylaws, and the time of one of its founders to assist Capital City Co-op Cab in Sacramento, California. Capital City Co-op Cab was created after a prolonged drivers' strike in that city. It began operating under a cooperative structure in the summer of 1982. DYCCA also provided advice to a group of drivers in Minneapolis, Minnesota, who had hoped to begin their own co-op, but were unable to do so because of lack of financial resources. Union Cab

Summary Evaluation of the Denver Yellow Cab Cooperative Association

Condition (see page 35)	Evaluation
Condition 1	Control at Denver Yellow Cab Co-op (DYCCA) rests with its membership. A voice in control of the co-op is available to all on the basis of a $40 initiation fee and an obligation to pay a membership fee. Management is largely based on representative democracy through an elected board of directors.
Condition 2	Income of DYCCA belongs to its members, and distribution is determined by the board and general membership. Wages are paid to inside workers based on collective bargaining through their unions. Cab drivers' (outside workers') income is based on lease fees negotiated between their union and the co-op.
Condition 3	Funding for the establishment of DYCCA involved the loan of a drivers' strike fund to the co-op as its seed money, and the rest of capitalization came from more traditional debt. Members retain individual claim on contributed membership fees. Further capitalization can take place from retained surplus.
Condition 4	Finance capital carries with it no right of control in this co-op. Lending institutions, however, can exert influence on management decisions. Outside debt receives a scarcity-reflecting rent, as does surplus retained and evidenced. Membership fee contributions do not receive a scarcity-reflecting rent.
Condition 5	Rents to capital are not recognized or accounted for other than through interest paid on members' retained surplus and that paid on outside debt. A significant amount of accumulation has taken place at DYCCA through debt retirement and growth of equity certificate accounts.
Condition 6	Information is available to members through the co-op newspaper, and it is also disseminated through a union newspaper. Minutes of board and committee meetings are posted in the drivers' room. Managerial and task skills are not widely shared; they are most readily developed by members who are elected to board or committee positions.
Condition 7	Basic liberties are not formally assured within the co-op. They are widely upheld in practice. Some members' rights are protected through union contracts.
Condition 8	The drivers' committee serves as the independent arbiter for disputes involving drivers' work rules. Drivers and all other employees use a conventional grievance process for infractions and for safeguarding rights. The board of directors is ultimately responsible for upholding the bylaws of the organization.
Condition 9	Development of democratic and participatory consciousness has not been a major organizational objective at DYCCA.
Condition 10	DYCCA is not a part of any organization that works for the development of self-management.

of Madison, Wisconsin, bears some resemblance to Denver Yellow Cab, although there was little or no contact between their founding members. Other cab co-ops have existed in name in the United States, but they have tended to operate with hired, and frequently nonunion, drivers. DYCCA offers a prototype for others who wish to create a unionized, worker-controlled, and more fully democratic form of cooperative.

Members of Denver Yellow Cab Co-op have made considerable progress in reshaping a traditional firm into one that is self-managed. To date they have relied heavily on forms of representative democracy in their organization, which is understandable for an organization in which the majority of its members work independently. For inside employees there will be opportunities to develop more cooperative work processes and perhaps to play a leading role in future development of self-management at Yellow Cab. The challenges facing the Denver Yellow Cab Cooperative Association are two: to continue developing as a democratic and cooperative workers' organization and to gain strength and vitality as a business. In this case a basis for meeting both challenges has been established.

Issue: Self-Management, Worker Takeovers, and the Role of Unions

There are several complex issues involved in the role of unions during and after worker takeovers. Some aspects of those issues will be reviewed here, first in terms of general labor strategy and then in terms of the role of a union in the firm that emerges from a takeover.

Labor unions are working people's primary defensive organizations in societies in which a labor market prevails. Unions' actions are intended to serve their members' best interest. There have been periods in the United States when union members concluded that their best interest would be served by abolishing capitalism. The past three decades have not been such a period; for the working lifetimes of a majority of American union members, labor unions have explicitly or implicitly accepted capitalism. Whether by resignation or forthright acceptance, workers' best interests have been identified with that system, rather than with an alternative system.

This acceptance has left unions attempting, at most, to constrain capital—to gain decent working conditions, a rising real wage, some measure of job security, and perhaps some lobbying power through unions that could affect labor and industrial policy at the state and federal levels.

These goals have become so ingrained that many workers, faced with the failure of the system to provide jobs or with its ability to take them away even if they have been provided, can imagine no alternative. Given the prospect of a plant shutdown, the first option for most union members and their leaders is to join the search for a new capital supplier, a new provider of jobs. If none is found, unemployment benefits allow the unemployed time to mount a job search or move to a new location "where they're hiring." Removal of capital's investment in a plant not only eliminates jobs, but usually also means the end of the local union. A work community is shattered, and a living community may be as well.

In the cases presented in this chapter, union locals thought out and acted upon strategies to change their relationship to capital. United Food and Commercial Workers Local 46 in Waterloo, Iowa, did so in fear for its members' future. The IDA in Denver took action based on the belief that the well-being of members would be best served by eliminating the conflict between them and an outside owner.

These changes came about because workers were organized. They had a mutual basis of action, and they had funds that could help effect a transition. Those funds were available because of the long-term success of unions in raising wages to levels where some savings are possible and more immediately because members agreed to curtail their consumption to build a pool of funds for collective action.

Did these unions act in their members' best interest? The answer to that question has to be yes. Local 46's gamble may not pay off in the long run, but members have saved relatively high-paying jobs for four additional years and have some hope for longer-run security. For a work force that was on average ten to fifteen years from retirement and most surely would have had to turn to far lower incomes either through public assistance or different work outside its craft, saving their jobs is one measure of success. If Rath workers had accepted large concessions in a search for a new investor for the company, their local union may well have been broken, and they would have had less control over the company's and their own future than they gained through their unusual action. For the IDA, the takeover of Yellow Cab has eliminated routine confrontation with owners and enabled workers to control more of the income they create.

One of the most vexing aspects of these cases is that even if worker takeovers do have positive outcomes for the members of union locals involved in them, they do not fit well with the aims and strategies of national or international unions. One of the cornerstones of union strategies in the era of collective bargaining has been industrywide negotiation of the basic provisions of a contract. That process has enabled union locals to stand together against employers' attempts to play them off against each other, and it has strengthened a union's strike threats. When a union local goes its own way attempting a takeover, that unified stance is endangered. If wage or benefit cuts are part of workers' attempts to make their own firm successful, those cuts can be used by employers in the next round of industrywide bargaining as examples of why *they* need concessions.

Another problem in local takeovers is that workers who begin to run their own firm throw themselves into a world of market forces that may tempt them to behave much like the capitalists that union leaders routinely confront across the bargaining table. The operation of a subsidiary firm made up of unrepresented employees would constitute a case in point. If workers yield to that temptation, the common interests shared by the international and the local may be eroded. With union membership declining in many industries, internal threats to the solidarity of the union are hardly welcome. These are complex problems. Most internationals have made little progress in developing strategies to respond to the threat of job loss through shutdown, and yet neither have they been able to devise constructive ways to support their local members' attempts to take over the firms that have employed them. Broader issues of the relationship between labor unions and workers' self-management will be addressed more fully in Chapter 7.

After a takeover is achieved, the role of a union local cannot help but change. Its new role is easier to assess in cases where complete control is achieved than in those where control of the firm is split between outside capital holders and workers. The latter situation can heavily undermine the traditional confrontational stance of the union. Its members' new interests as partial owners restrict their range of oppositional action at the same time that lack of full control limits the development of new forms of action. The issue of control will be explored separately below.

In cases where full workers' control is established, the union can expand its role as representative of members of the firm. It can act as a counterforce to natural tendencies of almost any organization's management to concentrate on the health of the organization, sometimes at the expense of immediate needs and rights of the firm's members. The union can become an advocate for expanded democracy in the organization—for education of all members, including management, to the processes and responsibilities of organizational self-management. Chances are that it can perform this function well only if it, too, is a broadly democratic organization.

New challenges that emerge for a union following a takeover may require changes in the focus of much of a local union's work, but not its overall objective. There may be parallels between confrontation with capital owners or their representatives and confrontation with managers of worker-controlled firms, especially over questions of policy and procedure. But the terrain of conflict is different once those who work in an organization control it. Conflict is not endemic to the organization itself. Union leaders are apt to find that their tasks involve working with managers to think out organizational solutions to persistent problems. By serving as a voice for the organization's members, the union can help solve a problem that exists for most co-ops: how to respond to multiple and often conflicting short-term demands of members. By bringing some unity to those demands, the union serves the interests of its own members, who are also, of course, the members of the self-managed firm.

The union in a self-managed firm also has the potential to help distill and verbalize workers' long-term desires for their firm. It is an organization through which values and aspirations can continue to be translated into a unified set of goals after the takeover. It can help guard against tendencies toward a group capitalist mentality and can encourage movement toward new collective work relationships. By providing an environment separate from daily work pressures where members can strengthen their work and nonwork bonds, the union can also strengthen ties between the firm's members and its broader community. This lofty proposal must, of course, coincide with maintenance of a front line of defense of workers' immediate rights in their firm. These new challenges clearly point to an expanding, not contracting, role for a union local.

Going beyond what has emerged in the Denver Yellow Cab Co-op, this proposal calls on the union to protect the short-term interests of members and also to play an ongoing role in shaping the long-term character of the new organization. That task could fall to a workers' council within a self-managed firm, but when a union has played a key role in a takeover, there is no reason it cannot perform this function. In sum, this proposal points to a situation in which the firm's management team carries out routine administrative chores, steering the firm under its board's supervision and in keeping with members' policy directives. Long-term goals that shape policy should be influenced by a commitment on the part of the union to expand the conceptualization and realization of workers' self-management within that firm.

An expanded role for union locals in takeovers and development of self-managed firms clearly points to a fundamental change in the thrust of their work. Collective bargaining has diminished the oppositional character of union locals; they may use oppositional rhetoric in their bargaining with individual firms, but most do not take an oppositional stance toward the economic system itself. The role of the union local as envisioned here entails a reversal of those positions, with the result that the local works closely with its worker-controlled firm to develop self-management. Completing the reversal, its oppositional energies would focus on the capital dominated market economy. It would become an advocate for worker-controlled production in a democratically controlled economy. Local unions of this type may in the short run be a thorn in the side of their internationals, but they may also bring some new life to those organizations. The shared bond of the local and international would be a common vision of a changed society with expanded power for workers. Their shared task would be development of strategies to achieve that vision at all levels of society, while maintaining and expanding other progressive gains already won.

Issue: The Significance of Workers' Control

Both cases described in this chapter are examples of workers buying control of the firms that have employed them. In both cases workers used established property rights to transform fundamentally their relationship to their work organization. Short of development of new forms of social or public ownership that would facilitate self-management, or gaining control of factories through physical occupations as has happened in Europe, buying control is the most likely way for workers to get it. Some of the opportunities and pitfalls of this practice will be explored here. Central to the issue of control for purposes of this study is that it is a precondition to development of self-management. Ownership is only a means of establishing that control, not an end in itself.

Several problems with ownership must be dealt with if it is to be an effective path to control and self-management. One of the most difficult is that of consciousness. Most employee ownership schemes have been constructed on premises of blue-collar capitalism, on Horatio Alger tales of economic and social mobility. Their basis in a capitalist ethic has been antithetical to development of workers' self-management. Development of a different consciousness is a long-term effort—one that is most likely to result from ongoing, effective, and politically aware labor organizing.

Second, schemes that involve ownership with minimal control must be rejected. These include most formulations of employee stock ownership trusts and even majority ownership situations in which future work toward transformation of the workplace can still be thwarted by outside stockholders. If there is a lesson in comparison of the Rath and Yellow Cab cases, it is that workers are best served by gaining full title to a firm's assets. If that is possible, they have the opportunity to modify or jettison the entire stock ownership financial structure. Rather than being caught between two worlds, they can complete a transition from an inherently conflictual to a fundamentally cooperative firm.

Finally, there is the question whether a firm is viable enough to meet its members' needs as a fully worker-controlled entity. Failing firms create opportunities for takeovers, but they may also have inherent obstacles to viability that will never be overcome. Obsolete products, uncompetitive production technologies, lack of essential raw materials or forward marketing linkages, or plant and equipment so worn out or obsolete that they cannot function productively are just a few of the pitfalls to be avoided. If workers wait to be buyers of last resort, this may be all they are able to get, and in that case, use of unemployment insurance may be a better option. The minimal but important security it provides at least allows a choice to be made.

Acquiring a firm is a complex process in the best of circumstances. Workers have little chance to gain control by acquiring publicly traded shares. At the local level workers do not have the funds that conglomerates have to make a public takeover offer, and any attempt to acquire shares more slowly may simply drive up the price of shares. If outside stockholders have no other option, they may assent to a new stock issue in return for capital supplied by workers, but it is highly unlikely that workers could end up with a controlling interest by that route.

There are two more likely targets for takeovers. One is a firm that is a relatively independent subsidiary of a conglomerate, one that the conglomerate would be willing to sell because of lower than desired profitability, incompatible product line, labor problems, or other reasons. If the firm's product can be produced and marketed without linkages to the parent firm, the firm is a candidate for worker control. The second and more likely target for takeover is the closely held firm—one in which negotiations can take place with representatives of few owners. Included in this group would be firms held by investors who may be seeking other opportunities or owners who want to retire and extract their capital from a firm that they have managed themselves.

In attempting to gain control of a firm, workers are faced with many tasks, but three stand out. The first, the need to be organized and committed, was discussed earlier. Second, workers need funds to help finance the deal. Rath workers were able to gain psychological and financial leverage in their quest for control through payroll deductions into an escrow account, and through the commitment of future earnings to stock purchase. If the company were not such a willing party to the takeover effort, funds would have to be pooled by workers who want to help create their own firm. Pledges have been used as an intermediate step; they help indicate a commitment on the part of workers, but when it comes to negotiating for both a purchase and supportive debt financing, nothing works better than tangible, committed funds. Even though the accumulated assets in IDA's strike fund amounted to less than 10 percent of the purchase price of the firm, they served as a basis for the transaction. The seller wanted the deal badly enough to finance himself, or "hold paper," on over 50 percent of the purchase price in that case.

The third essential component of the takeover is establishment of a structure that will "own" the firm in the name of its workers. The legal forms of organization best suited to that purpose are a cooperative corporation or a conventional corporation with cooperative bylaws. One or the other can be formed in any state in the union. Either could also be linked to some form of community development corporation. Another organizational form that could be used is a trust designed to hold the shares of a corporation. Although an employees' trust may have a slight tax advantage over a cooperative structure, it is more unwieldy in execution and more a facilitating vehicle for a hybrid corporate structure than one suited to a fully cooperative firm. Where high levels of capitalization are needed, the employee stock ownership plan may be the only alternative (Olson 1982). Attorneys working for Local 46 pushed ESOP legislation to its democratic limit in establishing the Rath Employee Stock Ownership Trust. Where outside stockholders are not involved, the same objective can be met much more directly by use of a cooperative structure.

Workers in the United States have to buy control of productive assets if they are creating a new firm or taking over a going operation. Both alternatives present practical problems: the first means that all aspects of the operation have to be defined in one major thrust, and the second means that ingrained and probably inappropriate ways of doing things will have to be changed quickly.

Gaining control is simply a beginning. Throughout that undertaking, there must be an ongoing effort to protect and develop ideas for transforming the workplace once workers' control is established. Workers operating their own firm in a market economy cannot control very much of what will affect that firm from the outside. They do have the opportunity, though, to modify profoundly the relations of production within the firm—hierarchy, methods of income distribution, oppressive labor process, and relationships between workers and much of their technology, to name a few. If these changes are to take place while a business continues to operate, there must be a clear commitment to a cooperative and more collective consciousness. That can be accomplished only if the people involved devote time and energy to educating and empowering each other, to developing new ways of relating to each other, and to democratic decision-making processes.

Workers who have gained control over their firm are in a position to deal with the question of how they want to share that control. Control may be shared with members of the community where the firm is located. It may be shared with members of other worker-controlled firms through joint agreements, nonmarket linkages, or shared control of a support organization that may have a voice in shaping a firm's policies. Ultimately control might be shared through a democratic planning process, one that overcomes the very notion of firms acting in isolation and solely for their own gain.

Workers' control is a necessary condition for workers' self-management. Until significant social change takes place, control at the level of the firm will have to be acquired. Even when workers' control is achieved, the development of viable forms of workers' self-management is a further challenge—one that requires a clear vision of the objective and concrete plans for reaching it. Much, but certainly not all, can be achieved at the level of the firm. The relationship between issues of workers' control of the firm, self-management, and broader questions of social change will be taken up in later chapters.

PART III

LESSONS AND BROADER
CONSIDERATIONS

CHAPTER 6

Conditions for Self-Management in the Firm and the Economy

The defining and facilitating conditions for workers' self-management developed in Chapter 2 were intentionally limited to those concerned with the firm. Strengths and shortcomings of these conditions will be assessed here, as will theoretical bases for better understanding self-management. This chapter will also broaden the focus of the study, shifting from emphasis on the firm and specific cases to emphasis on the economic, social, and political environment of the self-managed firm. Guidelines dealing with industrial, technological, and work process aspects of self-management will be outlined. Macroeconomic, social, and political conditions for an environment conducive to self-management are then introduced by a review of contributions in this area.

Evaluation and Further Development

The ten conditions (see Chapter 2) synthesized from previous studies of self-management and workplace democratization at the level of the firm have served as a framework for case analysis. Salient features of specific cases have been clarified in light of those conditions; the conditions enable us to pinpoint relationships that reflect the process and very existence of workers' self-management. These conditions represent a reasonable summary of current knowledge about the self-managed firm. They can be refined as experience with and knowledge of this form of production develops further. A summary evaluation of each of the conditions used in this study follows.

Condition 1 is central to the definition of the self-managed firm.

Whether members contribute financial resources to their own firm or not, their right to share in control and management stems from their work role in it. This condition is occasionally dismissed as utopian, as being unattainable in an economy in which capital ownership is the passport to control and management. Several of the cases cited in this study demonstrate that it has in fact been met by successful firms in the United States. It has also been met by firms in other countries where direct control by capital has customarily been the rule.

Condition 1 can be criticized as overly restrictive. It makes no mention of other forms of social and community control over production. The firm does not exist in isolation, and control may be shared with other constituencies. The basic premise remains that those who work in the firm, and not capital owners, enter into mediating and control-sharing relationships with others affected by that firm. Conditions 3 and 4 are closely related to and help clarify Condition 1.

Equality of voting power is both readily attainable and fundamental to sharing control within the firm. A more detailed statement might make allowances for degrees of work involvement in the firm, such as fractional voting for part-time workers.

Condition 2 is based on the assumption that income is derived by the firm itself from its sale of goods and services. Costs include those for raw materials and financial resources, as well as taxes. Taxes could run a wide gamut from the common federal, state, and local levies to self-taxation chosen by the firm as contribution to external groups or projects.

Distribution of income specified here is a clear departure from market principles. Cases indicate that the ratio of income distribution between the highest and lowest paid workers in worker-controlled firms in the United States is frequently less than 2:1. Member incomes are in some cases lower than prevailing wage rates for similar work, but in many cases they are higher. More crucial to most firms is the measure of internal solidarity gained by relatively egalitarian distribution of income. It is definitional that members determine the criteria for distribution of the firm's income.

Condition 3 recognizes a full range of sources of funding. Under present conditions in the United States, members' contributions and borrowed funds are most likely sources. This condition was modified from Vanek's original formulation to reflect recent changes in his and other researchers' thinking.[1] Members who contribute funds from previous income or from individually assigned current income should retain individual claim on them. However, past strictures against development of collectively held reserves are not necessary as long as those reserves are built from undistributed retained earnings. Then the continuity and stability provided by some portion of a firm's assets being held collectively constitute an important legacy from one generation of workers to the next.

Condition 4 states that finance capital has no voice in control of the firm. This condition might be deemed redundant given Condition 1, but since what is proposed here contradicts normal practice, this condition represents an important clarification and reinforcement of a fundamental principle of self-management.

Should finance capital be paid a scarcity-reflecting rent (interest)? As a normative issue, the answer to that question is heavily influenced by how finance capital is owned and controlled in a society. The actual basis for this condition lies in a mainstream economic concern for efficient allocation of a scarce resource. The rent paid for scarce finance capital is intended to assure that it will be used efficiently in society. For instance, it is intended to guard against members of a very successful firm combining more and more rent-free capital with diminishing amounts of their own labor, to the disadvantage of other workers who did not have the same original access to funding. The outcome might then be a few capital-intensive firms with members earning high incomes and others starved for assets with which to work. Payment of interest on finance capital has this argument in its favor under present conditions in the United States. The argument assumes, of course, that financial markets operate as capital's rationing device in a way that is compatible with social objectives. It should be one of the conditions most open to scrutiny and revision in conjunction with potential changes in property rights, development of democratic control of investment, changes in forms of inheritance, and expansion of publicly and socially controlled productive assets. Some of these issues will be addressed in Chapter 7.

Condition 5 corrects for distributional inequality in income that could be caused by some members of a firm supplying more fi-

1. See Appendix 1.

nancial resources than others and receiving greater nonwork income in the form of interest. It temporarily neutralizes the effect on current income of inequalities in wealth holding or abilities to save among members while they are working in the firm, but allows the full value of committed funds and accumulated rents to be regained on retirement or departure from the firm. This condition prematurely assumes that there are mechanisms available for lending and borrowing among and between self-managed firms.

Condition 6 calls for full availability of information to members, subject to brief and limited possible exceptions noted in Chapter 2. The sharing of managerial and task skills facilitates self-management, and this objective can be served by job rotation, rotation of members on boards and committees, on-the-job and outside training, and other programs. Specific managerial skills can be hired or shared among firms, although the long-range objective must remain development of a full range of skills among members. An issue not addressed by this condition is that development of skills may involve cost to the firm as a whole. A firm may choose some means to recover part of those costs should a member leave the firm before it has reaped sufficient benefit from training that took place at cost to the group.

Conditions 7 and 8 can stand with little need of alteration. A firm may find it helpful to specify a range of basic liberties. These would reflect trade-offs between the good of the individual and the collective, and they could be recorded and codified to facilitate their use.

Condition 9 is both essential and inadequate. Resources of the firm must be devoted to education for self-management and to consciousness raising within the organization. Yet this is one of the areas in which commitment at the level of the firm will never fully suffice; the issues involved are influenced by aspects of members' lives at work and away from work. This condition is one of several that connects closely to larger social and political elements of the firm's environment.

Condition 10 is essential because forms of institutional support are only meagerly available where self-managed firms are unusual in the economy and society. Support organizations help overcome the isolation of firms in general in a market economy and the isolation of self-managed firms from others of their kind. Because of the focus on the firm in these conditions, Conditions 9 and 10 appear grossly understated in the tasks that they suggest. That shortcoming will be addressed below.

At a very practical level, these conditions can guide people planning to organize themselves for self-managed production. The conditions provide a means of focusing that group's attention on crucial decisions to be made in structuring their firm. The conditions have been tested empirically against past successes and failures of groups with similar objectives, and they can diminish the need for trial-and-error learning. They are not a set of hard and fast rules for implementation, and a group may have good reason to modify them to suit its own circumstances. By understanding the rationale of each condition, a group can clarify its own reasoning should it decide to modify any of them.

On a theoretical level these conditions reflect considerable work yet to be done on the self-managed firm. They are a product of disparate theoretical foundations in what have developed as separate disciplines in the social sciences. The leverage they provide could be strengthened by more fully integrated analysis. For instance, conditions addressing appropriate financial structures for these firms are based on the assumption that firms act independently in a market economy and that members of the firm act in their own individual best interest. Further, much of the financial theory used to develop these conditions assumes that people define their own best interest in terms of their financial income. It is unlikely that the goal of people who take the initiative to form a self-managed firm can best be described as maximizing income alone or that this goal will guide all decisions. It can also be argued that the more successful the firm is in expanding members' participatory and democratic consciousness, the less appropriate will be theoretical foundations based on human motives of individual material gain.

Assuming that institutions influence human behavior, the theorist has to deal not only with values and levels of consciousness when members form a new firm, but also with how they will change under the impact of their subsequent experience in it. Research should help inform us of how people expand or limit development of democracy, share power, and develop collective versus individual consciousness and then how these and other changes affect members' future actions. Much of this work remains to be done. There is at minimum a need to specify quite clearly the behavioral assumptions that underlie theoretical models and discourse. Theory also grounds empirical investigation; assumptions must be enumerated and their appropriateness assessed. This precaution could help clarify any investigation in the social sciences, but it is doubly important when dealing with atypical organizations for which appropriate theory is far from developed.

Present economic theory of the self-managed firm is neoclassical in its roots, but eclectic in its application. For instance:

(*a*) A marginalist theory of the firm normally assumes the existence of a labor market and equilibrium conditions in which people at all levels of the firm are paid their marginal value product. Yet the self-managed firm does not hire and fire labor; it adds members. That process can be explained only partially on the basis of a new member's marginal value product. In addition, the self-managed firm does not fire workers when conditions change so that the marginal value product of some portion of members is less than a predetermined benchmark. The behavioral norms of the self-managed firm are not likely to allow for decisions that would cannibalize the collective, and decisions to vary its size are not well explained by theories derived for more traditional firms.

(*b*) Methods of income distribution proposed in these conditions clearly violate precepts of neoclassical economics and labor markets within that theory. People in a self-managed firm base their distributional decisions on a wide range of considerations that cannot be explained by marginalist theory.

(*c*) Neoclassical theory embraces capital as a factor of production, and the theory of the self-managed firm does as well. But neoclassical theory assumes that when capital suppliers also organize the firm, they are rewarded with the category of income called profit. For the self-managed firm, the entrepreneurial effort is socialized in the work collective, and the category of profit does not exist. In the case of the self-managed firm, capital is rented at its prevailing price, and the firm's value added in production belongs to all who work in it.

The economic theory of the labor-managed firm is no small achievement; it has aided development of the self-managed firm as a viable alternative to the traditional capitalist firm. However, the economic theory of the labor-managed firm is also stretching the limits of its neoclassical foundations, and the results of some empirical research based on it are open to question. A case in point is production function studies common to research on traditional and self-managed firms. These studies are based on the assumption that a factor of production receives an income share that in some way indicates its productive power at the margin. Both this assumption and the way in which the studies are reported take no account of power—of politics, conflict, and bargaining—as more likely indicators of relative shares of income in the real world. Equally significant is the fact that the capital theory that grounds this work in neoclassical economics remains in doubt. Since the late 1960s it has been known that a fund (in value terms) of capital does not have any direct relationship to production; capital goods or instruments of production do.[2] Yet studies of both traditional and labor-managed firms have continued to refer to the contribution to production of "capital", regarded as a fund of money values, as determining the profit rate on that capital. This premise has far outlived any claim to scientific rigor.

Theoretical work in other disciplines—for example, political science, sociology, and organizational theory—does not necessarily provide a more comprehensive understanding of the self-managed firm. Recent developments in theories of participatory democracy and of nonbureaucratic organization offer some hope of better resources with which to carry on research. The fact that most theory is developed in separate disciplines is itself a barrier to further development of appropriate theory for self-managed forms of production. Interdisciplinary investigation could lead to a better understanding of the self-managed firm, but a reintegration of the social sciences does not come easily. Work in political economy has been productive in this area because some barriers between supposedly separate disciplines have been removed. The past decade has seen gradual development of a political economy with an emphasis on the firm. That body of thought provides a fertile base for further work.[3] Not only is it broadly integrative of the social sciences, but it develops understanding of the firm without erroneously isolating the firm from a social context: from class, power, and the macroeconomy.

2. There is an extensive and often neglected literature on the controversy over capital theory in neoclassical economics. An excellent summary can be found in Harcourt 1969.

3. This literature includes, at minimum, Braverman 1974; Burawoy 1979, 1981; Edwards 1979; and Marglin 1974.

This study points to challenging work to develop a unified and consistent theoretical understanding of the self-managed firm. This work cannot progress in a vacuum; it must parallel further development of the firms themselves. The conditions used in this study will ultimately be improved by theory grounded in people's action to create more cooperative forms of production. That action serves as a basis for theoretical formulation, for testing theories against reality, and for modification of action in light of lessons from theory. Praxis ignorant of the insight of theory will be impoverished, but in the case of the self-managed firm, theoretical tinkering devoid of practical grounding, testing, and application will be of no consequence whatsoever.

Organizational and Industrial Guidelines

Many of the ten conditions used in this study are largely definitional in nature. Conditions that deal with facilitating self-management are more difficult to specify, in part because they are closely related to issues beyond the bounds of the firm, many of them dealing with how supportive an environment exists for self-managed firms. Despite the impossibility of establishing any complete list of facilitating conditions, it is clear that decisions on industrial and technological characteristics and work process can affect chances for success. These areas of concern have not been addressed in the conditions used for this study, even though case analysis in preceding chapters and other research suggest possible guidelines, particularly for a less hospitable environment. The word *guideline* is used here in a suggestive and less emphatic sense than the word *condition*. Six guidelines in the areas of industry, technology, and work process that could facilitate development of self-managed firms are summarized in the following chart and discussed below.

The first of these guidelines involves the amount of funds needed to finance a firm in relation to the number of jobs that are created in it. In mainstream economics this relationship is summarized in the capital-labor ratio of the firm, or its *capital intensity*. Case studies of workers' co-ops and self-managed firms suggest a common dilemma for the capital-poor firm; one that stems from the fact that higher incomes for members are generally possible if the labor of

Organizational and industrial guidelines that facilitate development of workers' self-management

---

Guideline A   Industries of moderate capital intensity offer the greatest potential for successfully starting self-managed firms under conditions in which members face a constraint of limited financial resources. For conditions in the United States today, moderate capital intensity can be characterized by capital expenditures of $10,000 to $20,000 per job.

Guideline B   If economies of scale can be reached in production units of less than 300 to 350 workers, the firm can be competitive in its industry while also remaining a size that facilitates self-management.

Guideline C   The technology used by a self-managed firm should not preclude members from full participation. Development of self-management will be facilitated when technologies can be readily learned by incoming members.

Guideline D   Work processes that lend themselves to collective work around common goals facilitate development of the process of self-management.

Guideline E   Ecologically sound products or services and production methods diminish chances of antagonistic relationships among the community of workers in the firm and between the workers and the community in which the firm is located. Members of the self-managed firm can be expected to derive most satisfaction from making products or delivering services that meet basic human needs, rather than those that are frivolous or available only to the wealthy.

Guideline F   Development of self-management can be facilitated if the type of firm created can be reproduced in multiple locations—that is, if technologies, work processes, and products or services can be implemented by self-managing groups of workers in other communities.

---

those working in a firm is combined with relatively large amounts of sophisticated plant and equipment. That has been the case historically in production of goods, and it can be true for firms that provide services. Since self-managed firms tend to be initiated by people with limited funds, they are faced with a need either to invest a large amount of money or to reinvest a large enough portion of the firm's initial earnings to raise its capital intensity and its ability to generate adequate future incomes. As long as people attempting to create these firms have limited access to private and public funds, they must carefully assess the capital intensity of the operation they have in mind, both in absolute terms and in terms of the characteristics of the other firms that they will compete with in the same industry.

In recent years, new jobs in goods-producing industries have been capitalized at a cost of approximately $50,000 per full-time worker. Creators of any new firm rarely supply all of those funds. Much of the start-up funds are borrowed, and plant and equipment are often leased. For the self-managed firm, questions of capital intensity and scale are related to other questions, such as how many people will constitute the working collective, an issue addressed in Guideline B. If the prospective firm faces a shortage of assets and yet seeks to provide jobs that pay well, a sensible guideline is to start with moderate capital intensity. By current American standards that means a capital intensity in a range of $10,000 to $20,000 per job. That range still allows members to consider a broad range of activities. At minimum, this guideline focuses the attention of those who wish to create a self-managed firm on this important determinant of relative economic performance within an industry.

Economies of scale is a term used by economists to indicate the tendency, up to a point, of lower unit cost for a product through larger-scale production. Optimal economies of scale exist at the level of production at which unit costs are lowest. Both national and international experiences with self-management suggest that its democratic process works best in a firm of a few to an upper limit of 300 to 350 people. If economies of scale in an industry required more than 300 to 350 people, then methods of decentralizing the operation to allow for direct human interaction in dialogue and decision making would have to be devised. Many activities do not require more than 300 to 350 people for competitive economies of scale. Choosing an activity that reaches economies of scale within that range means that a firm can be competitive in its industry and can be a size that lends itself to self-management.

Technology used in a firm can serve to exclude members of the firm from full participation. If the technology requires a very high degree of training, then those with that training can be in more powerful positions than those without it. An extreme example is the medical services industry, in which not only are high levels of technological expertise required, but on-the-job training is hampered by regulation and licensing requirements for practitioners. Creation of a self-managed firm can be facilitated if the technology is reasonably accessible so that all members of the firm can participate in its work.

Work processes and the human interrelationships that accompany them are related to technological determinants. For instance, how individualized or collectivized is the actual day-to-day process of work in the firm? It can be argued that relatively individualized work lends itself to formation of cooperative ventures. Taxicab and tree-planting cooperatives are examples. Yet individualized work processes may inhibit development of sufficient collective bonds that are important for more complete development of self-management. Work that is relatively collective can enable people involved in it to modify more readily processes and technologies to suit their needs as self-managed producers. Incentives can be shaped to that same end. Guideline D favors work processes that allow and encourage at least some work in groups, where consultation and dialogue are a part of the collective production or delivery of goods and services.

The cohesion of a self-managed firm may be enhanced by broad agreement on the *desirability of the product or service* it produces or delivers. It seems reasonable to suggest that a product should be ecologically safe for members of the firm who will work with it, as well as for the community where they live and work. Agreement on the desirability of the product also seems more likely if it meets a basic human need in areas such as food, shelter, transportation, health care, or energy. Production of frivolous or luxury goods may limit members' satisfaction with the work they have created.

Reproducibility is an attribute that can facilitate development of self-management on a regional or national scale. The fact that a proven kind of firm could be reproduced in multiple locations would be of particular concern to support organizations that serve and advise people involved in enterprise formation. The advantages can be seen in traditional franchise operations, which serve local markets with the assistance of a centralized staff to develop products or services, help with planning, and provide advice. Often the franchises have considerable local autonomy. For self-managed firms, a reproducible technology, labor process, and scale of operation could allow a support group, perhaps structured as a second level co-op as described in Chapter 2, to help other groups plan and create new firms.

These guidelines represent preliminary thinking on many of these issues, and no claim is made for their exhaustiveness or their uniform applicability to all self-managed firms. They are intended simply to guide thinking about the kinds of activities that self-managed firms might undertake. They complement the ten conditions used earlier in this study, fitting with those that are largely definitional while augmenting the facilitating conditions. They also represent a shift in the level of discussion away from the internal operation of the firm itself and toward issues that cover a middle terrain between the firm and the macroeconomic, social, and political issues to be introduced next.

Conditions for a Supportive Environment

The conditions developed in Chapter 2 and used in the case analysis of this study were drawn from a larger group. Their selection was restricted to those addressing issues within the firm. The authors who developed those conditions addressed macroeconomic, social, and political issues as well. The following review and evaluation of Vanek's and Bernstein's suggested macro conditions[4] will set the stage for a discussion in Chapter 7 of social change that could facilitate self-management in the United States.

Macro elements from Vanek's conditions[5] can be summarized as follows:

(*a*) Any self-managed economy must rest on a philosophical and moral basis of control, management and income belonging to the people who work together in an enterprise.

(*b*) Funding of assets should preferably be based on national ownership.

(*c*) Returns to capital and land should be earmarked for accumulation and for creation of new capital assets.

(*d*) The proposed shelter organization should be national in scope, with appropriate decentralization. It is tied by his Conditions 7, 8, and 9 to national planning, supervision of capital markets, and coordination of investment.

(*e*) The ideal macroeconomy for self-management is a modified market economy.

(*f*) Education for self-management and participatory democracy is essential in society as well as in the firm itself.

(*g*) The combined rights of "economic self-determination," the right to employment and to self-management, are fundamental human rights.

---

4. Horvat's writings on self-management are excluded from this review in order to keep it a manageable task. Horvat has not specified a set of conditions in the same way that Vanek and Bernstein have, even though his writing on self-management in general and Yugoslav self-management in particular is extensive.

5. See Appendix 1 or Vanek 1975a, pp. 33–36.

The macro elements in Bernstein's suggestions for facilitating conditions[6] can be summarized as follows:

(*a*) A democratic consciousness must be fostered both in the firm and in people's larger environment.

(*b*) Job, status, and pay equalization obviously have macro as well as micro implications.

(*c*) Abolishing private ownership serves to overcome property rights that limit democratization.

Conditions that were used for the case analysis of this study focus on processes and relationships within the unit of production. They do not take into account the specific conditions of a country, its economic system, or related social and political reality. The macro conditions of Vanek and Bernstein address this larger environment. Three common themes emerge from them:

1. These conditions reflect the fundamental problem for self-management of lack of material resources that can be used for this form of production. Vanek points to a need for national funding of assets for the firm, and Bernstein more sweepingly suggests that abolishing private ownership could facilitate democratization. These and other writers have analyzed the complex elements involved in the bundle of rights attributed to ownership of capital. Forms of national, social, community, and worker ownership have been suggested as alternatives to vesting rights of ownership of the means of production in private hands. Development of a fully self-managed economy would require both a sufficient magnitude and appropriate forms of material resources for this form of production.

2. These conditions reflect an ambivalence toward allocational and distributional patterns that result from market mechanisms. At minimum they call for modification of market-determined investment priorities by some form and amount of planning and by an investment policy that would mandate resources for self-managed firms. They also advocate income equalization, another modification of market outcomes. Vanek is careful to point out that a labor market would not exist in a self-managed economy, but the economy he envisions does include many aspects of a market economy for the apparent autonomy it allows the firm. The question of how that autonomy can be maintained while larger social ob-

6. See Appendix 1 or Bernstein 1980, pp. 118–120.

jectives are also met is not fully addressed in either author's conditions.

3. Development of a human basis for self-management is considered as vital as assuring a material base for its development. These conditions stress the role of education in that process. The word *education* is used here in its broadest sense. It does not refer simply to what takes place in educational institutions, but to ways in which consciousness is shaped throughout society. The conditions recognize important interrelationships among people's expectations about participation in economic decision making, growth of their will to participate, and development of their ability to do so.

Helpful as they may be, these authors' macro conditions lack social, political, and economic specificity. Some of their conditions are explicitly oriented to Third World economic situations, and others address Western industrialized democracies. Berstein's conditions for facilitating democratization are purposely abstract; they are part of the summary of his study. Both sets of conditions share disparities in their scope, the level of change they suggest from any existing conditions, and their premises. At times those premises are moral or philosophical, at other times political.

Creating a detailed, cross-cultural, and universal set of macro conditions for self-management would be neither possible nor useful. Self-management is a practical and viable process for the organization of production, and it does not demand one specific form of macroeconomic, social, or political organization. Yet it is clear that the continued existence and quality of self-management will be shaped and conditioned by specific aspects of its macroeconomic, social, and political environment. The three themes just outlined are most helpful in pointing to broadly defined areas for development of an environment that is conducive to self-management. Those areas—freeing material resources for development of self-managed production, fostering human consciousness for its further development, and locating it in a viable and supportive macro economy—will be considered in the specific environment of the United States in Chapter 7.

Self-Management, Reform, and Social Change

Economic, social, and political changes that would provide an environment more consistent with the self-managed organization of work will not occur automatically. At a minimum, they will be the product of people who share goals and work together for reforms that would create that environment. And if this form of production is to be generalized throughout the economy, far more fundamental change will be necessary. This chapter outlines general criteria for reforms and explores a number of reforms that would help facilitate the expansion of self-management. It then addresses problems inherent in a reform strategy and the limits of reform as a path to an environment that would be broadly supportive of self-management.

The subject of this study is inevitably intertwined with issues of social change. Small and isolated cases of self-managed production may be capable of survival in a capitalist economy, but the proliferation of self-managed firms is unlikely unless financial assets are readily available and new forms of democratically controlled resources are developed. Equally important, development of people's ability to practice direct democracy in their work relationships can result only from changing patterns of social interaction, authority, and gender relationships. The latter portion of this chapter looks beyond the question of reform to analyze whether and how the concept of self-management, and self-managed firms themselves, may contribute to larger social tansformation. That inquiry is based on a summary of the historical practice of self-management in the United States and on a vision of a more fully supportive economic, social, and political arena for worker-controlled and self-managed production.

Reforms in Support of Self-Management

The objective of reforms in support of workers' self-management were summarized in the three macro themes discussed at the end of Chapter 6. Beginning with the most concrete, reforms are needed to make material resources available for creation of self-managed firms. Equally important are reforms that would broaden and deepen knowledge of this way of organizing work, and develop a macroeconomic setting that would be conducive to development of these firms. The third category, consciousness, is not easily shaped by reform. It is more clearly the product of values, cultural conditioning, and forms of awareness shaped by human interaction. Reform efforts in this category would stem from and reinforce forms of consciousness that favor more cooperative production, and those reforms might thereby encourage further social change.

Obviously, gains are possible through reforms that succeed. It is crucial to determine, though, what reforms would be worth the effort it they are won; how much time and energy should be devoted to a particular reform effort; and when to abandon it if its cost becomes too high in terms of time and energy, potential for dividing a progressive coalition, or compromise on basic principles. Even if a reform is not won, working for it may unite people into a political force capable of other gains.

Some criteria that may be useful in selecting reforms are: Do they advance the class interests of those who produce in society? For those who are disenfranchised to the point of not having a job, would a reform diminish oppression and lead to greater control over their lives or to greater opportunity for meaningful work? Does a reform help establish conditions under which the next important reform can be won? If changes are won, what form of reaction will they bring, and how can it best be counteracted? Reform efforts carry with them the constant chance of failure and, with failure, potential loss of direction or momentum. Thus it is crucial for the nucleus of any reform effort to consist of a group committed to a vision *beyond* reform, even if that group is willing to try multiple paths of change *through* progressive reform.

Forms of workplace democracy are currently advocated by a wide range of political groups, including liberal Democrats, grass-roots citizens' organizations, and socialist groups. They advocate worker and community ownership, economic democracy, or more fundamental change. They would presumably find common cause with others working specifically for reforms aimed at workers' control over production and self-management. So little now exists in the way of legal and institutional support for self-managed production that reforms that could facilitate its development could win substantial support across this spectrum of interests. Reform efforts are shaped by the economic and political reality of their moment. The following reforms are suggested and evaluated in light of the depressed economy and depressing political situation of the early 1980s.

First, there are several alternatives for creating material resources for self-managed firms. Social funds channeled through federal programs have proven helpful to groups attempting to gain worker and community control of firms in the past, and they can prove helpful in the future if they are expanded. If job creation is an objective for use of federal funds, then those funds can presumably be made available to self-managed as well as conventional firms. Expansion of grant and loan programs such as those of the Economic Development Administration, HUD's Urban Development Action Grant and community development funds, and Small Business Administration loan guarantee assistance are cases in point. Before those programs were curtailed, many of them were just becoming accessible to worker-controlled firms. To assist the development of self-management, their renewal and expansion would have to be accompanied by not only a mandate but also a programmatic emphasis on worker and community initiated job creation, and provision of outreach and technical assistance to help make those efforts bear fruit. None of these programs has been of a magnitude to provide substantial funding on a scale necessary for large industrial projects. Most of them do not have provisions for equity funding of any kind, leaving the challenge of initial equity formation to those attempting the venture. Progressive reforms would have to expand the availability of debt financing and also establish new forms of revolving debt and "social ownership" categories of financing that would constitute a new use of social surplus for noncapitalist enterprise formation. Rather than using public dollars simply to support the creation of additional conventional firms, the funds would be used to create jobs through worker- and community-controlled firms, with products and services potentially geared to local and regional markets. There is historical precedent for programs of this nature in development of port authorities (Lynd 1982, pp. 213–218) and in the conceptualization and implementation of rural electrification during the New Deal. The latter program was developed with the provision of low-cost federal credit to locally controlled cooperatives. Despite later problems, it was very successful in spreading a basic service throughout rural areas and in putting people to work.

Legislative battles for public resources can be fought at local, state, and regional levels as well as at the federal level. A "new federalism" may reinforce the importance of fighting and winning increasing numbers of these reform battles at less central levels of government and community, where organizing for them may be less costly and complex. The threat to these efforts lies in the potential for communities that make progress toward nontraditional public resource accumulation and usage to be "punished" by the flight of privately held investment capital.

Other resources can be captured without the legislative effort required for new program creation. Union pension funds, for example, might be invested in worker-controlled production (Rifkin and Barber 1978; Carnoy and Shearer 1980, ch. 3). Some portion of these private funds could be redirected gradually into forms of equity and debt financing for worker-controlled jobs and regional development rather than simply invested for the highest return at least risk. Until more complete income and retirement security can be won for all people in this country, a large portion of pension funds will have to be tagged for essentially conservative, system-based investment. One of the common problems of reforms is their lack of programmatic coherence. If reforms do not develop around a unified program, each can be neutralized by the lack of another. Freeing a portion of pension funds for worker-controlled resource development must, for now, be tempered by more traditional investment programs to "protect" the pensions themselves. Even traditional pension investments can still be reoriented toward more progressive concerns such as domestic job creation and conversion from production for military use, with some portion targeted to self-managed jobs.

Other kinds of legislative reform than financial can help shape an environment more consistent with worker- and community-controlled production. A significant example is the recent passage of legislation that recognizes the workers' cooperative as a legal entity in the state of Massachusetts (Industrial Cooperative Association 1982). Efforts toward similar gains in other states are under way. Since these proposals do not require any funding, they generate little opposition in financially pressed statehouses. Legal statutes that simplify the process of incorporation for self-managed firms ease the task of setting up such firms and cut the legal cost of doing so. Accompanying tax rulings that recognize and do not subvert the unique nature of these firms can also simplify the process.

Trusteeship programs offer a means of converting privately held resources to quasi-public ones. They are an option for people who own property and are willing to transfer or bequeath it to trusts to be managed for collective or public use (Institute for Community Economics 1982). Trusts are one response to a need for new categories of property, and they could help stimulate further thinking about other new forms of property in this country. As a voluntaristic method of generating resources through conversion of privately held assets at the option of sympathetic property holders, they could be a significant resource only after fundamental changes in consciousness.

An important indirect outcome of reform efforts is reshaping people's perceptions of how the economy could be organized. There are victories to be won in opening people's thinking to fundamentally different ways of producing and distributing the goods and services they require. Community-based jobs resulting from an expanding public sector or cooperatives linked to a community development corporation or property in public trusteeship can contribute to that process. Every successful firm run democratically by the people who work in it can affect many more lives than those of its work force. Over the last ten years worker takeovers have set an example for others: "If they can do it, why can't we?" By and large, these takeovers have been isolated cases and partial victories, but important ones nonetheless if like-minded people are going to formulate new ideas and join together to realize them.

The support organization described in Chapters 2 and 4 is a partial and reformist solution to problems of self-managed firms in unsupportive environments. In its fullest form it can increase public awareness of self-management, a possible first step in changing consciousness. It can also help generate resources for use in loan programs and in technical assistance and educational work.

Support organizations that can perform this broadly developmental role constitute a potentially important product of reform efforts—one that could contribute directly to the development of self-management.

Each of the reforms suggested here would be helpful in implementing self-management; each would strengthen the ability of people to create self-managed firms or to use forms of self-management in responding to the threat of economic and social dislocation. Even if all of these reforms were won, though, they would not create an environment fully supportive of self-managed production. The dominant way of organizing work and allocating its product in society would remain capitalist in nature. Any dominant form of production by nature contains both structural and cultural barriers to significant alternatives; active resistance to those alternatives is frequently unnecessary. If with the help of reforms such as these, fully self-managed production gained a toehold in any part of the country, sector, or industry, it would likely be seen as contrary to the interests of capital. It might at least be viewed as eliminating some amount of production in service to private accumulation and as exemplifying a potentially subversive alternative to control systems within the traditional firm. If more active resistance were judged necessary, that resistance might take the form of restricted access to finance capital, markets, or raw materials or to other requisites for production and distribution which remained under capitalist control. A less than neutral state has the ability to administer mandated programs restrictively or press unfavorable tax rulings for self-managed firms. These and other possible forms of resistance to self-management raise nagging questions. Can solidly progressive reforms that favor self-management be won and then sustained? If not, is the effort worthwhile? Or can these efforts somehow be joined to a strategy for more fundamental economic, social, and political change toward an environment more consistent with self-managed production of goods and services? These questions are addressed in the following sections of this chapter.

The Limits of Reform

Reforms typically have as their object modification of social, political, and economic structures, rather than fundamental change.

Given that limited objective, each reform still must be won in an unending contest against the rights, privileges, and power of those interested in maintaining the existing order. When reforms seem to be won, the contest is not necessarily over; many of them turn out to be gutted in a last-minute attempt to win support for their legislative enactment, constrained by a lack of funding, administered in a manner that neutralizes them, or killed off by a subsequent legislature or administration. The National Consumer Cooperative Bank provides a reminder of the many ways that reform can be frustrated. Through a combination of several of the pitfalls facing reform, it has been turned into a conservative shadow of the institution that was envisioned and worked for by its co-op advocates. If it is ever to play a constructive role in the development of workers' co-ops, it will have to be both recaptured and in a sense recreated. Judged by those seeking progressive social change, it is a reform gone wrong.

The frustration of reform has been summarized well in the following passage on the arena of the state in capitalist society where "government takes on a life of its own and is not simply an 'instrument' of capital.... (I)t is a battle ground in which popular forces, if they are massively and effectively mobilized, can make incremental gains of considerable value. But then the long term tendency reasserts itself, and victories of the organized workers and/or of the poor, the minorities, and the middle class advocates of social change are taken over and turned to ruling class purposes" (Harrington 1976, p. 318). The author of that depressingly accurate picture is one of this country's leading advocates of reformist struggles within the established political system. Harrington sees them as the rallying point around which political forces "that might make irreversible structural changes and eventually transform the system itself" (ibid.) could be assembled. That may be the case, and given the current weakness of political forces posing alternatives to capitalism in the United States, it is an avenue worthy of consideration. But transformation will require a unifying vision and forms of political organization that are not currently present here. Reforms may help assemble political forces, but it is crucial that those forces be guided by more than reformist objectives if they are to achieve significant social change.

Reform efforts in Western democracies frequently embrace the objective of social democracy. Social democratic movements are characterized by work through the political institutions of capitalist society rather than directly or solely confrontational tactics, and by their willingness to work for improvements or reforms in capitalism, rather than full commitment of their energy to transformation.[1] They raise long-debated questions of whether participation in the system serves only to strengthen it, to emphasize the economic over the political aspects of the struggle for change, thus diminishing direct action and foreclosing an ultimate objective of social transformation. Despite their ability to make a difference in the quality of life for workers and the disenfranchised, even relatively successful movements for social democracy remain questionable vehicles for further transformation. Most fundamentally, they require the sacrifice of direct workplace reorganization to the constant need to strengthen and renew parliamentary representation. Not only does that cut short work to develop forms of workers' control and self-management (witness the diminished postelection importance given *autogestion* under the Mitterand regime in France), but it contains its own impediment to change. In order to deliver on promises of improvement in the economic position of those they represent—in order to get their representatives reelected—social democratic regimes must make every effort to increase the productivity of the existing economic system (Przeworski 1980, pp. 54–56). If the means of production remain in private hands, that effort only strengthens the position of the class whose dominance was to be overcome. More radical change threatens the onslaught of crisis in the established system, and with crisis there is the probable loss of even limited economic gains won earlier in the contest. Such a loss is precisely the condition that would have a social democratic majority thrown out of power. Promising near-term economic gains as a means of winning political power can result in an impasse. Threatened with loss of wage-earner support and electoral defeat because of crisis in the economic system, the likely avenue for social democrats is programmatic retreat. Social democratic regimes must ultimately turn away from transformation and act to protect the profitability of private investment. Reforms turn out to be noncumulative in nature, and their end result is

1. This discussion draws heavily on the work of Adam Przeworski (1979, 1980). See also the recent debate over labor and socialist strategy in England (D. Coates 1981, 1982; Ali and Hoare 1982; Hodgson 1982).

likely to be at most a constrained or mediated capitalism. And even if social democracy is achieved, its conditions of continued private appropriation of surplus, hierarchical organization of work, and wage labor run counter to workers' control and self-management.

The United States remains far from conditions of mediated capitalism today. Despite their shortcomings as direct instruments of change, reform efforts *may* provide a means, a starting point, for building a progressive political movement. Programmatic efforts to constrain capitalism might bring together forces in society that see their interest served best through noncapitalist alternatives. A reform strategy could then be significant to workers' self-management primarily as a means of joining consciousness, agency, and organization—of linking ideological, grass-roots, and spontaneous resistance to capitalism with organizations, a program, and a movement of people that would more precisely define an alternative to capitalism and work to achieve it. Although there are no specific precedents for such a development in the United States, it may offer the potential for creation of a new socialist politics that would outgrow reformism and yet avoid sectarianism, and one that could programmatically incorporate self-management. Investigation of that potential can be informed by an analysis of the firms that have been largely worker-controlled and democratically managed in the United States to date.

Lessons from the History of Self-Management in the United States

The history of self-managed firms in this country is contained largely in the history of U.S. workers' cooperatives. It is an erratic history, one of individual firms and clusters of similar firms scattered in time and geography over a nearly 200-year period. Researchers have attempted to explain the appearance of these firms in several ways. One has linked formation of workers' co-ops to the business cycle, arguing that they have been formed most often during periods of persistent and substantial unemployment or in the aftermath of unsuccessful strikes, which also tend to occur more frequently in periods of economic stagnation (Shirom 1972). This argument differs from the contention that industrial co-ops were simply mutations of craft guilds (Commons et al. 1918) and says that many later nineteenth-century co-ops were the products of groups of urban wage workers who sought to promote self-management (Shirom 1972). A more recent analysis identifies specific clusters of co-ops, both chronologically and by industry (Jones 1979). It calls the economic deprivation hypothesis into question by documenting cluster formations in both stagnant and buoyant economic times.

A characteristic common to the formation of workers' cooperatives is their founding members' hope of overcoming dependency and subservience in the wage relationship. Nineteenth-century strikes and lockouts occasionally sparked workers' attempts to escape their status as employees by creating their own firms. The more egalitarian and democratic of these people became cooperative producers, rather than simply employers. For example, the original plywood cooperative was formed by people seeking a form of work that avoided both routine confrontation between labor and capital and periodic unemployment in the timber industry. More recent waves of workers' co-ops in forest services and food distribution have resulted from people's efforts to create organizations that they control as workers in them. They represent rejection of many aspects of the employer-employee and wage relationships.

This history cannot support an argument that these efforts attained political significance in and of themselves. With the exception of the Knights of Labor co-ops in the mid-1800s, these efforts were unrelated to more significant aspects of the labor movement in this country. In fact, one of the most striking characteristics of co-ops has been their relative isolation—from the larger thrust of organized labor, from each other, and from any organized political activity.

The lack of linkages between workers' cooperatives and the organized U.S. labor movement deserves particular attention. Where workers' co-ops were formed by people acting to break out of wage labor, the concerns of their members differed from those of workers still confronting capital. When unions with socialist objectives were active in the United States, workers' co-ops were criticized as a form of labor capitalism—an attempt at "socialism in one firm" before the conditions for its survival had been won through traditional objectives of public ownership of the means of production and workers' control of the state. Workers' co-ops were deemed by those unions to be utopian experiments that, at best, threatened to interfere with a unified working-class strategy for political change. Given their historical tendencies to employment of nonmember workers, their occasional antiunion biases, and their inward-looking behavior, many co-ops created barriers to any fruitful relationship with the radical labor movement in this country.

Workers' co-ops have had different, but equally difficult, problems with more conservative and more recently familiar trade union movements in the United States. For unions that had accepted the wage labor system, setting their goals within it, co-ops were seen as a disquieting diversion. They had no place in an increasing shift toward the industrial democracy of collective bargaining within the capitalist system. When co-ops advocate decentralization and democratic practice in general, they could also be perceived as troublesome by unions that were adopting centralized and bureaucratic structures designed to combat big business. In sum, workers' co-ops had little chance for a fruitful relationship with either kind of labor organization.

Workers' cooperatives have also been isolated from each other in at least two ways. First, they have tended to be geographically scattered, even during periods of relatively high numbers. Second, when clusters of similar co-ops have been concentrated geographically, their firms have been in competition with each other in the same industry. Clusters were often sparked by a successful prototype firm, and individual firms within the cluster were sometimes able to attain remarkable levels of internal cooperation. Their competitive position in industry, however, meant that they competed with other co-ops as well as with capitalist firms. Through their lack of cooperation among themselves, they missed opportunities to share scarce knowledge and resources and to share the burden of defending their tenuous position on the edge of mainstream industry and commerce. These kinds of isolation have contributed to the paucity of workers' co-ops in the United States. Isolation has also perhaps prevented these co-ops from significantly influencing others to develop alternative forms of production.

Self-Managed Firms and Social Change

Development of workers' co-ops and self-managed firms today can be encouraged with two objectives in mind. One is the creation of more firms as a continuing firm-by-firm alternative to traditional employment or substitution for lost employment, although the record demonstrates that those firms will be hard-pressed to survive in a fully self-managed form. This objective is generally the one promoted by advocates of co-ops, workplace democracy, and participative firms, that is, people who believe in and seek to expand upon liberal alternatives within democratic capitalism. The case studies in Chapters 3 through 5 demonstrate that these firms can be created. Reforms that would make that task easier are generally advocated by this group.

A second objective, and the alternative to be explored more fully in the rest of this chapter, embraces worker-controlled and self-managed firms as an important but not singular element in a broader movement for social change. The goals of such a movement derive from a vision of a different society, one that would be conducive to self-management. That vision will be only sketched here; to do more would deny the role of the movement just outlined.

Workers' control and self-management are most consistent with a society that would take as fundamental people's right to be fully involved in the decisions that affect their lives. Such a society would encourage open, nonhierarchical, and nonbureaucratic economic, social, and political organizations, and it would commit resources to developing an informed citizenry capable of critical thought, cooperative work to meet life's needs, and development of opportunities for human growth and enrichment. It would not be a society that glorified work as an end in itself, but one that was able to specify common objectives and determine collectively how to meet them with minimum human and material costs. This would be a society that reflected the macro facilitating conditions summarized at the end of the last chapter. That is, it would make resources available to its members so that they could cooperatively attend to their material well-being; it would be committed to encouraging consciousness and human development that would reinforce that objective and in turn be reinforced by it; and it would locate those characteristics in a larger economic and political setting that also balanced collective needs with individual and group autonomy.

Discussion of social change also requires specification of what the change is from—in other words, what is to be overcome. Since this topic received considerable attention early in this study, a brief summary will suffice. For the United States it would involve changing an economic system that places control over production in the hands of those who own productive assets and finance capital. Making resources available for cooperative production would mean ending the right of a minority of citizens to control investment decisions, the way in which work is organized, and ultimately the division of the product of that work. Accompanying changes would expand the application of democratic decision making and change its character from a largely representative form to more participatory forms. Participatory democracy would require a transition from education that serves to condition a work force for acquiescence to a hierarchical work organization. New forms of production would call for changing incentive systems that are presently biased toward ever greater individual material consumption.

Can a fully democratic and self-managed workplace be the dominant form of production under capitalism? The answer is clearly no. At the heart of that economic system is wage labor and the appropriation of surplus from production based on the legal rights and power of private capital ownership. Fully self-managed firms negate the relationships that sustain this process.

Capitalist "mixed economies" exhibit multiple arenas of conflict. They include the workplace, the focus of this study, where income levels, working conditions, and job security have traditionally been fought over or negotiated. Another is the family, in which male ties to jobs in the economy have provided the material source of their power in another hierarchical social organization. Confrontation also takes place at the level of the state, where capital enjoys the privilege of institutions that serve to further private accumulation and to convince citizens that private capital accumulation is the best and most logical way of dealing with social surplus. The international economic and political spheres are also important arenas of conflict as countries compete to provide favorable greenhouses for capital.

Conflicts within the capitalist firm and competitive pressure among capitalists at the international level can bring about temporary solutions, such as participation programs, that constitute some movement in the direction of self-management. It is worth considering whether firms that approach, but do not meet, the conditions for full workers' control and self-management could prove compatible with a new form of capitalism. It is conceivable that "enlightened" capital owners, faced with ongoing resistance in the workplace itself and international competitive pressure, would turn over the day-to-day management of production to all people who work in the firm. The firm could "manage itself," but private accumulation would continue primarily through capital's and the capitalist state's control over finance capital and its price, raw material sources and prices, marketing channels and access to them, and patent and production rights. Workers would manage production at the level of the firm, meeting most conditions for self-management. The accumulation process and economic policy would go on serving those who privately control productive wealth. Capital would continue to be capital, rather than social surplus that had been brought under democratic control.

The theoretical bases for this development in capitalism's future are open to debate. They contain enough plausibility, however, to reinforce the importance of self-management at the level of the firm being *minimally* defined by conditions enumerated in Chapter 2 of this study. They also strengthen arguments for understanding the self-managed firm as one part of an integrated quest for a more democratic and egalitarian future.

What determines whether self-managed firms can be an integral part of a process of social change? Perhaps the most crucial determinant of whether change at the level of the firm could be incorporated into broader transitional strategies has to do with the character and actions of the firms being created. There can be little that is progressive about a firm that claims to be cooperatively and democratically managed if it has not overcome an employee-employer relationship and wage labor. Firms that are fully worker-controlled and self-managed have made that transition. They must be seen as distinct from firms with participation and quality-of-worklife programs, which are the hallmark of attempts to coerce cooperation from employees. Those programs are organized, sanctioned, and can be terminated, by capital and its managers who remain in charge of the firm. As programs initiated by management, they have more in common with actions to prevent significant change than to bring it about.

Second, worker-controlled and self-managed firms can play a role in social change only by distant example unless they are themselves actively committed to change. Most U.S. workers' co-ops have been simply alternative, but not oppositional, organizations.

The distinction is important. Alternative organizations are those that have found a different way to live (produce) and want to be left alone with it. Oppositional organizations, on the other hand, have found a different way to live and want to change society in its light (Williams 1973). Alternative organizations offer a different way of living, but they do not necessarily represent an attempt to confront established powers and relationships with a desire for social change (Moberg 1979). Oppositional organizations do that. The U.S. plywood co-ops can be seen as examples of alternative economic organizations. The forest workers' co-ops, and particularly Hoedads in its activist periods, have demonstrated oppositional character.

Members of oppositional organizations may choose varying levels of individual activism at different times. What is important is a binding consensus on the oppositional character of the organization as a whole and on the commitment of some level of its resources (time, members' energy, material resources, etc.) to oppositional activities. The oppositional organization is defined, then, by a desire for social change that mirrors some of its important attributes, by a willingness to confront established powers, and by a commitment of resources to those ends. This activity clearly involves an added burden to alternative organizations that already fall outside the economic and organizational mainstream. A compensating benefit for these firms is that oppositional activity can serve as a check against tendencies to slip into mainstream business practices. An organization that is committed to social change should find heightened political consciousness affecting its own internal methods and relationships.

Politically committed, fully self-managed firms do have the potential to contribute to the development and outcomes of progressive social change. The ways in which they can do so include the following:

(*a*) They can serve as magnets for like-minded men and women who, for whatever reason, find themselves outside traditional labor organizations. They provide a unique setting for developing a thorough analysis and critique of mainstream organizations of production and for attempts to work out alternatives to them.

(*b*) Self-managed work organizations can serve as educational centers for their members. They provide social training for participatory democracy at the same time that they affirm the political and cultural goal of direct citizens' control over the institutions that affect their lives. Their chances for doing this are limited by their larger social and economic setting, but enlarged by their fully self-managed character.

(c) Lessons learned from the work environments of these organizations reach a wider population than their members. These organizations demonstrate to others the possibility of nonalienating work relationships based on democratic and egalitarian values. At the same time they help clarify the critical difference between capitalist firms, even if run in an enlightened fashion, and worker-controlled and managed production.

(d) The resources created by successful practice of worker-controlled production can assist in the creation of more jobs outside capitalist relations of production.

Each of these contributions is dependent on the oppositional character of alternate organizations. Organizations that are simply alternate in character can attract the disaffected, but they are unlikely to serve as forums for social analysis. They are crippled in educating others about direct democracy if they somehow restrict their own democratic practice. Alternate organizations that remain purposely anonymous limit dissemination of information about their work environment, and little or none of their resources will be used to foster similar organizations of production.

Oppositional organizations are unlikely to exist in isolation. Self-managed firms that choose oppositional paths can seek linkages of at least two kinds: among themselves and between themselves and other groups committed to change. Linkages among themselves have proven attractive for the reforestation co-ops. They allow sharing of scarce resources such as managerial skills, and they provide shared staffs for political work, mutual assistance, or common education and outreach programs. Firms from more than one industry that are committed to promoting self-management, and conditions that could facilitate self-management, could similarly share benefits in joint action.[2]

Linkages between self-managed firms and other organizations

2. See, for example, discussion of the Northwest Forest Workers' Association and possible linkages between reforestation co-ops and other groups in the issues sections of Chapter 3 above.

with an interest in social change present both opportunities and challenges. One such challenge is cooperation between self-managed firms or their advocacy groups and more traditional labor organizations. In the current era of capital flight and negotiation of "givebacks" an implicit social contract with capital, an era of "negotiated class struggle" is called into question and that may lead to new thinking on labor goals and strategy (Metzgar 1980). What could be substituted for decades of emphasis on bread-and-butter demands in collective bargaining? Most fundamentally, the prerogative of capital owners to move their resources at will would come under attack. Collective bargaining has been based on the assumption of plants to work in. Relocation and export of capital have prompted demands for a union voice in decisions concerning plant location and new technologies and for accounting records to be opened for workers so they can better assess the health of firms they work in. The growing awareness of union pension funds as sources of wealth and power could encourage new thinking on the ownership, control, and uses of productive property on the part of unions. People involved with self-managed firms are concerned with these same issues. Their response has been different in nature from that of labor unions, but not necessarily in spirit. Self-managed firms could be well served by a more supportive environment for their development, as could labor organizations. They share the objectives of loosening capital's grip on the nation's wealth and strengthening the decision-making power of working people. Given those common interests, mutually appealing programs for change might be found.

Other opportunities for linkages between self-managed firms and other organizations can be imagined more easily. Worker-controlled firms are by definition community-based firms. They share with grass-roots and citizens' groups, for example, a quest for locally controlled economic and social development, freedom from the coercive control of distantly held capital, and development of open and responsive local government. As democratic, egalitarian, productive organizations that empower their members through skills development, they also lend themselves to alliances with feminists, particularly feminist groups that challenge both capitalism and patriarchy. Minority groups may see in self-managed firms opportunities for community-controlled economic development through egalitarian institutions. Ecologists who see little hope for controlling destruction of the environment under capitalism are another activist group with which linkages could be formed.

The problems inherent in these potential linkages cannot be minimized. The groups are diverse; they include portions of a deeply divided working class as well as people who fall outside of that class, either because they have no job or because of their work in managerial or professional positions. Uniting elements of these groups as agents of change remains a challenge. If linkages are to be developed into a meaningful political movement, it will require more than simply a short-term coalition of interest groups. A "politics of linkages" is a potential starting point for development of a broader range of political alternatives in the United States.[3] It would bring together portions of groups mentioned here, and others, around a set of goals that would benefit all of them and that would transcend the special interests of each. The key to that set of common goals lies in the oppositional character of segments of each of these groups and movements. A politics of linkages in the United States would have to shape that opposition into a more clearly articulated alternative to capitalism and then into program. The outcome of that process could be a revitalized politics in the United States—one based on current conditions and visions of a different future. It is possible for self-managed firms to contribute to that process as alternate and oppositional organizations and for self-management to be a part of that future.

Self-Management and More

Most of this discussion has dealt with the role of self-managed firms in social change. This chapter would be incomplete without consideration of what significance the concept of self-management holds in shaping development of alternatives. The topic is a complex one. Two of its many aspects will be considered here. The first is the connection between the concept of self-management, people's lives at work, and resistance to the capitalist workplace. The second is the potential importance of self-management in defining the form and content of an alternative vision.

3. The use of linkages between groups on the left as an initial strategy for development of a new political movement has been discussed by Rowbotham, Segal, and Wainwright (1979) and by Rustin (1980), among others.

Workers' control and self-management can result only from the action of people engaged in the struggle for democratic control over the organizations they work in. Theorizing, cataloguing case studies, and attempting to enumerate conditions that have facilitated the practice of self-management are of practical significance only if they serve people in their collective actions toward control over their productive activity. Those actions are legitimate and ongoing for working people, and they offer a means by which a political initiative can gain concreteness. Programs that have addressed the needs of working people with one-dimensional proposals for public ownership of the means of production or a dictatorship of the proletariat appear irrelevant to the lives of many in modern capitalist societies. A program that addressed contemporary problems of the workplace could help overcome the remoteness of more traditional proposals.

Workplace action can be encouraged and informed by what people who have gained control, even at the micro level, have done to reorganize the way they work. Examples of fully self-managed firms can serve as reminders that new structures and processes are possible as people change and that the process of change has many dimensions, some coming together to encourage—others to retard—further transformation. Efforts to realize change at the workplace are close to people's lives; they take place in an arena where people can see progress and where they can understand barriers to change and confront them. There is a continuum here that is frequently not recognized in the United States. It consists of the logical extension from the best of trade union struggles for workers' power on the factory floor—those to retain control over process, fight speedups, and keep jobs—to those that have to do with workers controlling and then organizing the workplace as they think best (Gorz 1973; Panitch 1978). Achievement of those goals could be truly liberating, and those objectives could be made more a part of a program of change, not a vague ideal to be acted upon only after other gains are in place. A progressive politics of linkages developed in the United States today that embraced workplace initiatives could build upon aspects of them that reflect people's dreams and needs for liberation from oppressive conditions of production. Integrated into strategies for change, self-management can be a logical extension of oppositional trade union activity—of activity aimed not at bargaining over the price of wage labor, but at abolishing it. Bringing together a revitalized labor movement, autonomous rank-and-file initiatives, and legitimate efforts toward workers' control and self-management wherever they occur in the economy lies at the heart of workplace programs for any progressive politics in this country.

Self-management could also make a conceptual contribution in the definition of objectives for this progressive politics. For instance, self-management fits poorly with the institutions of social democracy, and it could help to safeguard an oppositional movement from retreating into social democratic objectives. Social democracy was described above as a highly mediated form of capitalism. Its institutional form is one that relies on national and largely centralized institutions to represent the interest of ongoing classes of labor and capital. Self-management raises questions about levels of autonomy for firms in an economy and about mechanisms other than the market that can assure levels of local control sufficient for self-managed production to take place. Those questions encourage work on tasks such as developing a practical range of proposals for democratic planning and for new relationships between firms and their communities.

To summarize, this chapter has presented policy reforms that could be beneficial to the development of self-management in the United States. It has also outlined some of the problems of reform strategies and argued that self-managed firms could play a significant role in social change, but only if they are oppositional in character. If they are oppositional, they could contribute directly to change and also contribute to a politics of linkages with other organizations to confront capitalism. That politics of linkages may serve as a starting point for the necessary definition of a viable alternative to capitalism and for development of a movement to realize that alternative. Self-management recommends itself as an important concept—one that can be a part of that vision.

CHAPTER 8

Getting Started

The emphasis of the preceding chapters has been on the workplace. Self-management offers a way of organizing the production of goods and services that reflects ideals of egalitarianism, democratic decision making, and direct involvement. Studies demonstrate that self-managed firms can be as efficient as more traditional firms, even when the measures of efficiency are narrowly defined. By human and social criteria, self-managed firms offer bold advantage over firms whose structures reflect the class conflict of their larger society. Recent cases indicate remarkable progress toward self-management, even in a less than supportive environment. Much remains to be learned about this form of organization, although what is known now should reinforce, not retard, further successful development of these firms.

Advocates of self-management have occasionally treated the firm as if it could be isolated from its surroundings. Similarly, people creating these firms have sometimes attempted to deny the continual impact of their larger social, political, and economic environment upon their project. As experience with these firms has grown, it has become clear that neither tendency is justified. At times full energies must be devoted to launching or maintaining a firm, but if successful implementation of these firms is to be assured in the long run, their development must coincide with development of an environment in which they will more readily fit.

Given the state of oppositional politics in the United States, it seems premature or even pretentious to speak of a political movement reflective of goals compatible with self-management. Yet a crucial objective must be precisely to get that movement started. Linkages among progressive groups can provide a basis for sorting out alternatives that will shape future programs, strategy, and tactics.

One relationship that will be central to development of a revitalized oppositional politics is that between the workplace and the state. The vision sketched above is shaped by the notion of collective self-regulation of society (politics) combined with the creative transformation of nature (labor) by relatively autonomous work organizations. Politics and labor must be more fully understood as interrelated elements both in present advanced capitalism and in the transformed world to be created. There is a conceptual linkage between the "politics of production" of the labor process and "global politics, whose object is the state" (Burawoy 1981). Simply put, worker-controlled and self-managed production cannot exist in the global realm of capitalist relations of production. Worker-controlled and self-managed forms of production may or may not be compatible with socialist "global politics." One of the many challenges facing a vital oppositional politics is to think out how worker control of production can be joined with rational, collective, and minimally centralized direction of society. What could emerge from that undertaking might include a (more or less) "centralized administrative body [that] may stipulate the external conditions of production (inputs and outputs), [while] direct producers themselves manage the organization of work" (ibid., p. 120). Equally important is the stipulation that direct producers participate in shaping the plan itself, collectively through their role as producers and also with citizens of the broader society, rather than simply receiving it from above.

To expand on these ideas at much greater length would be inappropriate here. Suffice it to say that there are concrete past and present attempts to learn from as this discourse proceeds. China under Mao experimented with limited forms of "planning from below." More recently Yugoslavia has sought expansion of decentralized planning and production agreements in a tentative but significant shift from extensive reliance on markets. Both cases provide insight that can help ground theoretical and practical inquiry on this important question. Even tentative answers will begin to fill the void between prescriptions for change in how work is organized and carried out and prescriptions for changes in the macro economic, political, and social setting that would enable worker-controlled and self-managed production to be the logical norm.

Getting started is the issue, and problems abound. Bringing what there is of the left together has never proven easy. The desperate landscape of current conservative and liberal nonalternatives provides added incentive to produce fresh alternatives, rather than factional splits. Current conditions can make it easier to rally people to a well–thought out, well-articulated alternative. But at the same time, economic crisis also deeply divides the working class and its potential allies. The transition of the past decade in economic and political conditions within the United States, and in other countries as well, calls for a rethinking of the mix of interests that can hold a politics of linkages on the left together long and productively enough to serve as the embryo of a broad and deep new movement. The Keynesian strategies of the postwar period favored a cautious reform program based on growth to be shared among labor, some other constituents, and capital. Today capital has returned to a predepression strategy based on the logic of a higher rate of exploitation as the path to greater private accumulation. Market anarchy and the rigors of international competition inspire various corporatist proposals. A weakened labor movement is not presently able to lead a counterattack, although it must be an important part of one as it regroups and rethinks its goals. What remains to be worked out on the left is a new program of broad appeal—one that encompasses labor and reaches well beyond the confines of traditional labor activity. At its root must be a new sense of what can be won, based on a reintegrated and nonreformist conception of economic, social, and democratic imperatives and a new model of how we want to live.

This argument holds both a place and a message for people involved with workers' self-management. Most important, it calls on them to recognize and insist upon self-management's anticapitalist character and to recognize the difficulty of creating worker-controlled and self-managed firms in even a liberal and democratic, but capitalist environment. In confronting economic, social, and political limitations facing self-managed firms, one recognizes the need to work with others for social change—to form the linkages that can begin development of a movement for transformation. By insisting on the importance of worker-controlled and self-managed production in programs for the future, advocates of self-management can help stimulate new visions and programs for that movement.

Sources of Defining and Facilitating Conditions

The Sources

The conditions presented in Chapter 2 are a synthesis of the firm-specific elements of Jaroslav Vanek's "necessary conditions of an optimal and viable self-managed economy (or, implicitly, of an isolated self-managed firm)" (Vanek 1975a, p. 33); Paul Bernstein's "minimally necessary components" for workplace democratization (Bernstein 1976, p. 45); and Branko Horvat's "general principles of an adequate distribution policy" for the labor-managed enterprise (Horvat 1976c, p. 187). Other authors have combined two of these sets of conditions in the past. I have combined the conditions of Vanek and Bernstein (Gunn 1980); Jones has used Vanek's conditions and some of Bernstein's (Jones 1980); and Thomas has used Vanek's and Horvat's together (Thomas 1982). To my knowledge, this is the first synthesis of all three sets of conditions. The original text of each set of conditions appears in this appendix.

Condition 1 combines most of Vanek's first necessary condition with the less emphatic first of Bernstein's necessary components. The portion of Vanek's first condition which refers to income is excluded here for clarity and appears in Condition 2. Condition 1 more than satisfies Bernstein's first component, which calls for participation in decision making.

Condition 2, which states that income generated by the firm after payment of costs and taxes should belong to those who work in it, is drawn from Vanek's first condition. It also satisfies Bernstein's second component, making feedback of economic results as direct as possible. This condition also incorporates Horvat's principles stipulating that as much income as possible remain under the direct control of the working collective and that decisions on earnings differentials should be left to the jurisdiction of the worker-managed organization.

Condition 3 is from Vanek's second condition. It stipulates that members retain individual claims on capital contributions, but it modifies Vanek's strong stand against use of collective retained earnings for reinvestment. This modification also takes into account a change in Vanek's views based on theory and on empirical evidence gathered since 1975.

Condition 4 is from Vanek's third condition. Since for Horvat capital resources are socially owned, the scarcity-reflecting rent on them would compensate society for the fact that the firm ties up some of society's scarce resources.

Condition 5 reflects both Vanek's fifth condition and Horvat's stipulation that only labor income be distributed as wages. That stipulation coincides with Vanek's emphasis on accumulation and creation of new capital assets.

Condition 6 is based on Bernstein's third necessary component for workplace democratization. It also reflects an observation by Horvat that determination of labor incomes is closely related to the way that work is organized. A sharing of skills and expertise will have distributional consequences within the firm.

Conditions 7 and 8 are, respectively, Bernstein's components four and five.

Condition 9 combines Vanek's eleventh necessary condition and Bernstein's sixth component.

Condition 10 is based on Vanek's seventh necessary condition.

As noted in the text of Chapter 2, only conditions at the level of the firm have been assembled to derive the ten conditions employed in this study. These authors' macroeconomic, social, and political conditions are addressed more generally in Part III of this book.

Original Texts

The full texts of Vanek's, Bernstein's, and Horvat's conditions are presented here. They are included because none of this writing has been widely distributed, and because the book in which Vanek's conditions appear (Vanek 1975) is no longer in print.

Vanek's "necessary conditions" are:

1. All control, management and income (after payment of all costs and taxes) should always remain in the hands of those who work in a given enterprise, whatever their number; the underlying operational principle being a fully democratic rule on the basis of equality of vote. The philosophical and moral basis of this must always remain work in common of a group of men and nothing else, in particular not, as was often the case with traditional producer cooperatives, some kind of ownership of shares or basic contributions. This is nothing but an expression of a fundamental humanist principle upon which any viable self-managed economy must be based.

2. Whenever, on grounds of static or dynamic economies of scale, division of labour and cooperation among two or more men in an enterprise are necessary,* funding of capital assets other than through collective retained earnings must be brought about. Funding should preferably be based on national ownership, administered by a shelter agency, or otherwise as explained in point 8 below. Of course funding does not imply control, which by condition 1 above remains in the hands of the working collective. If members of the self-managed enterprise contribute through their savings, this should be done freely, and in some way retain the individual claims of the savers.

3. While capital, or more precisely the source of financial capital, does not command any right of control, it is entitled to adequate remuneration at a rate reflecting the relative scarcity of that factor in the economy. Such a rate in real terms can be quite high in developing countries, perhaps well in excess of ten per cent.

4. Conditions 1, 2, and 3 are equally applicable to productive land, which for all practical purposes can be treated as capital. The only exception here is that the payment of rent or income of land should be conditioned by the attainment of necessary minimum subsistence of those who work on the land.

5. The returns on capital and land should in their entirety or at least predominantly be earmarked for accumulation—that is, creation of new capital assets—and not for individual consumption of any kind. In this way the fundamental problem of accumulation facing especially the developing economies is resolved, while at the same time the objection to personal capital income (nonlabour income) on

---

*Collective exploitation of land is sometimes justified in developing countries by such dynamic economies of scale; modernization and technological change are impossible on traditional, very small, and sometimes fragmented, individual holdings.

distributional grounds is eliminated.* It can be shown that the rates of accumulation attainable through this method are quite considerable. In [the] case of an isolated self-managed firm, it is imperative that the firm itself perform on its own behalf this accumulation function, at a fixed rate of return to capital.

6. In principle, the returns charged on capital should be the same for all users. This guarantees an optimal allocation of capital resources.

7. It is imperative to establish a shelter organization or institution on the national level (which can be decentralized according to need), whose express function would be to fund and promote the self-managed sector or economy. More specifically, this agency would be charged with the supervision but not the control of the capital market, the promotion and expansion of new firms or sectors according to national plans, the coordination and spreading of information regarding alternative investment projects, technical and other assistance to new groups desiring to form self-managing firms, and supervision designed to secure in the long run the equalization of income per worker (of course, of equal skill) among industrial branches. The shelter organization is the active arm of the national planning agency or ministry, if such a thing exists. Its fundamental objective must be the promotion of the social good of the participatory sector and of the whole economy. In the absence of a nationally endorsed self-management policy, in a western economy, the shelter organization can assume the form of one or more nonprofit supporting corporations. Such corporations can then be given the additional task of accumulating and using for investment pension funds within the sector and other savings of individuals belonging to the self-managing sector.

8. To minimize the need for the services of the sheltering institution, it is advisable that existing firms be given the priority of using the funds which they are paying as interest on capital for the purposes of their own expansion or creation of new firms. The projects must pass accepted criteria of viability, and funds thus re-invested must yield the normal rate of return as all other investments.

9. In general, but especially in young countries interested in rapid accumulation and the efficient flow of resources, the depreciation allowances of the self-managed firms should also be collected and added to the national investment fund and allocated according to optimality criteria. To protect the interest of the firms contributing their depreciation allowances, the authorities and the shelter orga-

---

*A significant exception to this rule can be permitted if capital assets are generated through workers' own savings and not through inheritance. A case in point here is one which played an important role in many successful self-managed firms where old-age insurance (pension) funds are used as a source of investment funds, and at retirement paid out together with accumulated interest income.

nization must guarantee automatic availability of the real value of these funds when actual replacement of plant and/or equipment (on which the depreciation allowances were paid) is called for.

10. The optimal form of the self-managed economy or sector is one based on the market mechanism, in the sense that all firms act to the best advantage of their working collectives and whoever else they may be concerned with, while using prices in all product and factor markets* as objective signals in their decision making. But of course, the authorities, planning institute or the shelter organization can and ought to exercise influence over the individual firms of the partici-patory sector by means of nondiscriminatory tools (tax policies of all kinds, price ceilings and other price controls). Price regulation in particular should be used whenever a significant degree of monopoly power exists in a given industry.

11. At all times, but especially in its early stages, the effort of introducing self-management must be accompanied by an educational effort focusing on both the basic philosophy of economic self-deter-mination and the specifics of self-management. This effort should be cooperative to the greatest possible degree as much as self-manage-ment itself.

12. On the political plane, especially in countries having or aspiring to political democracy, it is most constructive, honest, and effective to place the struggle for self-management on the philosophico-ide-ological base of *fundamental rights of the working man*. These rights, which must be guaranteed by society, are broadly defined as eco-nomic self-determination and include, most importantly, the right to employment and the right to self-management. To use the traditional platforms and categories of socialism-communism-capitalism can be most divisive and can frustrate efforts for democratization in the economic sphere for many years. It is not good to pour new wine into old skins. [Vanek 1975a, pp. 34-36]

Bernstein's "necessary components" for workplace democrati-zation are developed in Chapters 4–9 of his book (1980), and are summarized as follows:

1. Participation in decision-making,
2. Economic return to the participants based on the surplus they produce,
3. Sharing management-level information with employees,
4. Guaranteed individual rights,

*Note, however, that the labour market is no longer a market in the traditional sense, labour remuneration being given by the performance and effort of each particular firm.

5. An independent appeals system, and
6. A complex participatory/democratic consciousness. [Bernstein 1980, p. 116]

Bernstein adds the following as candidates for facilitating but not essential components for democratization:

1. Job equalization
2. Status equalization
3. Pay equalization
4. Forbidding individual rewards, in favor of collective consumption, and
5. Abolishing private property. [Ibid., p. 119]

Horvat's "general principles of an adequate [income] distribution policy" are:

1. As great a part of the income generated as possible should remain under the direct control of the working collective.
2. Only labor income should be distributed in wages. [Horvat 1976c, pp. 179–188]

These two conditions briefly summarize a lengthy article by Horvat on a theory of distribution (Horvat 1976a). That article has been summarized by Thomas (1982, pp. 147–148).

Economic and Financial Theory of the Labor-Managed Firm

Neoclassical economic theory has long recognized the capitalist firm operating in a fully competitive market economy as its paragon of efficiency. Economists have questioned the ability of a firm run by those who worked in it to allocate scarce resources as efficiently as its capitalist counterpart. Their questions of theory were largely answered with the publication of Jaroslav Vanek's *General Theory of Labor-Managed Market Economies* in 1970. This appendix summarizes the neoclassical[1] economic theory of the labor-managed firm[2] and some of the lessons derived from a related theory of finance. It assumes a basic knowledge of the neoclassical (mainstream) economic theory of the firm.

Modifying and developing earlier work of Ward (1958) and Do-

---

1. The premises, assumptions and language of the analyses of this appendix are those of neoclassical economics. In this context the word *capital* is used to denote the funds used to finance a firm, or the stock of productive capital used in an actual firm or in the production function in the theory of a firm. It is, of course, a matter of debate whether capital is productive at all. An alternate view based on the labor theory of value understands fixed capital or capital equipment as embodied labor. Finance capital is value in a liquid form; in the capitalist mode of production it is value that has been expropriated from those who produced it (labor as a class) by those who "own" it (capital as a class).

Use of neoclassical tools requires clear and critical recognition of the premises and assumptions that shape that body of thought, i.e., the firm as a price taker in a market economy, perfect information, individuals acting in their own rational best interest, etc. It is questionable whether these assumptions would form a very realistic basis of analysis of the behavior of a noncapitalist firm, particularly if it were operating in a noncapitalist environment. However, until a more appropriate theory of the self-managed firm is developed, the theory of the labor-managed firm operating in a modified market economy yields results that are worthy of consideration.

2. The economics of the labor-managed firm deals with the autonomous enterprise in which management and control rest with the total work force.

mar (1966), Vanek argued that workers in the labor-managed firm (LMF) could most fundamentally seek to maximize net revenue (value added) per worker. This theory demonstrates that in the short run, with only one variable factor, labor (L), and with capital (K) stock fixed, using a simple production function

$$X = f(L,\bar{K})$$

where X is output and diminishing marginal returns exist, and with prices of capital (P_k) and of the product (P_x) both constant, then the labor-managed firm seeks to maximize income (Y) where

$$Y = (1/L) (P_xX - P_kK).^3$$

Based on this maximand, the operating rule for the firm is to set income per worker equal to the marginal value product of labor (Vanek 1970, pp. 20–22). A more realistic short-run production function (ibid., pp. 22–27) with variable inputs of both labor and a substitutable material M could be

$$X = f(L,M,\bar{K}).$$

Here the operating rule that maximizes income per worker is to employ M up to the point at which its marginal value product just equals its price and add workers until the income per worker is just equal to the marginal value product of the last person joining the collective.[4] The methods for achieving these equilibrium levels of employment of substitutable factors naturally differ from those of the capitalist analogue in that labor, the working collective, is making managerial decisions.

Much of the early literature on the economics of the labor-man-

---

3. The assumption of a labor-managed firm maximizing dollar income per worker is convenient for theoretical analysis, but it obviously does not reflect the broad variety of "incomes," such as leisure time or education, that members may choose. Steinherr (1978) provides a discussion of maximization of a generalized utility function. Furubotn (1976) added intertemporal considerations to an objective function, even though his analysis was affected by rather unusual assumptions (Berman and Berman 1978).

4. More exactly in the generalized short-run case variable inputs of labor and a substitutable material M are combined with a nonsubstitutable material N to the level of output such that

$$N = nX$$

where n is a constant input-coefficient that brings use of N into line with the product X (Vanek 1970, p. 23).

aged firm gave particular attention to its short-run response to changes in its exogenous variables of output price (in a fully competitive market the firm is a price taker) and the cost of capital. It was found that in theory the LMF would reduce its labor force in response to a rise in the price of its output or a fall in the rental price of capital. These findings were the opposite of those for the short-run behavior of the capitalist firm. The results were found to be partly mitigated in short-run cases where multiple inputs or outputs were posited (Vanek 1970, ch. 3). They were also considered to be poor reflections of the actual behavior of people working in a cooperative firm (Robinson 1967). In sum, this theoretical debate over the behavior of the LMF confirms that in the short run it will exhibit a relatively inelastic supply curve relative to its theoretical analogue of the conventional firm under similar conditions (Meade 1972). For an economy made up of labor-managed firms, these results point to a critical need for ease of entry into markets experiencing a rising price of product.

Long-run equilibrium conditions are developed from the model outlined here, but with all inputs, of course, variable. In the case of a production function of the increasing-decreasing-returns-to-scale (IDRS) type, operating rules of setting marginal value product added (MVPA) of factors equal to their prices

$$MVPA_m = P_m$$
$$MVPA_m = P_k$$
$$MVPA_l = (1/L) (P_x X - P_m M - P_k K)$$

lead to long-run equilibrium solutions. Unlike the capitalist firm (for which the optimality conditions are described in similar terms) the labor-managed firm will reach long-run equilibrium at only a limited set of points on its production function. Because of the conditions that all income is distributed among the factors of production and that each substitutable factor earns its MVPA, those points are those for which (with constant factor prices) the long-run average cost curve of a capitalist firm would be at its minimum point. This set of points constitutes the locus of maximum physical efficiency (see Figure 7), and in long-run equilibrium the labor-managed firm will operate on that locus (Vanek 1970, pp. 28–34).

In the short run, with capital stock fixed and equal for both the labor-managed and the capitalist firm, the level of optimal employment in the labor-managed firm is less than or equal to the employment level of the capitalist firm. The capital-labor ratio of the labor-managed firm is greater than or equal to that of the capitalist firm. In the ideal case in which the competitive capitalist firm is making zero profits, the marginal and average revenues of the capitalist firm are equalized, and labor employment is the same for both types of firms. In that case the income per worker in the labor-managed firm is equal to the wage for workers in the capitalist firm. If the capitalist firm is making more than normal economic profits, its wage rate will be lower than the income per worker of the labor-managed firm.

In the long-run case, with the capitalist firm again making normal economic profit, the two firms are equally efficient allocators of scarce resources. The labor-managed firm tends to reach an equilibrium at smaller size, since it maximizes average net revenue rather than total net revenue. This is a positive attribute in the abstract world of neoclassical economics. If the capitalist firm should deviate from the theoretical ideal and make profits in the long run, then it will expand beyond a scale corresponding to lowest average costs. The labor-managed firm, operating in both short- and long-run situations under the rule of equating marginal and average revenue per unit of labor, is not subject to that inefficiency (Vanek 1970, p. 31). Perhaps the fullest conventional economic test of the potential of the labor-managed firm rests with general equilibrium analysis for an economy composed of many labor-managed firms and sectors. That analysis shows the labor-managed economy, under conditions of multisectoral, perfectly competitive general equilibrium with free entry, to be Pareto-optimal in the long run (ibid., pp. 134–139). In the language of conventional (capitalist) economics, an "ideal" labor-managed economy operates as efficiently as an "ideal" capitalist economy. Arguments against the labor managed firm cannot be made on grounds of pure economic efficiency.

Research on financing of the labor-managed firm follows from this model. Vanek (1975b) identified four economic forces that acted destructively on these organizations. These forces stemmed from holding assets in a collective and nonrecoverable form rather than retaining individual members' claim on them and from failure to pay scarcity-reflecting rent on capital employed.

This analysis is based on the firm's operation in a market economy, and, again, the standard assumptions of neoclassical theory are employed. Vanek (1975a, p. 15) distinguishes a pure collectively financed, worker-managed firm (WMF) from a pure labor-managed firm (LMF). Jones and Backus (1977, p. 488) point out that this distinction is somewhat less confusing than the distinction between internally and externally financed firms used in Vanek's original analysis. The distinction can be further clarified if the term *collectively financed* is dropped. The key issue is whether invested funds are compensated by a scarcity-reflecting rent and recoverable by whoever provides them. Both WMFs and LMFs are autonomous and controlled by their work force on a basis of equality, but the WMF is one in which investment is provided from social funds (as in Yugoslavia) or members' investment (as in many historical examples of workers' cooperatives), with no claim applying to funds from either source or on any portion of reinvestment from earnings. Members cannot, therefore, recoup their investment. In addition, they do not receive a scarcity-reflecting rent on any funds they may invest. Capital rents accrue to members as part of their working income, and not to capital suppliers as a rental payment for use of that capital. By contrast, in the LMF a scarcity-reflecting rent *is* paid to capital, whether the capital is supplied by members or external sources. In addition, suppliers retain a claim on all funds supplied. The maximands of the two firms, then, differ; the collectively financed WMF maximizes average income because no charge is made for capital, whereas the LMF maximizes average net (of capital costs) income.

The destructive behavior of a WMF is analyzed first under conditions of a constant returns to scale (CRS), linear-homogeneous production function. All members of the firm are assumed to have some time preference R for their assets; they prefer that the assets grow to 1 + R the next year. R can be thought of as the market rate of interest. Members are also expected to act in their own self-interest. The first of the four forces that limit both the growth potential and the ability to employ capital to best advantage for the WMF, called the "first self-extinction force" (Vanek 1975b, p. 448), results from the tendency of members to let their numbers diminish through retirement, attrition, or voluntary withdrawal. Given capital held constant, this reduction in work force increases the capital-labor ratio of the firm, thus increasing income per worker. In Figure 7, this force is illustrated by movement outward on the capital-labor axis. If the technology would allow, the absurd end result of this process would be one member left operating the

FIGURE 7. Financing under conditions of constant-returns-to-scale, linear-homogeneous production functions.

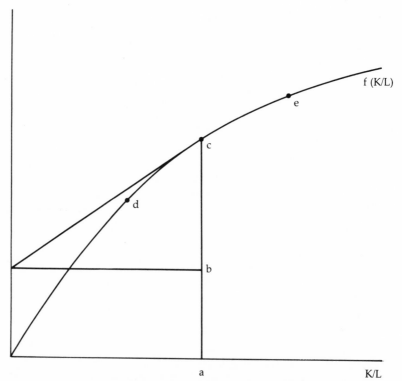

capital equipment of the collectively financed WMF. If departing members took their funds with them, at the time of their departure or over some extended time period, then this force would be nullified. The capital-labor ratio of the firm would remain constant, *ceteris paribus*, and the incentive to reduce membership would be eliminated.

A second self-extinction force (Vanek 1975b, p. 448) is related to the first. In Figure 7, function f(K/L) expresses output per worker in both physical and value terms. Its slope at any point measures the marginal product of capital. If labor and capital were both paid their marginal products segment ab would measure the wage rate, and bc the income share of capital per worker. In the case of the WMF all of ac is income divided among working members of the collective. As point *a* moves to the right in response to the first force, the slope of the function (K/L), the marginal product of capital, diminishes. If the WMF has some preference for the investment level represented by point *a*, then as the number of remaining members diminishes and the K/L ratio increases, remaining members might return to point *a* by gradually disinvesting or by consuming the firm's capital. This force would also be eliminated in a firm with recoverable funding.

Next, Vanek identified an "underinvestment force" (1975b, pp. 449–450) attributable to nonrecoverable funding with no rental payment to capital. This force is demonstrated by conventional investment theory, which argues that an individual will invest up to the point at which the rate of return is just equal to the individual's time preference. The theory assumes that the invested principal is recovered at the end of the investment period, so that the present value of an invested dollar would be

$$V = A \sum_{i=1}^{T} (i + R)^{-i} + (1 + R)^{-T}$$

where V is the present value of the total returns, A is the annual returns from the invested dollar, R is the rate of time preference, i is the i'th time period of the investment, and T is the total investment time period. To reach the point where A = R, extra dollar investment takes place until V = 1.

In the case of the WMF, invested funds are not recoverable, and the present value of a dollar invested becomes

$$V' = A \sum_{i=1}^{T} (1 + R)^{-i}$$

or simply the annual incremental return to the investment. With no payment of interest on invested funds, the member benefits from investing only through the potential for increasing income per worker. The member would rationally invest, then, only when the marginal productivity of capital, A, is at a level A* at which it is higher than R by some positive amount D that would compensate for the nonrecoverable invested principal:

$$A^* \geq R + D, D \geq o$$

The magnitude of D is inversely related to T, the amount of time that the member plans to remain with the firm. McGregor (1977, p. 480) points out that if the member is young, plans on remaining with the firm for a period of 30 years, and has a rate of time preference R of 6 percent, then she or he would be willing to invest if

$$A \sum_{i=1}^{30} (1.06)^{-i} \geq 1$$

or if A = 7.2 percent. D in this case is a relatively low 1.2 percent.[5] But the same calculation for a member with a planning horizon of two years would be

$$A \sum_{i=1}^{2} (1.06)^{-i} \geq 1$$

with A = 54.5 percent. The D factor required to compensate for the nonrecoverable principal is now 48.5 percent,[6] and investment opportunities that promise returns of that magnitude are rare. The result is that the firm tends to underinvest, and that tendency grows stronger as the age of members increases. The impact of the underinvestment force could be diminished by a pension fund that draws heavily on the firm's annual income (ibid., p. 481), but even under that condition it remains a significant force.

The last of the destructive forces that can be identified in the case of a WMF with a CRS production function is called the "never employ force" in Vanek's analysis (Vanek 1975b, p. 450). Again in Figure 7, a firm might find itself at point *d*, when in fact the equilibrium level of the marginal product of capital is at point *c*, and the ideal condition where the marginal product of capital would be equal to members' time preference is at point *e*. Members would then choose to invest in order to expand production up to point *a*, but once at that point, any additional member admitted would reduce the capital-labor ratio and diminish income per worker. To expand membership, investment would have to take place at a rate that would at least maintain the capital-labor ratio. But the lack of

5. $A = R + D$
$.072 = .06 + D$
$D = .012$

6. $54.5 = .06 + D$
$D = 48.5$

a mechanism for recovering invested capital makes that additional investment unlikely, as the other three forces have demonstrated. This fourth force, then, results from the previous three.

All four of these negative forces could be reversed if the firm were Vanek's ideal LMF type rather than the WMF type. With recoverable financing at some rate equal to members' time preference R, an equilibrium at point *e* in Figure 7 could be reached. The first self-extinction effect would be removed because if membership were reduced and the K/L ratio increased with a constant payment to capital R, members would find their income reduced because fewer of them would be servicing the capital costs. The second self-extinction force, a desire to reduce capital stock, would also be eliminated as this would cause movement back toward the origin on the K/L axis, away from optimal income per worker. The investment level at *e* would be optimal, as the marginal productivity of capital at that point would just equal the rate of time preference. And given the assumed constant-returns-to-scale technology, employment could be increased as long as additional investment was also made at the level of capital per worker corresponding to point *e* on the K/L axis. Assuming a constant price of capital, both factors could be increased proportionally, and the firm could grow while maintaining its optimal level of income per worker.

If we analyze a firm with a production function that exhibits increasing and then decreasing returns to scale (IDRS), similar results are obtained. With a WMF the principal of any investment would not be recoverable, and investment of only very high rates of return would be undertaken. Compared to Vanek's ideal-type LMF, the WMF would tend toward equilibrium in the increasing returns to scale zone of the production function at a lower level of output, and with a lower capital-labor ratio, than the LMF.

Figure 8 illustrates these forces for the case of an IDRS production function for both types of firms. This figure represents the capital-labor input plane, with increasing returns to scale evident at low levels of output, constant returns to scale in the area of the EE locus, and either constant or decreasing returns to scale beyond the EE locus. The EE locus is the locus of maximum physical efficiency; points along it represent the situation in which average productivities for the factors capital and labor are maximized for the given capital-labor ratios. In addition, along locus EE Euler's theorem holds; that is, with marginal product pricing of both fac-

FIGURE 8. Financing under conditions of increasing-decreasing-returns-to-scale production functions.

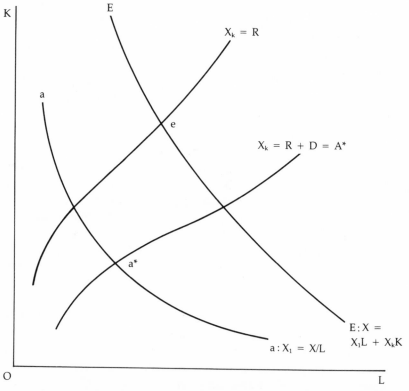

tors of production, the total product will be exactly exhausted by payments to both inputs. This is the locus on which both the pure LMF and the perfectly competitive firm will operate in the long run (Vanek 1970, pp. 30–31). The WMF, however, will not attain this level of efficiency.

Locus aa in Figure 8 is the locus along which the average product of labor is maximized for various levels of fixed amounts of capital. It is also the locus along which the average product of labor equals the marginal product of labor, and thus the locus that the WMF, maximizing average income per worker, will operate upon. It lies in the increasing-returns-to-scale zone of the IDRS production function.

Based on his analysis of the labor-managed market economy,

Vanek (1970, ch. 2) has shown that an efficient labor-managed firm will operate along locus $X_k = R$ in Figure 8. On this locus the marginal productivity of capital (X_k) is equal to the marginal rate of time preference (R) of investors or the market rate of interest for investment capital. The pure LMF will be in equilibrium at point *e*, where both capital and labor are paid their respective marginal products. Workers in the WMF, unable to recoup any investment of capital they may make, will rationally choose to have their firms operate on locus $X_k = R + D = A^*$. The collectively financed WMF, then, will be in equilibrium at point *a**, where the marginal product of capital is equal to something more than the scarcity-reflecting remuneration of capital and labor is receiving its average product. This would be a stable equilibrium, since movement to the right of aa would cause employment to decline and income per worker to increase, and movement to the left would cause the reverse. Below $X_k = R + D = A^*$ the firm would accumulate capital, and above it it would consume it.

Point *a** represents the historic position of workers' cooperatives that have followed a WMF model; they have traditionally been small relative to comparable capitalist firms, and they have usually been undercapitalized. Workers' cooperatives or worker-owned and -controlled firms formed today to operate in market economies may not be able to neutralize all the negative forces they face, but they can eliminate the destructive forces illustrated in this analysis by their own choice of financial structure.

The theoretical arguments for retention of individual claim on invested capital and retained earnings in workers' cooperatives are strong, and empirical evidence to date, although not conclusive, supports those arguments. Given the historically poor record of cooperatives that have attempted capitalization based upon non-recoverable and uncompensated members' contributions of the WMF model, this explanation warrents serious consideration.

The theoretical argument for payment of a scarcity-reflecting rent on capital follows from neoclassical economic theory. Aspects of that body of thought, however, are modified here in that capital is not in control of productive enterprises and is not necessarily privately owned. Whether capital is socially owned, owned by the state, or privately held, in this analysis it is considered a scarce resource, and on that basis it can be paid a scarcity-reflecting rent to assure its efficient allocation, to compensate for its use, and to guarantee against its loss in value (Vanek 1970, p. 5). Further, capital is assumed to have a price and to be available through some form of capital market. These assumptions are consistant with the current U.S. economic environment.

Self-managed firms that use productive land have been found to exhibit problems of financial structure that parellel those described here (McGregor 1977, Roca 1975). If those firms are operating in market economies, solutions to problems of financial structure lie in treating land as a scarce resource, paying a scarcity-reflecting rent on it, and financing through recoverable investments.

Bibliography

Alaska Consulting Group, Inc. 1981. "Report on General and Northwest Plywood Industry Trends, Methods for Evaluating Worker Acquisitions, and a Review of the Westfir Acquisitions Attempt" (draft). Anchorage, Alaska, Sept. 30.

Alchian, Armen A., and Harold Demsetz. 1972. "Production, Information Costs, and Economic Organization." *American Economic Review* 62(5):777–795.

Ali, Tariq, and Quintin Hoare. 1982. "Socialists and the Crisis of Labourism." *New Left Review*, no. 132, pp.59–81.

Alvarado-Greenwood, William; Steven Haberfeld; and Lloyd C. Lee. 1978. *Organizing Production Cooperatives: A Strategy for Community Economic Development*. Berkeley: National Economic Development and Law Center.

American Plywood Association, 1982a. *Management Bulletin*, no. FA-215. Tacoma, Wash.: APA, Mar. 12.

———. 1982b. Plywood Statistics: Weekly Report, no. 82–27. Tacoma, Wash.: APA, July 10.

"An Acid Test for Worker-Owners." 1982. *Business Week*, Aug. 2, pp. 67, 70.

Anderson, Perry. 1976. "The Antinomies of Antonio Gramsci." *New Left Review*, no. 100, pp. 5–78.

Andors, Steven. 1977. *China's Industrial Revolution*. New York: Pantheon.

Argyris, Chris. 1964. *Integrating the Individual and the Organization*. New York: Wiley.

Aronowitz, Stanley. 1973. *False Promises: The Shaping of American Working Class Consciousness*. New York: McGraw-Hill.

Arrow, Kenneth. 1964. "Control in Large Organizations." *Management Science* 10(3):397–408.

Barkai, Haim. 1977. *Growth Patterns of the Kibbutz Economy*. New York: North Holland.

Bellas, Carl J. 1972. *Industrial Democracy and the Worker-Owned Firm*. New York: Praeger.

Ben-Ner, Avner. 1982. "Changing Values and Preferences in Communal Organizations: Econometric Evidence from the Experience of the Israeli

Kibbutz." In *Participatory and Self-Managed Firms*. See Jones and Svejnar 1982.

Berle, Adolph, and Gardner Means. 1968. *The Modern Corporation and Private Property*. Rev. ed. New York: Harcourt, Brace.

Berman, Katrina V. 1967. *Worker-Owned Plywood Firms: An Economic Analysis*. Pullman: Washington State University Press.

————. 1982a. "The Worker-Owned Plywood Cooperatives." In *Workplace Democracy and Social Change*. See Lindenfeld and Rothschild-Whitt 1982.

————. 1982b. "Worker Management in U.S. Plywood Manufacturing Cooperatives: A Cooperative Model for Labour Management." In *The Performance of Labor-Managed Firms*. See Stephen 1982.

Berman, Katrina V., and M. D. Berman. 1978. "The Long-Run Analysis of the Labor-Managed Firm: A Comment." *American Economic Review* 68(4):701–705.

Bernstein, Paul. 1974. "Run Your Own Business: Worker-Owned Plywood Companies of the Pacific Northwest." *Working Papers* 2(2):24–34.

————. 1980. *Workplace Democratization: Its Internal Dynamics*. New Brunswick, N.J.: Transaction Books.

Bettelheim, Bruno. 1969. *Children of the Dream*. New York: Macmillan.

Bluestone, Barry, and Bennett Harrison. 1982. *The Deindustrialization of America: Plant Closings, Community Abandonment, and the Dismantling of Basic Industry*. New York: Basic Books.

Bluestone, Barry; Bennett Harrison; and Lawrence Baker. 1981. *Corporate Flight: The Causes and Consequences of Economic Dislocation*. Washington, D.C.: The Progressive Alliance.

Blumberg, Paul. 1968. *Industrial Democracy: The Sociology of Participation*. New York: Schocken.

Bookchin, Murray. 1980. *Toward an Ecological Society*. Montreal: Black Rose.

Bowles, Samuel, and Herbert Gintis. 1976. *Schooling in Capitalist America: Educational Reform and the Contradiction of Economic Life*. New York: Basic Books.

Boyer, Richard O., and Herbert M. Morais. 1972. *Labor's Untold Story*. 3d ed. New York: United Electrical, Radio and Machine Workers of America.

Bradley, Keith, and Alan Gelb. 1982. "The Mondragon Cooperatives: Guidelines for a Cooperative Economy." In *Participatory and Self-Managed Firms*. See Jones and Svejnar 1982.

Brand, Stewart, ed. 1981. *The Next Whole Earth Catalog*. 2d ed. New York: Random House.

Brandow, Karen, and Jim McDonnell. 1981. *No Bosses Here!* 2d ed. Boston: Vocations for Social Change.

Braverman, Harry. 1974. *Labor and Monopoly Capital: The Degradation of Work in the Twentieth Century*. New York: Monthly Review.

Brecher, Jeremy. 1972. *Strike!* Boston: South End Press.

Brody, David. 1980. *Workers in Industrial America. Essays on the Twentieth Century Struggle*. New York: Oxford University Press.

Brous, Ira, et al. 1977. *Democracy in the Workplace: Readings on the Implementation of Self-Management.* Washington, D.C.: Strongforce.

Burawoy, Michael. 1979. *Manufacturing Consent: Changes in the Labor Process under Monopoly Capitalism.* Chicago: University of Chicago Press.

———. 1981. "Terrains of Contest: Factory and State under Capitalism and Socialism." *Socialist Review* 58, vol. 11, no. 4, pp. 83–124.

Burns, Thomas R.; L. Erik Karlsson; and Veljko Rus, eds. 1979. *Work and Power.* London: Sage Publications.

Cable, John R., and Felix R. Fitzroy. 1980a. "Cooperation and Productivity: Some Evidence from West German Experience." *Economic Analysis and Workers' Management* 14(2):163–180.

———. 1980b. "Productivity, Efficiency, Incentives, and Employee Participation: Some Preliminary Results from West Germany." *Kyklos* 33(1):100–121.

Carnoy, Martin, and Derek Shearer. 1980. *Economic Democracy: The Challenge of the 1980s.* White Plains, N.Y.: M. E. Sharpe.

Case, John, and Rosemary C. R. Taylor, eds. 1979. *Co-ops, Communes and Collectives.* New York: Pantheon.

Coates, David. 1981. "Labourism and the Transition to Socialism." *New Left Review* no. 129, pp. 3–22.

———. 1982. "Space and Agency in the Transition to Socialism." *New Left Review,* no. 135, pp. 49–63.

Coates, Ken. 1976. *The New Worker Cooperatives.* Nottingham: Spokesman.

Commons, John R., et al. 1918. *History of Labor in the United States.* Vols. 1 and 2. New York: Macmillan.

Curl, John. 1980. *Work Cooperation in America.* Berkeley: Homeward Press.

Denver Yellow Cab Cooperative Association. 1981. *Bylaws,* rev. Nov. 30, 1981.

Derber, Milton. 1970. *The American Idea of Industrial Democracy: 1865–1965.* Urbana: University of Illinois Press.

Dolgoff, Sam, ed. 1974. *The Anarchist Collectives: Workers' Self-Management in the Spanish Revolution, 1936–1939.* New York: Free Life Editions.

Domar, Evsey. 1966. "The Soviet Collective Farm as a Producer Cooperative." *American Economic Review* 56(4):734–757.

Dubofsky, Melvyn. 1971. *We Shall Be All: A History of the Industrial Workers of the World.* Chicago: Quadrangle Books.

Edwards, Richard. 1979. *Contested Terrain: The Transformation of the Workplace in the Twentieth Century.* New York: Basic Books.

Espinosa, Juan G., and Andrew S. Zimbalist. 1978. *Economic Democracy: Workers' Participation in Chilean Industry, 1970–1973.* New York: Academic Press.

Fine, Ben, and Laurence Harris. 1979. *Rereading Capital.* New York: Columbia University Press.

Fiori, Giuseppe. 1970. *Antonio Gramsci: Life of a Revolutionary.* New York: Schocken.

237

Foote, Donna. 1981. "When Employees Take Over." *Newsweek*, June 1, p. 74.

Freire, Paulo. 1972. *Pedagogy of the Oppressed*. New York: Herder and Herder.

Furubotn, Eirik. 1976. "The Long Run Analysis of the Labor-Managed Firm: An Alternative Interpretation." *American Economic Review* 66(1):104–123.

Fusfeld, Daniel R. 1979. "Workers' Management and the Transition to Socialism." *Economic Analysis and Workers' Management* 13(4):463–471.

Gascoyne, Steve. 1978. "Denver Cabbies Vote to Buy Company." *In These Times*, Dec. 6–12, p. 4.

Gintis, Herbert. 1972. "Activism and Counter-Culture: The Dialectics of Consciousness in the Corporate State." *Telos* 12 (summer):42–62.

Gordon, David M.; Richard Edwards; and Michael Reich. 1982. *Segmented Work, Divided Workers: The Historical Transformation of Labor in the United States*. Cambridge: Cambridge University Press.

Gorz, Andre. 1973. "Workers' Control is More than Just That." In *Workers' Control*. See Hunnius et al. 1973. Also in *Workplace Democracy and Social Change*. See Lindenfeld and Rothschild-Whitt 1982.

Gramsci, Antonio. 1971. *Prison Notebooks*. New York: International.

———. 1977. *Selections from Political Writings: 1910–1920*. New York: International.

Greenberg, Edward S. 1979. "The Political Effects of Self-Management." Boulder: Institute of Behavioral Science, University of Colorado.

———. 1981a. "Industrial Democracy and the Democratic Citizen." *Journal of Politics* 43(4):964–981.

———. 1981b. "Industrial Self-Management and Political Attitudes." *American Political Science Review* 75(1):29-42.

———. Forthcoming. "Producer Cooperatives and Democratic Theory: The Case of the Plywood Firms." In *Worker Cooperatives in America*. See Jackall and Levin forthcoming.

A Guide to Cooperative Alternatives. 1979. Louisa, Va.: Community Publications Cooperative.

Gunn, Christopher. 1980a. "Plywood Cooperatives of the Pacific Northwest: Lessons for Workers' Self-Management in the United States." *Economic Analysis and Workers' Management* 14(3):393–416.

———. 1980b. "Toward Workers' Control." *Working Papers* 7(3):4–7.

———. 1980c. "Workers' Self-Management in the United States: Theory and Practice." Ph.D. dissertation, Cornell University.

———. 1981a. "The Fruits of Rath: A New Model of Self-Management." *Working Papers* 8(2):17–21.

———. 1981b. "Worker and Community Response to the Threat of Economic Dislocation: The Rath Packing Company." In *Financing Community Economic Development*. See Schramm 1981.

———. Forthcoming. "Hoedads Co-op: Democracy and Cooperation at Work." In *Worker Cooperatives in America*. See Jackall and Levin forthcoming.

Gutman, Herbert G. 1977. *Work, Culture and Society*. New York: Vintage.

Harcourt, Geoffrey C. 1969. "Some Cambridge Controversies in the Theory of Capital." *Journal of Economic Literature*, no. 7, pp. 386–395.

Harrington, Michael. 1976. *The Twilight of Capitalism*. New York: Simon and Schuster.

Hodgson, Geoff. 1982. "On the Political Economy of the Socialist Transition." *New Left Review*, no. 133, pp. 52–66.

Hoedads Co-op. Inc. 1978. "By-laws of the Hoedads: An Oregon Cooperative." Rev. Dec. 17. Eugene, Oreg.

Horvat, Branko. 1976a. "Fundamentals of a Theory of Distribution in Self-Governing Socialism." *Economic Analysis and Workers' Management* 10(1–2):24–42.

———. 1976b. "Workers' Management." *Economic Analysis and Workers' Management* 10(3–4):197–214.

———. 1976c. *The Yugoslav Economy: The First Labor-Managed Economy in the Making*. White Plains, N.Y.: International Arts and Sciences Press.

Horvat, Branko; Mihailo Marković; and Rudi Supek, eds. 1975. *Self-Governing Socialism: A Reader*. 2 vols. White Plains, N.Y.: International Arts and Sciences Press.

Hunnius, Gerry; G. David Garson; and John Case, eds. 1973. *Workers' Control: A Reader on Labor and Social Change*. New York: Vintage Books.

Industrial Cooperative Association. 1982. "The New Massachusetts Law for Worker Cooperatives: MGL Chapter 157A" (photocopy). Somerville, Mass.: ICA.

Institute for Community Economics. 1982. *The Community Land Trust Handbook*. Greenfield, Mass.: ICE.

Jackall, Robert. Forthcoming. "Paradoxes of Collective Work: A Study of The Cheeseboard, Berkeley, California." In *Worker Cooperatives in America*. See Jackall and Levin forthcoming.

Jackall, Robert, and Henry M. Levin, eds. Forthcoming. *Worker Cooperatives in America*. Berkeley: University of California Press.

Jensen, Michael C., and W. H. Meckling. 1979. "Rights and Production Functions: An Application to Labor-Managed Firms and Codetermination." *Journal of Business* 52(4):469–506.

Jones, Derek C. 1974. "The Economics of British Producer Cooperatives." Ph.D. dissertation, Cornell University.

———. 1979. "U.S. Producer Cooperatives: The Record to Date." *Industrial Relations* 18:342–357.

———. 1980. "Producer Cooperatives in Industrialized Western Economies." *British Journal of Industrial Relations* 18:141–154.

———. Forthcoming. "American Producer Cooperatives and Employee Owned Firms: An Evaluation." In *Worker Cooperatives in America*. See Jackall and Levin forthcoming.

Jones, Derek C., and David K. Backus. 1977. "British Producer Cooperatives in the Footwear Industry: An Empirical Evaluation of the Theory of Finance." *Economic Journal* 87:488–510.

Jones, Derek C., and Jan Svejnar, eds. 1982. *Participatory and Self-Managed Firms: Evaluating Economic Performance*. Lexington, Mass.: Lexington Books.

Jones, Derek C., and Alberto Zevi. Unpublished. "The Italian System of Producer Cooperatives."

Kessler, Lauren. 1982. "The Economics of Cool." *Oregon Magazine*, September, pp. 31–33, 65.

Knapp, Joseph G. 1969. *The Rise of American Cooperative Enterprise: 1620–1920*. Danville, Ill.: Interstate Press.

———. 1973. *The Advance of American Cooperative Enterprise*. Danville, Ill.: Interstate Press.

Kreitner, Phil. 1982. "The Co-op Bank: Two Eyes, Three Views." *Co-ops Today* 8(3):13–16.

Levin, Henry. 1982. "Issues in Assessing the Comparative Productivity of Worker-Managed and Participatory Firms in Capitalist Societies." In *Participatory and Self-Managed Firms*. See Jones and Svejnar 1982.

Lindblom, Charles E. 1977. *Politics and Markets: The World's Political Economic Systems*. New York: Basic Books.

Lindenfeld, Frank, and Joyce Rothschild-Whitt, eds. 1982. *Workplace Democracy and Social Change*. Boston: Porter Sargent.

Lynd, Staughton. 1982. *The Fight against Shutdowns: Youngstown's Steel Mill Closings*. San Pedro, Calif.: Singlejack Books.

McGregor, Andrew. 1977. "Rent Extraction and the Survival of Agricultural Production Cooperatives." *American Journal of Agricultural Economics* 59(3):478-488.

Machlup, Fritz. 1967. "Theories of the Firm: Marginalist, Behavioral, Managerial." *American Economic Review* 57(1):1–33.

Mandel, Ernest, ed. 1970. *Workers' Control, Workers' Councils, Workers' Self-Management: An Anthology*. Paris: Maspero.

Mandel, Ernest. 1971. *The Formation of the Economic Thought of Karl Marx*. New York: Monthly Review.

Marglin, Stephen A. 1974. "What Do Bosses Do?" *Review of Radical Political Economics* 6(2):60–112.

———. 1979. "Catching Flies with Honey: An Inquiry into Management Initiatives to Humanize Work." *Economic Analysis and Workers' Management* 13(4):473–488.

Martin, David A. 1982. "Participatory Management: The Road to 'Economic Democracy'?" *Northern Business and Economic Review* 1(1):8–20.

Maslow, Abraham. 1954. *Motivation and Personality*. New York: Harper & Row.

Meade, James E. 1972. "The Theory of Labour-Managed Firms and of Profit Sharing." *Economic Journal* 82:402–428.

Melman, Seymour. 1970. "Industrial Efficiency under Managerial versus Cooperative Decision Making." *Review of Radical Political Economics* 2 (1):9–34. Also in *Self-Governing Socialism*. See Horvat et al. 1975.

Metzgar, Jack. 1980. "Plant Shutdowns and Worker Response: The Case of Johnstown, Pa." *Socialist Review* 53, vol. 10, no. 5, pp. 9–49.

Minsky, Terri. 1981. "Workers Who Bought Iowa Slaughterhouse Regret That They Did." *Wall Street Journal*, Dec. 2, pp. 1, 23.

Moberg, David. 1979. "Experimenting with the Future: Alternative Institutions and American Socialism." In *Co-ops, Communes and Collectives*. See Case and Taylor 1979.

Montgomery, David. 1979. *Workers' Control in America: Studies in the History of Work, Technology, and Labor Struggles*. New York: Cambridge University Press.

Nagle, Greg. 1979a. "Hoedads." In *A Guide to Cooperative Alternatives*. See *A Guide to Cooperative Alternatives*.

———. 1979b. "A Report on Timber Resources and Timber Industries in Lane County." Prepared for the Lane Economic Development Council, Eugene, Oreg., May.

Nazario, Ruth. 1982. " 'We Interrupt This Dream. . .': A Personal View of NCCB." *Co-ops Today* 8(3):23–24.

Oakeshott, Robert. 1978. *The Case for Workers' Co-ops*. Boston: Routledge & Kegan Paul.

O'Connor, Harvey. 1964. *Revolution in Seattle*. Reprint. Seattle: Left Bank Books, 1981.

Olson, Deborah Groban. 1982. "Union Experiences with Worker Ownership: Legal and Practical Issues Raised by ESOPs, TRASOPs, Stock Purchases and Co-Operatives." *Wisconsin Law Review* 1982(5):729–823.

Panitch, Leo. 1978. "Workers' Control and Revolutionary Change." *Monthly Review* 29(10):37–48.

Pateman, Carole. 1970. *Participation and Democratic Theory*. New York: Cambridge University Press.

Perry, Stewart E. 1978. *San Francisco Scavengers: Dirty Work and the Pride of Ownership*. Berkeley: University of California Press.

Przeworski, Adam. 1979. "Material Bases of Consent: Economics and Politics as a Hegemonic System." *Political Power and Social Theory*, no. 1, pp. 21–63.

———. 1980. "Social Democracy as a Historical Phenomenon." *New Left Review*, no. 122, pp. 27–58.

Quality of Work Life. 1979. Ann Arbor, Mich.: Institute for Social Research.

Rhodes, Susan R. 1978. "The Relationship between Worker Ownership and Control of Organizations and Work Attitudes and Behavior." Ph.D. dissertation, University of Oregon.

Ridgeway, James, and Alexander Cockburn. 1981a. "Fear and Loaning at the Co-op Bank." *Village Voice*, Nov. 4–10, pp. 16–19, 34–35.

———. 1981b. "More Fear and Loaning at the Co-op Bank." *Village Voice*, Dec. 23, pp. 22–23.

———. 1982. "The Liberals' Bank: Conflict of Interest and Cover Up?" *Village Voice*, Mar. 9, p. 11.

Rifkin, Jeremy, and Randy Barber. 1978. *The North Will Rise Again: Pensions, Politics and Power in the 1980's*. Boston: Beacon Press.

Robinson, Joan. 1967. "The Soviet Collective Farm as a Producer Cooperative: Comment." *American Economic Review* 57(1):222–223.

Roca, Santiago. 1975. "The Peruvian Sugar Cooperatives: Some Fundamental Economic Problems, 1968–1972." *Economic Analysis and Workers' Management* 9(1–2):25–54.

Rothschild-Whitt, Joyce. 1976. "Problems of Democracy." *Working Papers* 4(3):41–45.

———. 1979. "Collectivist-Democracy: An Alternative to Rational-Bureaucratic Models." *American Sociological Review* 44(4):509–527. Also in *Workplace Democracy and Social Change*. See Lindenfeld and Rothschild-Whitt 1982.

Rowbotham, Sheila; Lynne Segal; and Hilary Wainwright. 1979. *Beyond the Fragments: Feminism and the Making of Socialism*. London: Merlin Press.

Rustin, Michael. 1980. "The New Left and the Crisis." *New Left Review*, no. 121, pp. 63–89.

Salinas, Nelson. 1977. "Education for Self-Management: The Case of a Farm Workers' Production Cooperative." In *Democracy in the Workplace*. See Brous et al. 1977.

Schaaf, Michael. 1977. *Cooperatives at the Crossroads*. Washington, D.C.: Exploratory Project for Economic Alternatives.

Schramm, Richard, ed. 1981. *Financing Community Economic Development: A Resource Guide for Community Planners, Organizers, Activists*. Ithaca, N.Y.: Cornell University Program in Urban and Regional Studies.

Schumpeter, Joseph A. 1942. *Capitalism, Socialism and Democracy*. Reprint. New York: Harper & Row, 1950.

Schweickart, David. 1980. *Capitalism or Worker Control?*. New York: Praeger.

Shirom, Arie. 1972. "The Industrial Relations System of Industrial Cooperatives in the United States, 1880–1935." *Labor History* 13(4):533–551.

Slentz, Gail. 1979. "Northwest Forest Workers' Association: How It All Got Started" (photocopy). Eugene, Oreg.: Northwest Forest Workers' Association, Aug. 20.

Smith, Adam. 1937. *An Inquiry into the Nature and Causes of the Wealth of Nations*. (E. Cannan, ed.) New York: Modern Library.

Smith, J. D. 1981. "The Hoedads." In *The Next Whole Earth Catalog*. See Brand 1981.

Steinherr, Alfred. 1978. "The Labor-Managed Economy: A Survey of the Economics Literature." *Annals of Public and Cooperative Economy* 49(2):129–148.

Stephen, Frank H., ed. 1982. *The Performance of Labour-Managed Firms*. New York: St. Martin's.

Stephen, Frank H. 1982a. "The Economic Theory of the Labor-Managed Firm." In *The Performance of Labour-Managed Firms*. See Stephen 1982.

Stiglitz, J. 1975. "Incentives, Risk and Information: Notes toward a Theory of Hierarchy." *Bell Journal of Economics* 6(2):552–579.

"Stonewalling Plant Democracy." 1977. *Business Week*, Mar. 28, pp. 78–82.

Tannenbaum, Arnold S., ed. 1968. *Control in Organizations*. New York: McGraw-Hill.

Tannenbaum, Arnold S. et al. 1974. *Hierarchy in Organizations*. San Francisco: Jossey-Bass.

Taylor, Frederick Winslow. 1911. Reprint *The Principles of Scientific Management*. New York: Harper & Row, 1947.

Thomas, Hendrik. 1982. "The Performance of the Mondragon Cooperatives in Spain." In *Participatory and Self-Managed Firms*. See Jones and Svejnar 1982.

Thomas, Hendrik, and Chris Logan. 1982. *Mondragon: An Economic Analysis*. London: Allen & Unwin.

Tigar, Michael, and Madeleine R. Levy. 1978. *Law and the Rise of Capitalism*. New York: Monthly Review Press.

Union for Radical Political Economics (URPE). 1979. "Toward the Development of a Model for Consensus Decision-Making." *URPE Newsletter* 11(3):40–43.

U.S. Bureau of the Census. 1981. *Statistical Abstract of the United States: 1981*. 102d ed. Washington, D.C.: U.S. Government Printing Office.

U.S. Congress. House. 1978. "Employment of *Fortune* 1,000 and Total U.S. Civilian Labor Force." *Congressional Record* H 1829, Mar. 8.

———. 1980. *Conglomerate Mergers: Their Effects on Small Business and Local Communities*. Report of the Committee on Small Business, Oct. 2.

U.S. Congress. Senate. 1979. *The Role of the Federal Government and Employee Ownership of Business*. Report of the Select Committee on Small Business, Jan. 29.

Vanek, Jaroslav. 1970. *The General Theory of Labor-Managed Market Economies*. Ithaca, N.Y.: Cornell University Press.

———, ed. 1975. *Self-Management: Economic Liberation of Man*. Harmondsworth: Penguin.

———. 1975a. "Introduction." In *Self-Management: Economic Liberation of Man*. See Vanek 1975.

———. 1975b. "The Basic Theory of Financing of Participatory Firms." In *Self Management: Economic Liberation of Man*. See Vanek 1975. Also in *The Labor-Managed Economy: Essays*. See Vanek 1977.

———. 1976. "Through Participation and Dialogue to A World of Justice." Unpublished manuscript.

———. 1977. *The Labor-Managed Economy: Essays*. Ithaca, N.Y.: Cornell University Press.

———. 1977a. "Uncertainty and the Investment Decision under Labor-Management and Their Social Efficiency Implications." In *The Labor-Managed Economy: Essays*. See Vanek 1977.

———. 1982. "A System for Worker Participation and Self-Management in Western Industrialized Economies." In *The Performance of Labour-Managed Firms*. See Stephen 1982.

Ward, Benjamin. 1958. "The Firm in Illyria: Market Syndicalism." *American Economic Review* 48(4):566–589.

Watts, Martin. 1982. "The Microeconomics of Conflict and Hierarchy in Capitalist Production: A Critical Note." *Review of Radical Political Economics* 14(3):57–60.

Wiles, P. J. D. 1977. *Economic Institutions Compared.* Oxford: Oxford University Press.

Williams, Raymond. 1973. "Base and Superstructure in Marxist Cultural Theory." *New Left Review,* no. 83, pp. 3–16.

Wilson, Harold B. 1974. *Democracy and the Work Place.* Montreal: Black Rose Books.

Wilson, James. 1975. "Self-Management, Participation and Organized Labor in American History." Paper presented at the Second International Conference on Self-Management, Cornell University, June.

Work in America: Report of the Special Task Force of the Secretary of Health, Education and Welfare. 1973. Cambridge: MIT Press.

Wright, Erik O. 1978. *Class, Crisis and the State.* London: New Left Books.

Young, John A., and Jan M. Newton. 1980. *Capitalism and Human Obsolescence: Corporate Control versus Individual Survival in Rural America.* Montclair, N.J.: Allanheld, Osmun.

Zevi, Alberto. 1982. "The Performance of Italian Producer Cooperatives." In *Participatory and Self-Managed Firms.* See Jones and Svejnar 1982.

Zwerdling, Daniel. 1974. "Looking for Workers' Control." *Working Papers* 2(3):9–18.

———. 1978. *Democracy at Work: A Guide to Workplace Ownership, Participation and Self-Management Experiments in the United States and Europe.* New York: Harper & Row.

Index

Library of Congress Cataloging in Publication Data

Gunn, Christopher Eaton.
  Workers' self-management in the United States.

  Bibliography: p.
  Includes index.
  1. Industrial management—United States—Employee participation.   I. Title.
HD5660.U5G86   1984   338.6   83-45937
ISBN 0-8014-1644-2 (alk. paper)